GCSE AQA
Music

There's a lot to be excited about in AQA GCSE Music, and CGP is
here at every step to make sure you know the score...

This brilliant CGP book explains everything you'll need to do well in your coursework
and exams. Musical knowledge, study pieces, compositions — you name it.

What's more, each section has plenty of warm-up questions and exam-style practice,
including online listening practice. And to help you finish the course on a high note,
we've even included a realistic practice exam at the end!

How to access your free Online Edition

This book includes a free Online Edition, including listening practice, for your PC,
Mac or tablet. You'll just need to go to **cgpbooks.co.uk/extras** and enter this code:

2662 0494 4496 6775

By the way, this code only works for one person. If somebody else has used
this book before you, they might have already claimed the Online Edition.

Complete
Revision & Practice
Everything you need to pass the exams!

Contents

This stamp means that there is an audio track available for the question. The audio is accessed via your Online Edition of the book (see the first page for your code).

Published by CGP

Editors: Sarah George, Ruth Greenhalgh, Caley Simpson.

Contributors: Catherine Baird, Christopher Dalladay, John Deane, Elena Delaney, Rob Hall, Angela Major, Peter Maries, Sam Norman, James Reevell.

With thanks to Hannah Totman, Ben Train and Karen Wells for the proofreading.
With thanks to Jan Greenway and Laura Jakubowski for the copyright research.

For copyright reasons, this book can only be sold in the UK.

ISBN: 978 1 78908 628 7

Clipart from Corel®
Printed by Elanders Ltd, Newcastle upon Tyne.

Based on the classic CGP style created by Richard Parsons.

What You Have To Do For GCSE Music

GCSE Music doesn't cover every single aspect of music — if it did it would take forever. Instead you focus on four main 'Areas of Study' (AoS for short).

You Learn About **Four Areas of Study**

For each Area of Study you'll learn the <u>basics</u> of that <u>style</u> or <u>period</u> — e.g. the musical <u>structures</u>, the <u>instruments</u> used, the <u>context</u> the music was originally <u>created</u> in, etc.

You have to be able to <u>answer questions</u> on <u>all four</u> Areas of Study, but you only need to look at <u>study pieces</u> for <u>two</u> Areas of Study. One of these has to be <u>AoS1</u>, but you (or your teacher) can <u>choose</u> which of the other pieces you study. The four Areas of Study are:

> **AoS1 — WESTERN CLASSICAL TRADITION 1650-1910** (covered in Section 6)
> Your study piece is the 3rd Movement of Mozart's *Clarinet Concerto in A Major*.

This is the compulsory piece — you have to study it.

> **AoS2 — POPULAR MUSIC** (covered in Section 7)
> Your study pieces are 'Prologue/Little Shop of Horrors (Overture)',
> 'Mushnik and Son' and 'Feed Me (Git It)' from the musical *Little Shop of Horrors*.

> **AoS3 — TRADITIONAL MUSIC** (covered in Section 8)
> Your study pieces are Paul Simon's 'Graceland', 'Diamonds on the Soles of Her Shoes'
> and 'You Can Call Me Al' from the album *Graceland*.

> **AoS4 — WESTERN CLASSICAL TRADITION SINCE 1910** (covered in Section 9)
> Your study pieces are Kodály's 'Battle and Defeat of Napoleon' and 'Intermezzo' from *Háry János*.

They Test You With a **Listening Exam...**

worth 40% of the total marks

At the end of Year 11 you do an <u>exam</u>. You listen to excerpts of pieces from <u>all four Areas of Study</u> and <u>answer questions</u> on what you hear. You'll also have questions on your <u>study pieces</u>.

...And With **Coursework**

The coursework is work done during the course. Obviously. It's split into <u>two chunks</u>:

PERFORMING

worth 30% of the total marks

1) You do <u>two performances</u>.
2) One has to be a <u>solo performance</u>. This can be a piece you <u>play</u> or <u>sing</u>, a <u>DJ performance</u> or a <u>realisation</u> using <u>music technology</u> (e.g. sequencing).
3) For the other, you have to perform as part of an <u>ensemble</u>. There must be <u>2 or more players</u> in the ensemble, with <u>distinct</u> and <u>separate</u> parts.

COMPOSING

worth 30% of the total marks

1) You compose <u>two pieces</u>. One is based on a <u>composition brief</u>. You'll be given a <u>choice</u> of <u>four composition briefs</u>, which might have a <u>stimulus</u> (e.g. a <u>poem</u>, <u>photo</u> or some <u>notation</u>).
2) Your second composition can be <u>anything you like</u> — it's a <u>free</u> composition.

Err, Miss... Is it too late to change to Physics?

Welcome to the wonderful world of GCSE Music. Breathe in the cool clear air. Listen to the birds. Relax.

Component 1 — Understanding Music

*At the end of the course, you have the joy of a **listening exam**. All **1 hour and 30 minutes** of it.*

The **Exam** Tests All Four **Areas of Study**

1) The listening and understanding music exam is worth 96 marks (40% of your total mark). It's divided into two sections — Section A and Section B.

2) Section A is the listening section — it's worth 68 marks and lasts for one hour. You have to listen to and answer questions on excerpts of music. You'll be told which Area of Study each excerpt is from and how many times it'll be played. You'll be given writing time for each question.

3) You have to answer all 8 questions in this section — they're on unfamiliar pieces from all four Areas of Study (most only need short answers). One question will probably require musical dictation.

4) Section B is the contextual understanding section — it's worth 28 marks and lasts for 30 minutes. You have to answer the first question, which is on the study piece from AoS1 (Mozart's Clarinet Concerto).

5) You then have to answer one of the next three questions — on whichever other AoS study pieces that you've looked at. There aren't any excerpts to listen to in this section — it's all based on your own knowledge. One part of each question needs a longer answer (it's worth 8 marks).

Some Questions are **Multiple Choice**

If you're stuck — guess the answer. There's a chance of getting it right.

Don't mess these up by rushing — read all the options carefully.

What is the texture of this excerpt? Put a cross in the correct box. *[1 mark]*

☐ homophonic ☐ monophonic ☐ contrapuntal ☐ antiphonal

Some Questions Just Need a **Short Answer**

These questions are only worth a few marks so don't waste time writing your answer out in a nice long sentence — just write down one good word for each mark.

Name two instruments playing the theme in this excerpt. *[2 marks]*

For questions worth 3 or 4 marks, you'll have to write a bit more.

They Sometimes Give You an **Outline** of the Music

You'll be given an outline of part of the music called a 'skeleton score'. It will just show part of the music — the melody, rhythm or lyrics, say. The skeleton score will help you with answering the question. You might be asked to fill in the pitch, rhythm or chords of a short section of the music.

Fill in the missing notes in bar 4. The rhythm is given above the stave. *[3 marks]*

Some Questions in **Section B** Need **Longer Answers**

There are a couple of questions where you have to write a longer answer — a few paragraphs of writing. Make sure you cover all the key points of the question in your answer.

Explain how the third movement of Mozart's Clarinet Concerto is typical of the Classical period. *[8 marks]*

Shiver me timbers — 'tis the skeleton score...

Concentrate on answering just a few of the questions each time the music's played — it's less confusing. Have a go at the Practice Exam on p.167 to give you an idea of what it'll be like.

Component 2 — Performing

Pick your pieces carefully and practise till your neighbours beg for mercy.

You Have To Do **Two Performances**

The combined time of both your performances must be at least four minutes.
Your ensemble performance must be at least one minute long.

SOLO PERFORMANCE

You simply play one solo piece of your own choice. It can be a traditional performance,
a DJ performance or a realisation using music technology (if you're using multi-tracking, you must
have a minimum of three tracks, at least one of which must be performed live). Your solo can be
accompanied (if it was written with an accompaniment, you have to perform it with accompaniment).

ENSEMBLE PERFORMANCE

For your ensemble piece, there must be at least two of you playing or singing, and your part can't
be doubled. Like the solo performance, this can be a traditional performance, a DJ performance
(with other DJs or live musicians) or a realisation using music technology. For a multi-tracked
performance, you must perform at least three tracks (one must be live), and there must be one or
more other parts (one has to be live). You have to play a different piece than your solo piece.

You have to hand in the music you've worked from for each performance. This can be
a score, a lead sheet or a recording of the piece made by someone else — a 'guide recording'.
(For music technology performances, you have to hand in an annotation, giving details of how
you produced your piece.) You also have to hand in digital recordings of your performances.

You Get Marks for the **Difficulty** of the **Piece...**

1) It's obvious really — a very simple piece will get fewer marks for difficulty than a complicated piece.
   But there's no point trying to play something that you're not capable of and then messing it up...

2) Choose your pieces carefully — ideally they should be the hardest level that you can
   play well. If you pick something too easy, you'll be throwing away difficulty marks.
   If you pick something too hard, you won't be able to play your best, and you'll lose marks
   for musicality. Get your music teacher or instrument teacher's advice on what to play.

3) If you choose an easy piece, you won't be able to get as many marks for the areas described below.

...And Marks for the **Quality** of Your **Playing**

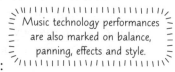
Music technology performances
are also marked on balance,
panning, effects and style.

You need to show off your 'musicality' and technique (how well you play your
instrument, including techniques specific to your instrument). You get marks for:

1) **ACCURACY:** Learn the notes, play them in time and in tune. Most importantly, keep going
   — your performance needs to be fluent. Lots of stopping and starting or slowing down for
   tricky bits will lose you marks. Don't worry about the odd slip, but start off well prepared.
   For DJ and music technology performances, this includes pitch and balance as well.

2) **EXPRESSION AND INTERPRETATION:** Your performance needs to be expressive — to make
   the audience feel something. Pay attention to stuff like dynamics, tempo, mood, articulation
   and phrasing. It's all about how well you communicate — i.e. how you interpret the music.

When you're playing in an ensemble, there are other things that you'll get marks for. Play in time and
in tune with the other players. Really listen to the other parts, so you know when you should be part of
the background and when you should make your part stand out — the ensemble should be balanced.

Practice makes perfect...

No doubt people have been going on at you about practising since you were knee-high to a piccolo.
It gets boring after a while. I expect you know that you need to do lots of practice. So I'll say no more.

Component 3 — Composing

For one composition, you can write whatever you like — but for the other, you have to follow a brief.

You Have to Write **Two Pieces** for **Coursework**

1) The <u>total</u> time for both pieces has to be <u>at least three minutes</u> (you'll <u>lose marks</u> if they're <u>less</u> than three minutes).

2) You <u>don't</u> have to perform your compositions <u>yourself</u> (but you can if you want to).

3) You can compose for <u>any</u> combination of <u>instruments</u>, <u>voices</u> or <u>DJs</u> and can use <u>technology</u> (unless the composition brief tells you otherwise).

4) One piece you write has to follow a <u>composition brief</u>:

   • The composition brief will be given to you by the <u>exam board</u>.
   • There will be <u>four different composition briefs</u> to choose from.
   • You can <u>choose</u> which one you do (though your <u>teacher</u> might suggest which one to pick).
   • The brief might include a <u>stimulus</u> — <u>written words</u> (e.g. a <u>poem</u> or some <u>text</u>), <u>images</u> (e.g. a <u>photo</u> or <u>film clip</u>) or some <u>notation</u> (e.g. a short <u>melody</u> or <u>rhythm</u>).

5) You should be given the composition brief <u>halfway</u> through your GCSE course — by which point, you should have <u>studied</u> the different areas (and looked at the <u>study pieces</u>) in detail.

6) The other piece you write is a <u>free composition</u> — it can be in <u>any style</u> you like.

Each Piece is Marked on **Six** Different **Categories**

Each composition is worth <u>36 marks</u>, based on two different categories (there are up to <u>18 marks</u> available for each category — you need to use <u>at least two</u> different elements to get all 18 marks).

RHYTHM, METRE, TEXTURE, MELODY, STRUCTURE AND FORM:
To get top marks in this category, think about things like <u>changing time signatures</u>, using <u>compound metres</u>, <u>syncopated</u> and <u>dotted</u> rhythms, <u>cross-rhythms</u> or <u>tempo changes</u> (including <u>rubato</u>) — see Section 2. Try using <u>homophonic</u> and <u>polyphonic</u> textures, <u>imitation</u>, <u>canon</u> or <u>antiphony</u>, <u>ostinatos</u> (or <u>riffs</u>), <u>conjunct</u> or <u>disjunct</u> melodies, different <u>ornaments</u> or <u>blue notes</u>. Texture is covered in Section 3 and melody is covered in Section 4. You could use <u>one</u> of the forms covered in Section 4, such as <u>ternary</u>, <u>rondo</u>, <u>theme and variation</u>, <u>ground bass</u>, <u>popular song form</u>, or <u>12-bar blues</u> (see p.130).

HARMONY, TONALITY, TIMBRE, DYNAMICS, PHRASING AND ARTICULATION:
Think about all four types of <u>cadence</u>, using <u>major</u> and <u>minor keys</u>, <u>modes</u>, different types of <u>harmony</u>, <u>changing key</u> (<u>modulation</u>), <u>dissonance</u> or <u>pedal notes</u>. This is all covered in Section 3. You should try and use both <u>solo</u> instruments/voices and <u>groupings</u> of instruments or voices, <u>synthesized</u> or <u>digitally-produced sounds</u>, <u>tremolo</u>, <u>vibrato</u>, <u>reverb</u> or <u>distortion</u> (for appropriate instruments or voices). You should also use a variety of <u>dynamics</u> (including <u>crescendos</u> and <u>diminuendos</u>), as well as a range of phrasing and articulation (e.g. <u>legato</u>, <u>staccato</u>, <u>tenuto</u> or <u>marcato</u>). See p.19-20 for dynamics and articulation and Section 5 for instruments and timbre.

For each composition, you have to produce a <u>programme note</u> — a <u>written report</u> that covers:
• The <u>purpose</u> or <u>intention</u> of the piece (you should specify the <u>audience</u> or <u>occasion</u> you wrote it for).
• The <u>musical elements</u> you chose (e.g. the texture, structure or rhythms you used — anything from the lists above).
• Any <u>equipment</u> you used to compose the piece.

Each programme note should be about 150 words long.

You have to hand in a <u>recording</u> of each composition, as well as a <u>written version</u> and your <u>programme note</u>. There's more information about these on p.7.

Component 3 — Composing

*Well, the **good news** is — the compositions you have to do for GCSE only need to be a total of **3 minutes** long. No one's expecting an opera. Something short will do.*

Here Are Some **General Things** To Think About...

DEVELOPING YOUR MUSICAL IDEAS

Don't just use a good idea once and then forget about it. Build up and develop the good bits — e.g. by changing the rhythm from short notes to long notes or the key from major to minor. See Section 3 for loads more techniques and devices for developing your ideas.

MAKING THE STYLE CONVINCING

Listen to lots of music from the style you're composing in. Make your piece sound like 'the real thing' by using similar musical ideas — e.g. in a Baroque gigue, use a lively tempo, regular beat and a harpsichord.

THE POTENTIAL AND LIMITS OF YOUR RESOURCES

Once you've chosen the instruments, think about all the ways they can make interesting and contrasting sounds — e.g. pizzicato bits for strings. But also remember the limitations — e.g. clarinet players need time to breathe. Think about the highest and lowest notes your chosen instruments can play — there's no point composing a brilliant piece if no one can play it.

One of your pieces will have to meet the composition brief, so there'll be extra things you have to bear in mind to match the brief.

STRUCTURE

Organise your music with a clear, definite structure (there's lots of information on different structures throughout this book). Even if your composition doesn't follow a traditional form, you'll need to make sure it doesn't just ramble on aimlessly.

When You're Composing, Make Plans **Before** You Start

1) Making a musical plan helps to organise your ideas — it's a bit like writing an essay plan. It'll also help when it comes to writing your composing log.

2) Music's got to be organised, or it just sounds like a load of random notes. The most basic bit of organisation is the timing (beats in a bar). The next biggest chunk is the phrasing.

3) The overall shape is called the structure or form. The structure could be the verses and chorus in a pop song, or the movements of a symphony. Composers usually decide on the structure of a piece of music before they get into the detail.

4) It's OK to design your own musical plan, but a lot of people use 'tried and tested' structures like the ones described throughout this book — because they know they'll work.

5) 'Tried and tested' structures are like templates. The general organisation of your ideas is decided for you — you just need to add the details.

6) For the piece that follows the composition brief, it's probably a good idea to use a 'tried and tested' structure as your composition will need to be in a particular style or form.

7) Your plan should include ways to vary the different sections — have a look on the next page for some ideas.

Clarinet players need time to breathe? Amateurs...

So the main thing to take away from this page is 'be organised'. I'm not expecting you to be organised in all aspects of your life, just in your compositions — and planning really helps.

Component 3 — Composing

There are lots of things you need to think about when composing. This is not a complete list (just a few general ideas), but it'll give you a few things to bear in mind.

Most Music Uses **Repetition** Repetition Repetition...

1) Repetition means using a musical idea — a chunk of tune — more than once.

2) Repeating bits is a really good way of giving music shape. A recognisable tune works like a landmark — the audience recognises that tune later in the piece. That's how choruses work.

3) If you're planning your own piece of music, try repeating the best part of the tune.

4) You can even repeat whole sections — in rondo form (see p.93), one section is repeated lots of times.

...and **Contrast**

Repetition is really important — but constant repetition is boring. Good compositions balance repetition with contrast. The aim is to do something different from the repeated bits to add variety. Here are some ways you can vary your compositions:

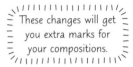
These changes will get you extra marks for your compositions.

PITCH AND TONALITY

You can create contrast by changing the organisation of pitch — e.g. changing the melody from a high register to a low register, and swapping between conjunct and disjunct tunes (see p.54). You can also change the tonality by modulating between major and minor keys.

TEMPO AND RHYTHM

Changing speed from fast to slow (or vice versa) is a good way of creating contrast. You can also change the rhythms — try a mix of dotted and straight rhythms, or long and short notes. You can change the articulation too — try legato, staccato, slurs and accents to vary your piece.

DYNAMICS

Changes in dynamics (loud to soft and vice versa, and crescendos and diminuendos) will instantly create contrast.

TEXTURE

Changing between a thin, monophonic texture to a thicker homophonic or polyphonic texture (see p.45) will create contrast.

Decide How To **Hand In** Your Work

For each piece, you give in three things — a written version, a recording (though you won't be marked on the quality of the recording, just the composition) and a programme note. There are a few options for how you present your written version.

1) The **WRITTEN VERSION** can be either a score (either handwritten or computer generated), a lead sheet (e.g. a vocal line with accompanying chords) or a written account (a guide to what the listener should hear in the piece).

2) Give as much information as possible. Dynamics, tempo, expression and articulation will all improve your mark. There should be enough detail for someone else to be able to recreate your piece.

The **RECORDING** must be saved digitally.

Even though you don't get marks for the quality of the recording, good recordings are easier to mark. It's also in your best interests to produce an accurate one.

The **PROGRAMME NOTE** is a written report. It should be about 150 words long.

The Basics

*These two pages give the **essential basics** you'll need to get through GCSE Music.*
Make sure you know everything here before you go on into the rest of the book.

❸ TWO LINES OF MUSIC

The top line of music has got a tune — it's the melody. The bottom line is the accompaniment.

❶ CLEF

These symbols at the start of a line tell you how high or low to play the notes. All the different clefs are covered on page 10.

❷ NOTE

Each note is shown by a separate oval. The symbol also tells you how long or short the note is. The symbols are shown on page 16.

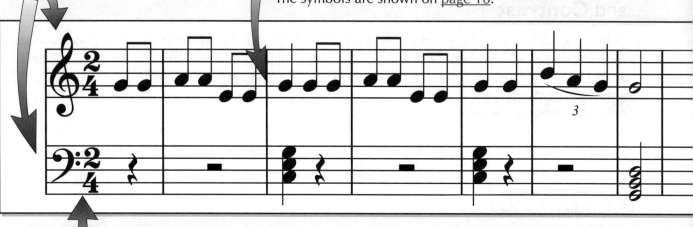

❼ TIME SIGNATURE

The numbers tell you about the beats in a bar. Time signatures are covered on page 12.

❾ KEY SIGNATURE

There are no flats or sharps, so this piece is in the key of C. Keys and scales are covered in Section Three.

❽ BEATS

Each bar has the same number of beats. Beats, bars and rhythm are covered on pages 13, 16 & 17.

THE PIANO KEYBOARD

Some of the diagrams in this book make more sense if you know what's what on a piano keyboard.
The white keys play natural notes.

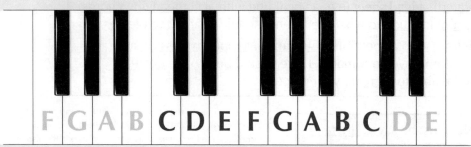

Note: The white notes from C to C make the scale of C major (p.24).

The black keys play SHARPS and FLATS. Sharps and flats are covered on page 11.
The C in the middle of a piano keyboard is known as MIDDLE C.

The Basics

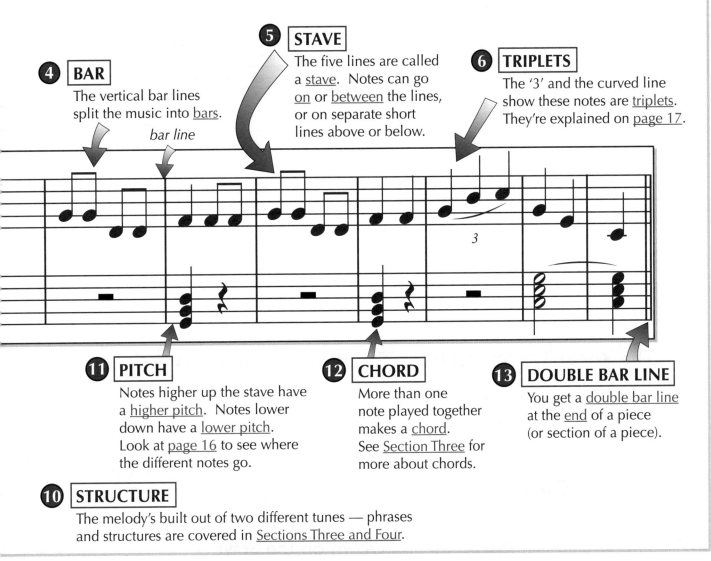

5 STAVE
The five lines are called a stave. Notes can go on or between the lines, or on separate short lines above or below.

4 BAR
The vertical bar lines split the music into bars.

bar line

6 TRIPLETS
The '3' and the curved line show these notes are triplets. They're explained on page 17.

11 PITCH
Notes higher up the stave have a higher pitch. Notes lower down have a lower pitch. Look at page 16 to see where the different notes go.

12 CHORD
More than one note played together makes a chord. See Section Three for more about chords.

13 DOUBLE BAR LINE
You get a double bar line at the end of a piece (or section of a piece).

10 STRUCTURE
The melody's built out of two different tunes — phrases and structures are covered in Sections Three and Four.

TONES AND SEMITONES

Tones and semitones are the gaps between notes.

On a piano, a semitone is the gap between any key, black or white, and its immediate neighbour.

The gap from any key to a key two semitone steps above or below is called a tone.

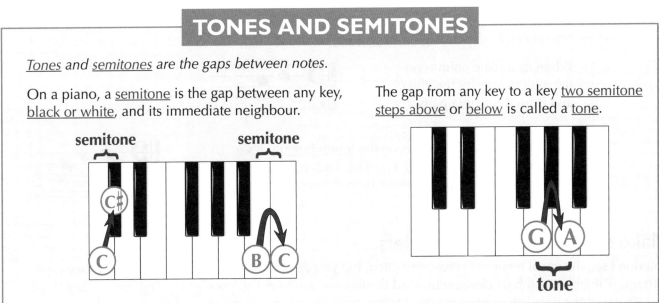

Clefs

*Clefs are the **curly symbols** that you find right at the **start** of most written music. The treble clef is used for high-pitched music. The bass and alto clefs are used for lower-pitched music.*

The **Treble** Clef is the **Most Common** Clef

1) The treble clef is used for <u>higher-pitched melody instruments</u>, e.g. flute, oboe, clarinet, violin, trumpet and horn.

2) Music for <u>soprano</u> and <u>alto</u> voices is written on the treble clef, too.

3) The sign always goes in the same place on the stave, with the curly bit wrapped around the line for the <u>G above middle C</u>.

MIDDLE C

The **Bass** Clef is used for **Low-pitched Instruments**

1) The bass clef is used for <u>lower-pitched instruments</u> like the tuba, trombone, bassoon, cello and double bass.

2) It's also used for <u>bass voices</u>.

3) The big blob always goes on the line for the <u>F below middle C</u>, and the two little dots go either side of the line.

MIDDLE C

The **Vocal Tenor** Clef is for **Tenor** Voices and **Lead Guitar**

MIDDLE C

Here's the 8.

1) Each line and gap in the vocal tenor clef stands for exactly the same note as it does in the <u>treble clef</u>, BUT that little '<u>8</u>' underneath means that the notes are played <u>one octave lower</u>.

2) It's used by <u>tenor voices</u> and <u>lead guitar</u> parts.

The **C** Clef can **Move** Up and Down on the Stave

The C clef always has its <u>middle point</u> on <u>middle C</u>. It can be used as two different clefs, depending on its <u>position</u> on the stave.

1) When its middle point is on the <u>middle line</u>, it's the <u>alto clef</u> and is used for <u>viola</u> parts.

MIDDLE C

2) When the middle point is on the <u>fourth line up</u>, it's called the <u>tenor clef</u>, which is used for the <u>higher notes</u> in <u>bass instruments</u> like trombones, bassoons and cellos.

MIDDLE C

Make sure you know your clefs...

You don't see the vocal tenor or C clefs very often, but you've got to know what they are when they <u>do</u> turn up. The treble and bass clefs are used all the time — aim to get so good at reading and writing them that it's easier than English. The only way is to practise. The notes are written in full on page 16.

Sharps, Flats and Naturals

*On a piano, **natural** notes are the **white** ones. **Sharps** are the **black** notes to the **right** of the white notes.*
***Flats** are the blacks to the **left** of the whites. So each black is both sharp **and** flat.*

♯ A **Sharp** Makes a Note One Step **Higher**

1) A sharp sign next to a note tells you to play it <u>one semitone higher</u>.

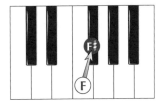

> *When you're writing on the stave, put sharps, flats and naturals before the note they affect. If you're writing text, put them afterwards — F♯.*

2) A <u>double sharp</u> — 🗙 — makes a note <u>two semitones higher</u>. If you see C🗙 you play <u>D</u> — it's the <u>same note</u> going by a different name. The fancy name for notes that sound the same but have different names is <u>enharmonic equivalents</u>.

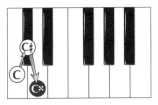

♭ A **Flat** Makes a Note One Step **Lower**

1) A flat symbol next to a note means you have to play it <u>one semitone lower</u>.

2) A <u>double flat</u> — ♭♭ — makes a note two semitones (a tone) lower.

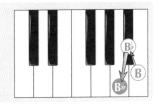

The **Key Signature** is Shown with Sharps or Flats

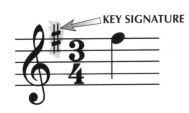

KEY SIGNATURE

1) Sharps or flats written at the <u>start</u> of a piece, straight after the clef, tell you the <u>key signature</u>.

> *There's more about key signatures on p.24-26.*

2) The key signature makes notes sharp or flat <u>all the way through</u> a piece of music.

3) Sharps and flats that you see by individual notes — but not in the key signature — are called <u>accidentals</u>. Once an accidental has appeared in a bar, it applies to all notes of the same pitch for the rest of the bar, unless it's cancelled out by a <u>natural sign</u>...

> *This key signature's got one sharp — on the F line. You have to play every F in the piece as an F♯.*

♮ A **Natural** Sign **Cancels** a Sharp or Flat

A <u>natural</u> sign before a note <u>cancels</u> the <u>effect of a sharp or flat</u> sign from earlier in the bar or from a key signature. You <u>never</u> see natural signs in the key signature, only in the music, as accidentals.

This stuff should all come naturally in no time...

Double sharps and flats are uncommon and quite peculiar — it doesn't seem that <u>logical</u> to write C🗙 when you could write D, but sometimes you just have to, I'm afraid. It all depends what key you're in.

Time Signatures

*Those **two numbers** at the beginning of a piece of music tell you **how many beats** there are in a bar and **how long** they are. Whatever you're playing, don't ignore them.*

Music has a **Regular Beat**

1) You can tap your foot along to the <u>beat</u> of any piece of music, as long as it hasn't got a horribly complicated rhythm. The beat is also called the <u>pulse</u>.

2) If you listen a bit harder, you can hear that some beats are <u>stronger</u> than others.

3) The strong beats come at <u>regular intervals</u> — usually every <u>2</u>, <u>3</u> or <u>4</u> beats.

4) The strong beat is the <u>first</u> beat of each <u>bar</u>. If the strong beat comes every 3 beats, then the piece of music you're listening to has <u>three beats</u> in a bar.

The **Time Signature** Shows **How Many** Beats are in a Bar

1) There's always a <u>time signature</u> at the beginning of a piece of music.

2) It goes to the <u>right</u> of the clef and the key signature.

3) It's written using <u>two numbers</u>.

TOP NUMBER
goes between the middle line and the top line

BOTTOM NUMBER
goes between the middle line and the bottom line

The <u>top number</u> tells you <u>how many beats</u> there are in each bar, e.g. a '2' means two beats in a bar, a '3' means three beats in a bar and so on.

The <u>bottom number</u> tells you <u>how long</u> each beat is (see <u>page 16</u> for the names of the different notes).

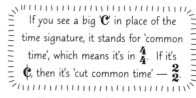

If you see a big '**C**' in place of the time signature, it stands for 'common time', which means it's in $\frac{4}{4}$. If it's **¢**, then it's 'cut common time' — $\frac{2}{2}$.

A <u>2</u> at the bottom means each beat is <u>1 minim</u> long.

$2 = \textsignificant{𝅗𝅥}$

A <u>4</u> at the bottom means each beat is <u>1 crotchet</u> long.

$4 = ♩$

An <u>8</u> at the bottom means each beat is <u>1 quaver</u> long.

$8 = ♪$

A <u>16</u> at the bottom means each beat is <u>1 semiquaver</u> long.

$16 = ♬$

If the **Beat Changes**, the **Time Signature Changes**

1) The time signature usually <u>stays the same</u> all the way through a piece of music. If it does, it's written just <u>once</u>, at the beginning.

2) Sometimes the beat <u>changes</u> during a piece. If it does, the new time signature's written in the bar where it <u>changes</u>.

3) Not all pieces start on the first beat of the bar — some start on an <u>unaccented beat</u> called an <u>anacrusis</u> (or <u>upbeat</u>).

You can practise listening for the beat any time...

Every time you listen to music, practise <u>listening for the beat</u> and work out the time signature.

Counting the Beat

*Counting the beat's fairly easy, but it's a crucial skill. It can help you work out how to **play** a new piece and how to **write a tune down** when you've only heard it played aloud or in your head.*

In **Simple Time** You Count **All the Beats**

1) <u>Simple</u> time signatures have <u>2</u>, <u>3</u> or <u>4</u> as their <u>top</u> number.

2) In simple time, if you're counting to the music, you count <u>every beat</u>.
For $\frac{4}{4}$ you'd count, "<u>One, two, three, four</u>." For $\frac{3}{2}$, you'd count, "<u>One, two, three</u>."

3) If you want to count out the rhythm of <u>smaller notes</u> as well as the beats, try using "<u>and</u>", "<u>eye</u>" and "<u>a</u>" — it seems to make the rhythm come out just right.

> Count "<u>One and two and</u>" for quavers, and "<u>One eye and a</u>" for semiquavers.

4) Any shorter notes are usually a <u>half</u>, a <u>quarter</u>, an <u>eighth</u> or a <u>sixteenth</u> of the main beat.

In **Compound Time** Only Count the **Big Beats**

1) Compound time signatures have <u>6</u>, <u>9</u> or <u>12</u> as their <u>top</u> number — you can always divide the top number by <u>three</u>.

2) If the music is fairly fast, it's too <u>awkward</u> to count to nine or twelve for every bar. You end up with so many little beats that the rhythm sounds <u>mushy</u>.

3) To make the rhythm <u>clear</u>, you can just count the <u>main beats</u>:

4) If you were counting out the main beats in $\frac{6}{8}$, you'd count "One, two". $\frac{9}{8}$ would go "One, two, three".

5) To count the <u>in-between notes</u>, use "<u>&</u>" and "<u>a</u>".

6) Shorter notes are made by dividing by three — so they're <u>thirds</u>, <u>sixths</u>, <u>twelfths</u>, etc. of the main beat.

7) Music in compound time <u>sounds different</u> from music in simple time because the beat is divided into threes — <u>practise</u> spotting the difference.

The **Patterns** the Beats Make are Called the **Metre**

Depending on the time signature, the beats make different <u>patterns</u>.
The pattern is known as the <u>metre</u>. Metre can be:

Regular

The strong beats make the <u>same pattern</u> all the way through.
<u>two</u> beats per bar = <u>duple</u> metre
<u>three</u> beats per bar = <u>triple</u> metre
<u>four</u> beats per bar = <u>quadruple</u> metre

Irregular

There could be <u>five</u> beats in a bar grouped in twos and threes, or <u>seven</u> beats in a bar grouped in threes and twos or fours.

Free

Music with <u>no particular metre</u>. This one's fairly unusual.

> You can describe a time signature based on its beat and metre — e.g. a piece in $\frac{4}{4}$ is in simple quadruple time, and a piece in $\frac{6}{8}$ is in compound duple time.

One and a, two and a, three and a, four and a...

Counting the beat's not really that hard. The tricky bit on this page is the stuff about <u>metre</u>.
You could get asked about the metre of a piece in your listening exam, so learn <u>all three sorts</u>.

Rhythms and Metres

*When **different rhythms** are played at the **same time**, some of them **fit together** well, but some of them **don't**. Rhythms that **don't fit** can create interesting and crazy **effects**.*

Hemiola Gives the Impression of a Different Metre

1) <u>Hemiola</u> is a <u>rhythmic device</u> used to create <u>contrast</u> within a piece. Music <u>written</u> in <u>duple</u> metre (see p.13) is temporarily <u>accented</u> to make it <u>feel</u> like it's in <u>triple</u> metre, or <u>vice versa</u>.

2) In $\frac{6}{8}$ time there are <u>two beats</u> in a bar, each the length of a dotted crotchet. <u>Hemiola</u> is created by playing a bar of <u>three crotchets</u>, giving the impression of $\frac{3}{4}$ time instead.

3) In $\frac{3}{4}$ time, <u>hemiola</u> is created by <u>accenting every other beat</u> for <u>two bars</u>. This gives the impression of <u>three bars</u> of $\frac{2}{4}$ time, rather than two bars of $\frac{3}{4}$.

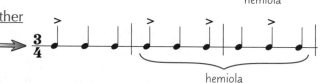

Different Rhythms Can be Played at the Same Time

1) When two or more <u>contrasting rhythms</u> are played at the <u>same time</u>, the music is <u>polyrhythmic</u>. A polyrhythm made up of just <u>two</u> different rhythms is known as a <u>bi-rhythm</u>. Lots of <u>African</u> music is polyrhythmic — see p.133.

2) <u>Polyrhythms</u> can be created by a number of performers playing <u>different instruments</u>. A drummer can also create polyrhythms by playing a <u>different rhythm</u> with <u>each hand</u>.

- The rhythms will often have <u>accents</u> in different places. <u>Hemiola</u> might be used in one or more parts, giving the impression of instruments playing in <u>different time signatures</u> (this is known as <u>vertical hemiola</u>).

- Another polyrhythmic device is to use <u>triplets</u> against <u>standard notes</u>, e.g. triplet quavers played at the same time as two normal quavers.

- <u>Cross-rhythm</u> occurs when the <u>accents</u> are 'out of sync' over a <u>number of bars</u>. This can be used to create <u>tension</u> in the music.

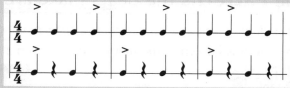

Drum Fills are Little Drum Solos

1) <u>Drum fills</u> are fairly <u>short</u> — they often only last for a <u>few beats</u>.
2) Fills are normally used to <u>build</u> the music up, or to <u>change</u> between <u>sections</u>.
3) They give the drummer a (very short) chance to <u>show off</u>.
4) Most <u>rock</u>, <u>pop</u> and <u>jazz</u> pieces will have drum fills in them.

Rhythms make me very cross...

Listen to 'Skyfall' by Adele and see if you can pick out the drum fills.

Warm-up and Exam Questions

Now have a crack at some questions to see how much you've learnt so far.

Warm-up Questions

1) Draw the symbols for a treble clef, bass clef, vocal tenor clef and C alto clef.

2) Explain what a sharp sign, a flat sign and a natural sign do.

3) Draw a time signature describing three minim beats per bar.

4) How many beats are there per bar if the time signature is $\frac{9}{8}$?

5) What's the difference between simple and compound time?

6) Name the three main types of metre.

Exam Question

This is the type of question you could get in your listening test. To access the tracks for the listening questions, go to cgpbooks.co.uk/extras and use your Online Edition code to log in.
Use this question to test your understanding of the last few pages and as practice for the real thing.

Play the following excerpt **four** times. Leave a short pause between each playing of the excerpt.

It's a good idea to read the whole question through before you listen to the track.

a) Fill in the **8 missing notes** from the vocal part, using the rhythm supplied.

Listen carefully for the direction of the notes — this really isn't as difficult as it seems at first.

[8 marks]

b) Draw a circle around the key signature.

[1 mark]

c) Fill in the time signature.

[1 mark]

d) Here is another part of the same excerpt.

Label the following features:

- the note A♯
- two notes a tone apart
- two notes a semitone apart

[3 marks]

Notes and Rests

*Let's face it, you'd be a bit lost reading music if you didn't know what all those funny little dots and squiggles meant. Make sure you know all this stuff **better than the alphabet**.*

The **Symbols** Tell You **How Long** Notes and Rests Are

1) <u>Notes</u> tell you how many beats to hold a <u>sound</u> for.

2) <u>Rests</u> tell you how many beats to hold a <u>silence</u> for.

3) Notes and rests have <u>names</u>, depending on how long they are.
   Two beats is a <u>minim</u> note or rest. A half-beat is a <u>quaver</u> note or rest.

The length of a note or rest is also called its duration.

Learn this table now — you need to know exactly how to <u>write</u> these out, and how to <u>play</u> them.

NAME OF NOTE	NUMBER OF CROTCHET BEATS	NOTE SYMBOL	REST SYMBOL
semibreve	**4**	o	—
minim	**2**	♩	—
crotchet	**1**	♩	𝄽
quaver	**½**	♪ or ♫ *if there are 2 or more*	𝄾
semiquaver	**¼**	♬ or ♬ *if there are 2 or more*	𝄿

The **Position** of the Note Tells You the **Pitch**

<u>Just in case</u> you don't know, this is where the notes go in the <u>bass</u> and <u>treble</u> clefs:

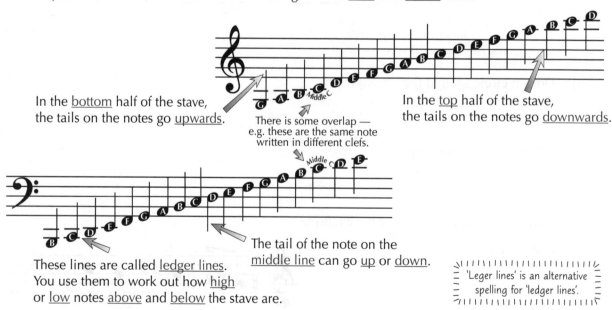

In the <u>bottom</u> half of the stave, the tails on the notes go <u>upwards</u>.

There is some overlap — e.g. these are the same note written in different clefs.

In the <u>top</u> half of the stave, the tails on the notes go <u>downwards</u>.

The tail of the note on the <u>middle line</u> can go <u>up</u> or <u>down</u>.

These lines are called <u>ledger lines</u>. You use them to work out how <u>high</u> or <u>low</u> notes <u>above</u> and <u>below</u> the stave are.

'Leger lines' is an alternative spelling for 'ledger lines'.

There's no excuse for not knowing this stuff...

Those of you who were playing the church organ before you could crawl might be feeling a bit like you know this stuff already and you don't need to be told. It's still worth <u>checking over</u> though, I reckon.

Dots, Ties and Triplets

*You can only get so far with the note lengths from **page 16**. If you use **dot**, **tie** and **triplet** symbols you can create more complicated, interesting and sophisticated rhythms.*

A **Dot** After a Note or Rest Makes It **Longer**

1) A dot just <u>to the right</u> of a note or rest makes it <u>half as long again</u>.

$$\text{♩} = \mathbf{1}\ \textbf{beat} \quad \xrightarrow[1 + ½ = 1½]{1 ÷ 2 = ½} \quad \text{♩.} = \mathbf{1½}\ \textbf{beats} \qquad \text{♩} = \mathbf{2}\ \textbf{beats} \quad \xrightarrow[2 + 1 = 3]{2 ÷ 2 = 1} \quad \text{♩.} = \mathbf{3}\ \textbf{beats}$$

2) A <u>second</u> dot adds on another <u>quarter</u> of the original note length.

$$\text{♩..} = \mathbf{1¾}\ \textbf{beats} \qquad \text{♩..} = \mathbf{3½}\ \textbf{beats}$$

Count these really carefully when you're playing — don't just "add a bit on".

3) In <u>dotted quaver rhythms</u>, you have a <u>dotted quaver</u> (worth ½ + ¼ = ¾ of a beat) followed by a <u>semiquaver</u> (worth ¼ of a beat). Dotted quaver rhythms are common in <u>marches</u>. They're usually written like this:

¾ beat   ¼ beat

4) In a <u>Scotch snap</u>, the rhythm is the <u>other way round</u> — the <u>semiquaver</u> is on the <u>beat</u> (and <u>accented</u>), followed by the <u>dotted quaver</u>, like this: Scotch snaps are used in <u>Scottish music</u> (e.g. <u>dances</u>) — hence the name.

A **Tie Joins Two Notes** Together

1) A tie is a <u>curved line</u> joining two notes of the <u>same pitch</u> together.

2) It turns them into <u>one note</u>.

3) Ties are often used to make a long note that goes over the <u>end of a bar</u>.

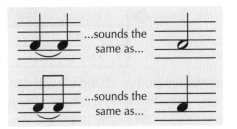

...sounds the same as...

...sounds the same as...

Ties are not the same as slurs. See page 19.

A **Triplet** is **Three Notes** Played in the Time of **Two**

1) A triplet is <u>three</u> notes, all the <u>same length</u>, squeezed into the time of <u>two</u>.

2) Triplets are marked with a '<u>3</u>' above or below the <u>middle</u> of the three notes. Sometimes there's a <u>square</u> bracket or a <u>curved</u> line as well as the three.

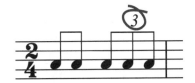

3) The notes don't all have to be <u>played</u> — part of a triplet can be <u>rests</u>.

Stick with it, even the tricky bits...

Triplets look so straightforward on the page, but they can be tricky to get just right. The only way to make sure you're playing them properly is to practise with a metronome. Have a go right now.

Tempo and Mood

*Composers don't just tell you the notes — they tell you **how fast** to play them, and what the **atmosphere** of the piece should be too. You need to understand all the different **terms** they use.*

The **Tempo** is the **Speed** of the Music

Tempo is Italian for "time". In a lot of music the instructions for how fast to play are written in Italian too. Here are the words you're most likely to come across:

> 60 beats a minute means each crotchet lasts one second. 120 beats a minute means each crotchet lasts half a second. And so on...

Italian word	What it means	Beats per minute
largo	broad and slow	40-60
larghetto	still broad, not so slow	60-66
adagio	bit faster than largo	66-76
andante	walking pace	76-108
moderato	moderate speed	108-120
allegro	quick and lively	120-168
vivace	very lively — quicker than allegro	168-180
presto	really fast	180-200

This is where you put the <u>tempo</u> and <u>beats per minute</u> on the stave. ♩ = 112 means there are 112 crotchet beats per minute. This is called a <u>metronome marking</u>.

These words tell you how to <u>vary</u> the speed. The <u>words</u> go <u>underneath</u> the stave. The <u>pause</u> symbol goes <u>above</u>.

> Rubato means 'robbed time' — you can slow some bits down and speed others up.

Italian word	Abbreviation	What it means
accelerando	accel.	speeding up
rallentando	rall.	slowing down
ritenuto	rit.	holding back the pace
allargando	allarg.	slowing down, getting a bit broader
rubato	rub.	can be flexible with pace of music
⌒		pause — longer than a whole beat
a tempo		back to the original pace

To give the <u>impression</u> that the tempo has changed (without actually changing it), composers can use <u>augmentation</u> or <u>diminution</u>. Augmentation is where note lengths are <u>increased</u> in a melody (e.g. by <u>doubling</u> the length of every note — so a <u>crotchet</u> becomes a <u>minim</u>). This has the effect of making the music sound <u>slower</u>. Diminution is the <u>opposite</u> — note lengths are <u>shortened</u>, so the music sounds <u>faster</u>.

Mood is the **Overall** Feel of a Piece

The <u>mood</u> of a piece is usually described in Italian too.

> Sometimes parts are marked obbligato, which means they are <u>really important</u> and can't be missed out (obbligato means 'obligatory').

Italian word	What it means
agitato	agitated
alla marcia	in a march style
amoroso	loving
calmato	calm
dolce	sweetly
energico	energetic

Italian word	What it means
giocoso	playful, humorous
grandioso	grandly
pesante	heavy
risoluto	strong, confident, bold
sospirando	sighing
trionfale	triumphant

To describe the <u>overall mood</u> put the word at the beginning of the piece.

To describe a <u>change of mood</u> write the word under the stave.

Yes, you do have to learn it all — even the Italian bits...

When you're learning this page, start with words that sound a bit like English — they're easy.

Dynamics and Articulation

*More ways for composers to tell players **exactly** how they want their music to sound...*

Dynamic Markings Tell You How Loud or Quietly to Play

Music that was all played at the <u>same volume</u> would be pretty dull.
To get a <u>variety</u> of different volumes you can use these symbols:

Symbol	Stands for	What it means
pp	pianissimo	very quiet
p	piano	quiet
mp	mezzopiano	fairly quiet
mf	mezzoforte	fairly loud
f	forte	loud
ff	fortissimo	very loud
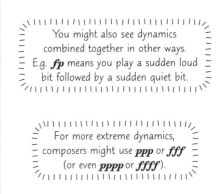 crescendo	crescendo	getting louder
diminuendo	diminuendo	getting quieter

You might also see dynamics combined together in other ways. E.g. *fp* means you play a sudden loud bit followed by a sudden quiet bit.

For more extreme dynamics, composers might use *ppp* or *fff* (or even *pppp* or *ffff*).

The markings go <u>underneath</u> the stave. → *p*

Crescendos and diminuendos are sometimes called <u>hairpins</u> when they're written like this.

Articulation Tells You How Much to Separate the Notes

In theory all the notes of a bar should add up to one <u>continuous</u> sound — but actually there are <u>tiny gaps</u> between them. If you <u>exaggerate</u> the gaps you get a <u>staccato</u> effect. If you smooth the gaps out, the notes sound <u>slurred</u>.

STACCATO  All the dotted notes are played slightly short.

SLUR  All the notes below or above the slur are played smoothly, with no breaks between.

 <u>Tenuto</u> marks (<u>lines</u> above or below a note) tell you that a note should be held for its <u>full length</u>, or even played slightly <u>longer</u>.

If the articulation goes <u>all the way through</u> a piece, there's an overall instruction at the <u>beginning</u>.
If this piece was marked <u>legato</u> you would have to play smoothly all the way through.

Staccato

Nothing to do with articulated lorries then...

Don't just learn the symbols, learn what they're <u>called</u> too — it'll sound far more impressive if you write about the "dynamics" and "articulation" in your listening exam rather than "loudness and quietness".

More Instructions

*Once a composer has told you how **fast** and how **loud** to play and how to **articulate** it, they sometimes put in **extra instructions**. Things like **accents**, **sforzandos** and **bends** make the music more **interesting**.*

An **Accent Emphasises** a Note

1) An <u>accent</u> is a type of articulation that tells you to <u>emphasise</u> (or <u>stress</u>) a note.

2) On a <u>wind</u> instrument, this is often done by <u>tonguing</u> a note <u>harder</u> than normal.

3) Accents are usually written like this **>** or like this **∧**.

4) If a whole <u>section</u> should be accented, it can be marked '<u>*marcato*</u>' (which means 'marked').

5) A <u>sforzando</u> is a <u>strongly accented</u> note. It's shown by writing *sfz* or *sf* underneath the note.

6) A sforzando is often a <u>sudden</u> accent — e.g. a <u>very loud</u> note in a <u>quiet section</u> of a piece. This makes the music more <u>dramatic</u>.

A **Glissando** is a **Slide** Between Notes

1) A <u>glissando</u> is a <u>slide</u> from one note to another. Usually you're <u>told</u> which notes to <u>start</u> and <u>finish</u> on.

2) A glissando can be played <u>effectively</u> on a <u>violin</u> (or other <u>string</u> instrument), <u>piano</u>, <u>harp</u>, <u>xylophone</u> (or similar instrument), <u>timpani</u> and <u>trombone</u>. Other instruments can play them too, but they often <u>won't</u> sound as <u>good</u>.

3) On some instruments (e.g. piano, harp and xylophone), <u>every note</u> is played in the glissando. Think about it — if you were to play a glissando on a xylophone, you'd run your beater over every note, so they'd all be played.

A portamento is similar to a glissando — it's more common in singing and on string instruments.

4) On other instruments, like the trombone and strings, the notes you hear <u>aren't fixed notes</u> — the glissando covers all the <u>tiny differences</u> in pitch between the two notes. For example, you <u>can't</u> pick out <u>individual notes</u> in a glissando on the trombone.

5) A glissando can be shown by writing *gliss.* underneath the stave, or by putting a <u>line</u> between <u>two notes</u>.

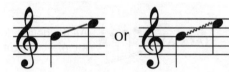

Notes can be **Bent**

1) A <u>bend</u> (or <u>bent note</u>) changes the <u>pitch</u> of the note slightly — it sounds a bit like a <u>wobble</u>.

2) They're often played by starting just <u>above</u> or <u>below</u> the note then <u>bending</u> to it.

3) Bends are often used in <u>jazz music</u>.

4) Bent notes can be played on <u>most</u> instruments — including <u>guitars</u>, <u>trumpets</u>, <u>trombones</u> and <u>harmonicas</u>. <u>Singers</u> can bend notes too.

Roundabouts, swings, climbing frames, glissandi...

All the things on this page are little <u>extras</u> composers can add to their music to make it more <u>interesting</u> — you could try adding some to your compositions too. I do love a good sforzando.

Warm-up and Exam Questions

Get your brain going with these warm-up questions before tackling the exam question below.

Warm-up Questions

1) Draw a 4-beat note, and write down its full name.

2) Draw a 4-beat rest.

3) Name the following notes and give the time value of each of them.

4) Explain the difference between a tie and a slur.

5) Look at the tempo words below. Write them out in order, fastest first.

   Andante   **Largo**   **Presto**   **Moderato**   **Allegro**

Exam Question

Here's another exam-style question for you to try.

Play the following excerpt **three** times. Leave a short pause between each playing of the excerpt.

Track 2

a) Listen to the rhythm of the opening melody.
   Tick one feature that matches what you hear.

   Staccato notes   ☐

   Triplets   ☐

   Dotted notes   ☐

   [1 mark]

   Turn over

Exam Question

b)   Which word best describes the tempo of this piece of music? Underline your answer.

largo   adagio   andante   allegro

[1 mark]

c)   Which word describes the dynamic at the opening? Underline your answer.

pianissimo   piano   forte   fortissimo

[1 mark]

d)   Which of the following describes the mood of this excerpt? Tick the box.

agitato   ☐

dolce   ☐

energico   ☐

pesante   ☐

[1 mark]

Revision Summary for Section Two

That's it for <u>Section Two</u> — better test yourself to find out <u>what you've learned</u>.

- Try these questions and <u>tick off each one</u> when you <u>get it right</u>.
- When you've done <u>all the questions</u> for a topic and are <u>completely happy</u> with it, tick off the topic.

The Basics (p.8-11) ☐

1) Draw a stave with a bass clef at the beginning.
2) Which voices read music from the treble clef?
3) Name two instruments that read music from the bass clef.
4) What's the difference between the symbol for a treble clef and the symbol for the vocal tenor clef?
5) Where does middle C go on a vocal tenor clef?
6) Draw staves showing the C clef in both positions and write the correct name by each one.
7) Draw a sharp sign, a flat sign and a natural sign.
8) What does a sharp do to a note?
9) What does a flat do to a note?
10) Draw each of these signs and explain what you do if you see them by a note:
   a) a double sharp   b) a double flat
11) Draw a treble clef stave and add a key signature with one sharp.
12) What do you call a sharp, flat or natural sign when it's in the music but not in the key signature?

Time Signatures and Rhythms (p.12-14) ☐

13) What do you call the two numbers at the start of a piece of music?
14) What does the top number tell you about the beats?
15) What does the bottom number tell you about the beats?
16) When a time signature changes in a piece of music, where's the new one written?
17) What's the difference between simple and compound time?
18) What's the difference between regular and irregular metre?
19) What is meant by a cross-rhythm?

Types of Notes and Rests (p.16-17) ☐

20) Draw the symbol for each of the following notes and write down how many crotchet beats it lasts:
   a) semibreve   b) semiquaver   c) crotchet   d) quaver   e) minim
21) What does a dot immediately after a note or rest do?
22) What's the time value of:
   a) a dotted crotchet   b) a dotted minim   c) a dotted semibreve   d) a double dotted minim?
23) What does a 'tie' do?
24) How much time, in crotchet beats, does a crotchet triplet take up?

Musical Instructions (p.18-20) ☐

25) Where do you put the tempo marking on a stave?
26) Which is slower, *allegro* or *moderato*?
27) Where would you write the word *agitato* on the stave?
28) How does a composer show on the written music that the notes should be played smoothly?
29) How are accents usually indicated in a piece of music?
30) What's a glissando?

Major Scales

*There are two main types of scales — **major** and **minor**. Once you've got the hang of how scales are put together, you should find keys and chords start to make a lot more sense.*

Ordinary Scales have **Eight Notes**

1) An ordinary major (or minor) scale has 8 notes, starting and ending on notes of the same name, e.g. C major goes C, D, E, F, G, A, B, C.

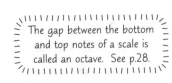

The gap between the bottom and top notes of a scale is called an octave. See p.28.

2) Each of the eight notes has a name.

1st note	2nd note	3rd note	4th note	5th note	6th note	7th note	8th note
tonic	supertonic	mediant	subdominant	dominant	submediant	leading note	tonic
I	II	III	IV	V	VI	VII	VIII

3) You can just use the numbers or the Roman numerals to name the notes too.

Major Scales Sound **Bright** and Cheery

Whatever note they start on, all major scales sound similar, because they all follow the same pattern. This pattern is a set order of tone and semitone gaps between the notes:

I tone → II tone → III semitone → IV tone → V tone → VI tone → VII semitone → VIII

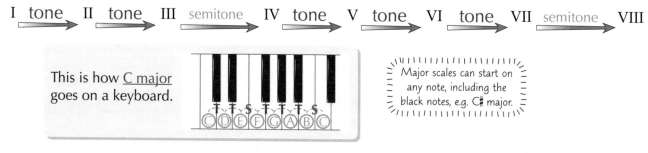

This is how C major goes on a keyboard.

Major scales can start on any note, including the black notes, e.g. C♯ major.

All Major Scales Except C have **One or More Black Notes**

C major is the only major scale with no black notes.
All the others need at least one black note to stick to the 'tone-semitone' pattern.

1) G major scale — you have to change F to F♯ to make the notes fit the major scale pattern.

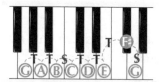

2) F major scale — you have to change B to B♭ to make the pattern right.

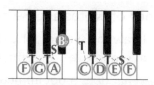

The **Set of Notes** in a **Scale** is Called a **Key**

The key signature goes between the clef and the time signature.

1) The key tells you what sharps and flats there are (if any).

2) Most music sticks to one key. To show what key it's in, all the sharp or flat signs from the scale are written on the beginning of every stave of the piece. This is called the key signature.

3) A key signature can have sharps or flats but NEVER both.

4) If a piece changes key, it's called a modulation — see p.44.

G major's got one sharp note — F♯. You put a sharp symbol on the F line.

Scales — dull but important...

Try playing some major scales starting on different notes. Even if you don't "know" them, you should be able to work out what the notes are, using the tone-semitone pattern and the sound. Give it a go.

Minor Scales

*Minor scales have fixed patterns too. There are **three** different kinds you need to know.*

Minor Scales All Sound a Bit Mournful

Minor scales sound <u>completely different</u> from major scales, because they've got a different tone-semitone pattern. There are <u>three</u> types of minor scale, and all of them sound a bit <u>mournful</u>.

1) The **Natural Minor** has the **Same Notes** as the **Relative Major**

These are easy. Start from the <u>sixth</u> note of any major scale. Carry on up to the same note an octave higher. You're playing a <u>natural minor scale</u>.

The sixth note of <u>C major</u> is <u>A</u>. If you play from <u>A to A</u> using the notes of C major, you're playing <u>A natural minor</u> (usually just called '<u>A minor</u>').

Pairs of keys like <u>A minor and C major</u> are called "<u>relative</u>" keys.
A minor is the <u>relative minor</u> of C major.
C major is the <u>relative major</u> of A minor.

<u>All the notes</u> in a natural minor are <u>exactly the same</u> as the ones in the <u>relative major</u>. The <u>key signature's</u> exactly the same too.

2) The **Harmonic Minor** has **One Accidental**

1) The <u>harmonic minor</u> has the same notes as the relative major, except for the <u>seventh note</u>.

2) The <u>seventh</u> note is always raised by <u>one semitone</u>.

3) You use the harmonic minor when you're writing <u>harmonies</u>. That <u>sharpened seventh note</u> makes the harmonies work much better than they would with notes from a natural minor. It's probably because it feels like it wants to move up to the <u>tonic</u>.

3) The **Melodic Minor** has **Two Accidentals**

1) The <u>melodic minor</u> is just like a natural minor, using the notes from the relative major scale, <u>except for notes 6 and 7</u>.

2) On the way <u>up</u>, notes <u>6</u> and <u>7</u> are each <u>raised</u> by <u>one semitone</u>.

3) On the way <u>down</u>, the melodic minor goes just like the natural minor.

4) The melodic minor is used for writing <u>melodies</u>. The accidental on note 6 makes tunes sound <u>smoother</u> by avoiding the big jump between notes 6 and 7 in the harmonic minor.

And not forgetting the Morris Minor...

All these scales have a <u>minor third</u> between the first and third notes in the scale — that's why they sound melancholy. You need to learn <u>all three</u> — names, notes and what they're used for.

The Circle of Fifths

*The circle of fifths looks complicated but it's very **useful** once you understand how it works — it tells you **all the keys**, all the **relative keys** and their **key signatures**.*

The **Circle of Fifths** Shows **All the Keys**

1) Altogether there are <u>12 major keys</u>. They're all shown on the <u>circle of fifths</u>.

2) Don't expect to fully get it if this is the first time you've seen it. Just <u>have a look</u>, then read on.

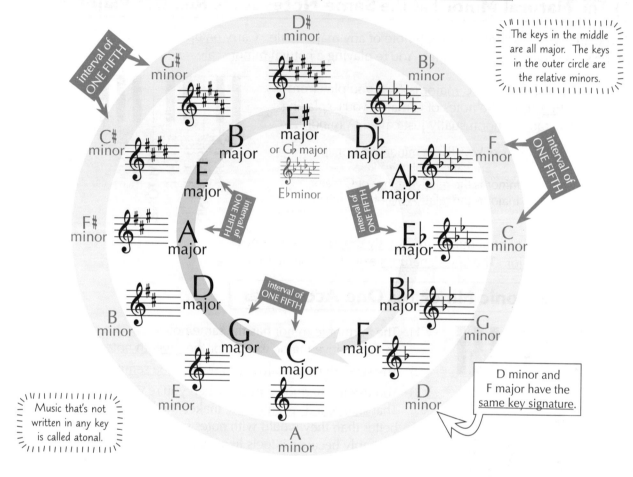

The keys in the middle are all major. The keys in the outer circle are the relative minors.

D minor and F major have the <u>same key signature</u>.

Music that's not written in any key is called atonal.

Each Key **Links** to the Next One

1) The circle <u>starts</u> with <u>C major</u> at the bottom. The next key round is <u>G</u>. G's the <u>fifth note</u> of C major.

2) The fifth note of G major is D, the <u>next</u> key on the circle. This pattern repeats <u>all the way round</u>. That's why the chart's called the circle of fifths.

3) As you go round the circle the number of <u>sharps</u> in the <u>key signature</u> goes up <u>one</u> for each key.

4) When you get to <u>F♯ major</u> at the top there are <u>six sharps</u>. From here, you start writing the key signature in <u>flats</u> — you don't need as many so it's clearer to read.

5) The number of <u>flats</u> keeps going <u>down</u> until you get back to C major, with no sharps and no flats.

The <u>relative minors</u> in the outer circle work just the same way as the major keys — the <u>fifth note</u> of <u>A minor</u> is <u>E</u> and the next minor key's <u>E minor</u>... and so on. Don't forget you can always work out the relative minor by counting up or down to the <u>sixth note</u> of a major scale, (see p.25) or the relative major by counting up to the <u>third note</u> of the minor scale.

REVISION TIP

Don't worry if it's making your head spin...

You need to be familiar with key signatures with <u>up to four sharps</u> or <u>four flats</u> (both <u>major</u> and <u>minor</u>). Don't worry too much about the others (but there's no harm in learning them too).

Modes and Other Types of Scale

*Most music uses notes from a **major** or a **minor scale** — and they're the **most important** ones to learn, but there are a few **more unusual scales** and **modes** that you need to know about too.*

Modes Follow Different Patterns of Tones and Semitones

Just like scales, you can start a <u>mode</u> on any note.

1) The most common mode is the one you get by playing a <u>major scale</u> (e.g. C major — just play the white notes on a keyboard from C to C). The pattern is <u>tone-tone-semitone-tone-tone-tone-semitone</u>.

2) Another mode can be formed by playing the notes of the same major scale, starting from the <u>second note</u>, e.g. D to D:

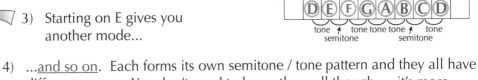

3) Starting on E gives you another mode...

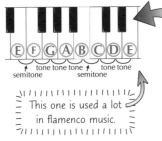

This one is used a lot in flamenco music.

4) ...<u>and so on</u>. Each forms its own semitone / tone pattern and they all have different names. You don't need to know them all though — it's more important that you <u>know what they sound like</u>. (E.g. playing the white notes starting from G forms a mode that sounds quite bluesy.)

5) For some examples of pieces written in modes, have a listen to the folk song <u>Scarborough Fair</u>, the theme tune to <u>The Simpsons</u> and REM's <u>Losing My Religion</u>.

Pentatonic Scales are Used a Lot in Folk and Rock Music

Pentatonic scales use <u>five</u> notes. They're really easy to compose with, because there are <u>no semitone steps</u> — <u>most combinations</u> of notes sound fine. There are <u>two types</u> of pentatonic scale.

1) The <u>major pentatonic</u> uses notes 1, 2, 3, 5 and 6 of a <u>major</u> scale.

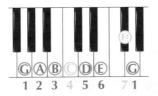

2) The <u>minor pentatonic</u> uses notes 1, 3, 4, 5 and 7 of the <u>natural minor</u> scale.

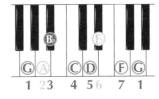

Whole Tone and Chromatic Scales Sound Spooky

Whole tone scales

Whole tone scales are pretty simple to remember — <u>every step is a tone</u>. From bottom to top there are only <u>six notes</u> in a whole tone scale.

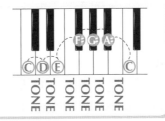

Major and minor scales are known as diatonic scales.

Chromatic scales

Chromatic scales are fairly easy too. On a keyboard you play <u>every white and black note</u> until you get up to an octave above the note you started with. From bottom to top there are <u>12 notes</u>. Basically, <u>every step</u> of a chromatic scale is <u>a semitone</u>.

You know the score...

You <u>could</u> get a piece of music in your <u>listening</u> that's written in a <u>mode</u> or one of the other <u>scales</u>. And you could get <u>asked</u> what kind of scale it's written with. So you'd better learn this page.

Intervals

*Not the break halfway through a concert, but the **distance** between two notes.*

An **Interval** is the **Gap** Between **Two Notes**

An interval is the <u>musical word</u> for the <u>gap</u> or <u>distance</u> between <u>two notes</u>.
Notes <u>close together</u> make <u>small</u> intervals. Notes <u>further apart</u> make <u>larger</u> intervals.
There are <u>two ways</u> of playing an interval.

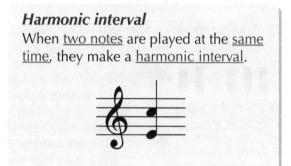

Melodic interval
When one note <u>jumps</u> up or down to another note, you get a <u>melodic interval</u>.

ASCENDING interval   DESCENDING interval

Harmonic interval
When <u>two notes</u> are played at the <u>same time</u>, they make a <u>harmonic interval</u>.

1) You can use the <u>melodic intervals</u> to describe the <u>pattern</u> of a <u>melody</u>.

2) In some melodies, there are only <u>small</u> intervals between the notes — no bigger than a <u>tone</u>.

3) When the notes are <u>close together</u> like this, the melody can be called <u>stepwise</u>, <u>conjunct</u> or <u>scalic</u> (because it moves up and down the notes of a <u>scale</u>).

4) Tunes with <u>big</u> melodic intervals (larger than a tone) are called <u>disjunct</u>.

An Interval has **Two Parts** to its Name...

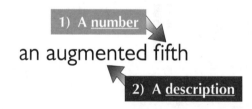

1) A <u>number</u>

an augmented fifth

2) A <u>description</u>

The **Number** Tells You **How Many Notes** the Interval Covers

1) You get the number by counting up the stave from the bottom note to the top note. You <u>include</u> the bottom and top notes in your counting.

2) C to E is a <u>third</u> because it covers <u>three letter names</u> — C, D and E.

3) C to F is a <u>fourth</u> because it covers <u>four letter names</u> — C, D, E and F.

4) The number of an interval is sometimes called the <u>interval quantity</u>.

The "description" bit is covered at the top of the next page...

The interval between G and D is a <u>fifth</u>.

G	A	B	C	D
1	2	3	4	5

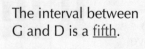

An interval covering eight letters (e.g. A to A) is called an octave.

The interval between D and F sharp is a <u>third</u> (you can just <u>ignore</u> the accidentals when counting).

D	E	F♯
1	2	3

Intervals

The **Description** Tells You How the Interval **Sounds**

There are <u>five names</u> for the five main sounds:

| perfect | major | minor | diminished | augmented |

1) To work out the <u>description part</u> of an interval's name, think of the <u>lower note</u> of the interval as the <u>first</u> note of a <u>major scale</u>.

2) If the top note of the interval is part of that major scale it's either <u>perfect</u> or <u>major</u>:

PERFECT MAJOR MAJOR PERFECT PERFECT MAJOR MAJOR PERFECT
unison 2nd 3rd 4th 5th 6th 7th octave

The perfect intervals are the ones that sound 'best' — the notes go together very cleanly.

3) If the top note <u>doesn't</u> belong to the major scale, then it's <u>minor</u>, <u>diminished</u> or <u>augmented</u>.
If the interval is <u>one semitone LESS</u> than a <u>major interval</u>, then it's <u>minor</u>.
If the interval is <u>one semitone LESS</u> than a <u>minor</u> or a <u>perfect interval</u>, then it's <u>diminished</u>.
If the interval is <u>one semitone MORE</u> than a <u>major</u> or a <u>perfect interval</u>, then it's <u>augmented</u>.

Work Out the **Full Name** of an Interval **Step by Step**

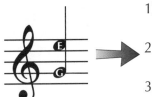

1) **HOW MANY LETTER NAMES DOES IT COVER?**
<u>Six</u> — G, A, B, C, D and E. So the <u>quantity</u> is a <u>sixth</u>.

2) **ARE THE NOTES FROM THE SAME MAJOR SCALE?**
The bottom note's G. E <u>is</u> in G major — it's the <u>sixth</u> note.

3) **WHAT TYPE OF INTERVAL IS IT?**
It's the <u>sixth note</u> of G major, and the sixth note always gives a major interval — so it's a <u>major sixth</u>.

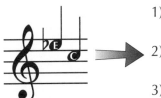

1) **HOW MANY LETTER NAMES DOES IT COVER?**
<u>Three</u> — C, D and E flat. So the <u>quantity</u> is a <u>third</u>.

2) **ARE THE NOTES FROM THE SAME MAJOR SCALE?**
No.

3) **WHAT TYPE OF INTERVAL IS IT?**
A third in the major scale is a <u>major</u> interval.
This interval's one semitone smaller, so it's a <u>minor third</u>.

The **Tritone** Interval **Sounds Odd**

1) The tritone is an interval of <u>three tones</u>. It's <u>dissonant</u> — i.e. it sounds awkward, some would say terrible. It's used in some twentieth century Western art music.

2) <u>Diminished fifths</u> (e.g. G to D flat) and <u>augmented fourths</u> (e.g. G to C♯) are both <u>tritones</u>.

3) Try playing some, so you know what they <u>sound</u> like.

Take it one step at a time and you'll get there in the end...

The tritone interval used to be called '<u>the Devil's interval</u>' — because it has such an awkward, clashing sound. It's supposed to be unlucky, so use it in your composition at your own risk...

Examples

You need to <u>hear</u> the difference between different types of scales and chords. Tracks 3-9 are practical examples of the theory on pages 24-29. Listen to the tracks as you read the info below.

Examples

Track 3   A <u>major scale</u>, with <u>F♯</u> as the tonic, played over two octaves. *(see p.24)*
Try writing out the notes of the scale on a stave. Remember — TTSTTTS.

Track 4   The <u>three</u> different types of <u>minor scale</u> with <u>D</u> as the tonic. *(see p.25)*
a) The <u>natural minor</u> scale
b) The <u>harmonic minor</u>
c) The <u>melodic minor</u>

Track 5   The two different types of pentatonic scale. *(see p.27)*
a) <u>Major pentatonic</u> scale starting on <u>C</u>
b) <u>Minor pentatonic</u> scale starting on <u>A</u>
These are relative scales, and because they're pentatonic all the notes are the same.

Track 6   A <u>whole tone</u> scale. *(see p.27)*
It starts off like the major scale, but the 4th and 5th notes are further apart (<u>harmonically distant</u>) than in a major scale, so it sounds odd.

Track 7   A <u>chromatic</u> scale. *(see p.27)*
This one starts on <u>G</u>, but all <u>chromatic</u> scales use all the notes, so they sound nearly the same.

Track 8   The <u>major</u> and <u>perfect</u> intervals. *(see p.29)*
They're played at the same time so they're <u>harmonic</u>.

Track 9   The <u>minor</u> and <u>diminished intervals</u>. *(see p.29)*
a) Minor 2nd
b) Augmented 2nd / minor 3rd
c) Augmented 4th / diminished 5th
d) Augmented 5th / minor 6th
e) Augmented 6th / minor 7th

Practice Questions

Now check you've got the hang of it all with these practice questions.

Practice Questions

Track 10   Listen to the four different types of scale. What are they?

a) ....

b) ....

c) ....

d) ....

You can play these tracks more than once — some of them are quite tricky.

Track 11   What type of scale does this tune use?

....

Track 12   Listen to these harmonic intervals. Write down what each of them is called.

a) ....   b) ....

c) ....   d) ....

e) ....   f) ....

g) ....   h) ....

Track 13   Now name these melodic intervals.

a) ....   b) ....

c) ....   d) ....

e) ....   f) ....

g) ....   h) ....

Warm-up and Exam Questions

Time for another round of questions...

Warm-up Questions

1) How many notes would you find in a normal scale?

2) What does a key or key signature tell you about the music?

3) What do the scales of C major and A minor have in common?

4) Name the **three** types of minor scales.

5) Which scale uses only notes 1, 2, 3, 5 and 6 from the major scale?

6) Why is a chromatic scale unusual?

7) What type of interval is formed when two notes are played together at the same time?

8) Which is smaller, a minor 7th or a diminished 7th?

Exam Question

This exam-style question includes a couple of questions on intervals to test your knowledge.

Play the excerpt **three** times. Leave a short pause between each playing.

a) Here are the first three bars.

Exam Question

i) How many beats are there in a bar?

....

[1 mark]

ii) What is the interval between the notes highlighted in red at letter **a**?

....

[1 mark]

iii) What is the interval between the two lower notes in the
left-hand chord indicated at letter **b**?

....

[1 mark]

b) What key is this excerpt in?

....

[1 mark]

c) What does the mark ‾ above a note tell the performer to do?

....

[1 mark]

Chords — The Basics

*A **chord** is two or more notes played together. Chords are great for writing **accompaniments**.*

Only **Some** Instruments **Play Chords**

1) A lot of instruments only play <u>one note at a time</u> — flutes, recorders, trumpets, clarinets, trombones... You can't play a chord with one note, so these instruments <u>don't</u> play chords.

2) You can <u>only</u> play chords on <u>instruments</u> that play <u>more than one</u> note at a time. <u>Keyboards</u> and guitars are both great for playing chords — you can easily play several notes together.

3) Other <u>stringed instruments</u> like violins and cellos can play chords, but not very easily, so chords are only played from time to time.

Don't play chords.
Do play chords.

Some Chords Sound **Great**, Others Sound **Awful**

1) The notes of some chords <u>go together</u> really well — like apple pie and ice-cream.

When you have nice-sounding chords it's called <u>CONCORDANCE</u> or <u>CONSONANCE</u>.

2) Other chords have <u>clashing notes which disagree</u> — more like apple pie and pickled eggs.

When you have horrible-sounding chords it's called <u>DISCORDANCE</u> or <u>DISSONANCE</u>.

The **Best-Sounding** Chords are Called **Triads**

1) You can play <u>any</u> set of notes and make a chord — but most of them sound <u>harsh</u>.
2) An <u>easy, reliable</u> way of getting nice-sounding chords is to play <u>triads</u>.
3) Triads are chords made up of three notes, with <u>set intervals</u> between them.
4) Once you know the intervals, you can easily play <u>dozens</u> of decent chords.

How to make a triad...

1) On a piano, start with any white note — this is called the <u>root note</u>. You <u>build</u> the triad <u>from the root</u>.

2) Count the root as 'first' and the next white note to the <u>right</u>, as 'second'. The <u>third</u> note you reach is the <u>third</u> — the middle note of the triad.

3) Keep counting up and you get to the <u>fifth</u> — the final note of the triad.

4) The intervals between the notes are <u>thirds</u>.

5) If the root note's a <u>B</u>, then you end up with a <u>B triad</u>. If the root note's a <u>C</u>, you end up with a <u>C triad</u>.

6) You can build triads on black notes too, so long as the intervals between notes are <u>thirds</u>.

Good things come in threes...

The next six pages will be useful when it comes to writing your compositions. You'll need to think about which instruments can play chords, and which notes sound nice together.

Triads

There's more than one type of triad...

Triads Use **Major** and **Minor Thirds**

1) All triads have an interval of a <u>third</u> between each pair of notes.

2) The intervals can be <u>major</u> or minor <u>thirds</u>.

A <u>major third</u> is <u>four</u> semitones.

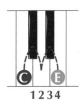

A <u>minor third</u> is <u>three</u> semitones.

3) Different <u>combinations</u> of major and minor thirds give different types of triad:

Major triads

- <u>Major triads</u> have a <u>major third</u> followed by a <u>minor third</u>.
- The <u>major third</u> goes between the root and the third.
- The <u>minor third</u> goes between the third and the fifth.

Minor triads

- <u>Minor triads</u> use a <u>major</u> and a <u>minor third</u> too, but in the opposite order.
- The <u>minor third</u> goes between the root and the third.
- The <u>major third</u> goes between the third and the fifth.

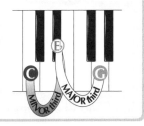

DIMINISHED TRIADS use <u>two minor thirds</u>.
AUGMENTED TRIADS use <u>two major thirds</u>.

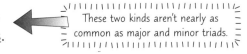
These two kinds aren't nearly as common as major and minor triads.

You Can **Add a Note** to a Triad to Get a **7th Chord**

1) <u>7th chords</u> are triads with a fourth note added — the <u>seventh</u> note above the root.

2) The interval between the root and the 7th can be a <u>major seventh</u> or a <u>minor seventh</u> — see p.29.

These **Symbols** Stand for Chords

A special <u>notation</u> is used to represent the various <u>chords</u>. For a triad starting on a <u>C</u>:

C = C major

Caug or **C+** = augmented C chord

C7 = C major with added minor 7th

Cmaj7 = C major with added major 7th

Cm = C minor

Cdim or **C-** or **Co** = diminished C chord

Cm7 = C minor with added minor 7th

Cm maj7 = C minor with added major 7th

For chords other than C, just change the <u>first letter</u> to show the <u>root note</u>.

It's not as hard as it looks and it's VERY useful...

If you play the guitar or play in a band you need to learn these symbols <u>right now</u>. Even if you only ever play classical music they're still worth learning — they're really useful as shorthand.

Fitting Chords to a Melody

There are some basic rules about fitting chords to a melody:
*No.1: All the notes in the chords have got to be in the **same key** as the notes in the melody.*

The **Melody** and **Chords** Must be in the **Same Key**

1) A melody that's composed in a certain key <u>sticks</u> to that key.

2) The chords used to <u>harmonise with</u> the melody have got to be in the <u>same key</u> or it'll <u>clash</u>.

3) As a <u>general rule</u> each chord in a harmony should <u>include</u> the note it's accompanying, e.g. a <u>C</u> could be accompanied by a <u>C chord</u> (C, E, G), an <u>F chord</u> (F, A, C) or an <u>A minor chord</u> (A, C, E).

There's a Chord for **Every Note** in the **Scale**

You can make dozens of triads using the notes of <u>major</u> and <u>minor</u> scales as the <u>roots</u>. <u>Every note</u> of <u>every chord</u>, not just the root, has to belong to the scale. This is how <u>C major</u> looks if you turn it into chords:

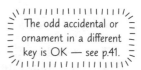

The odd accidental or ornament in a different key is OK — see p.41.

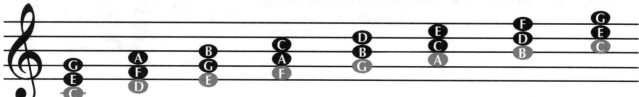

Chord I	Chord II	Chord III	Chord IV	Chord V	Chord VI	Chord VII	Chord I
Tonic	Supertonic	Mediant	Subdominant	Dominant	Submediant	Leading Note	Tonic

1) Chords I, IV and V are <u>major triads</u>. They sound <u>bright and cheery</u>.
   A <u>7th</u> can be added to <u>chord V</u> to give a <u>dominant 7th</u> chord (written V^7).

2) Chords II, III and VI are <u>minor triads</u>. They sound more <u>gloomy</u>.

3) Chord VII is a <u>diminished triad</u>. It sounds <u>different</u> from the major and minor chords. Another name for Chord VII is the <u>leading note chord</u> — it sounds like it should lead on to another chord.

4) Chords built on <u>any</u> major scale, not just C major, follow the <u>same pattern</u>.

5) A <u>series</u> of chords is known as a <u>harmonic progression</u> (also called a <u>chord progression</u> or <u>chord sequence</u>).

6) The <u>speed</u> at which the chords <u>change</u> is called the <u>harmonic rhythm</u>.

The **Primary Chords** are Most **Useful**

1) The three major chords, <u>I</u>, <u>IV</u> and <u>V</u>, are the <u>most important</u> in <u>any</u> key. They're called <u>primary chords</u>. Between them, the primary chords can harmonise with <u>any note</u> in the scale.

2) This is how it works in <u>C major</u>:

note...	C	D	E	F	G		A	B
goes with...	Chord I	Chord IV	Chord V	Chord I	Chord IV	Chord I Chord V	Chord IV	Chord V
	G	C	D	G	C	G D	C	D
	E	A	B	E	A	E B	A	B
	C	F	G	C	F	C G	F	G

Minor Chords Make Harmony **More Interesting**

1) Primary chords can get a bit <u>boring</u> to listen to after a while — the harmonies are fairly <u>simple</u>.

2) Composers often mix in a few of the other chords — <u>II</u>, <u>III</u>, <u>VI</u> or <u>VII</u> — for a <u>change</u>.

3) Instead of just having endless major chords, you get a mixture of minor and diminished chords too.

Inversions

Inverting triads means **changing the order** of the notes. It make accompaniments more **varied**.

Triads with the **Root at the Bottom** are in **Root Position**

These triads are all in <u>root position</u> — the <u>root note</u> is at the bottom.

● = fifth
● = third
● = root

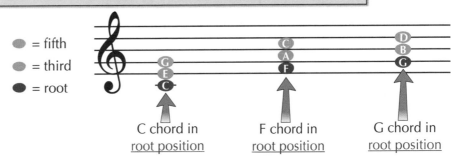

C chord in <u>root position</u>   F chord in <u>root position</u>   G chord in <u>root position</u>

First Inversion Triads have the **Third** at the **Bottom**

These chords are all in <u>first inversion</u>. The root note's moved up an octave, leaving the <u>third</u> at the bottom.

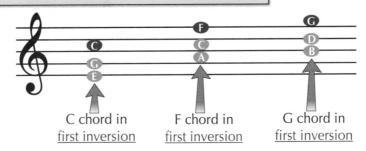

C chord in <u>first inversion</u>   F chord in <u>first inversion</u>   G chord in <u>first inversion</u>

Second Inversion Triads have the **Fifth** at the **Bottom**

Chords can be played in <u>second inversion</u> too.

From the first inversion, the third is raised an octave, leaving the <u>fifth</u> at the bottom.

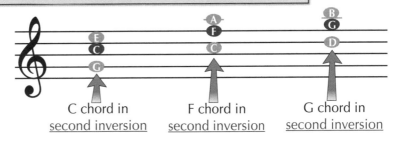

C chord in <u>second inversion</u>   F chord in <u>second inversion</u>   G chord in <u>second inversion</u>

7th Chords Can Go into a **Third Inversion**

1) 7th chords can be played in root position, first inversion or second inversion — just like triads.

2) But there's also a <u>third inversion</u> — where the <u>7th</u> goes <u>below</u> the standard triad. They have a third inversion because they're <u>four-note</u> chords.

There's a **Symbol** for Each **Inversion**

> This means a C chord with E at the bottom.

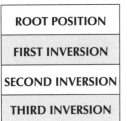

ROOT POSITION		5/3 chords	because there's a <u>fifth</u> and a <u>third</u> between the notes
FIRST INVERSION	...also known as...	6/3 chords	because there's a <u>sixth</u> and a <u>third</u> between the notes
SECOND INVERSION		6/4 chords	because there's a <u>sixth</u> and a <u>fourth</u> between the notes
THIRD INVERSION		6/4/2 chords	because there's a <u>sixth</u>, a <u>fourth</u> and a <u>second</u> between the notes

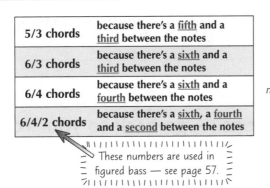

...and in Roman numerals...

Ia	
Ib	...and in good old chord symbols...
Ic	
Id	

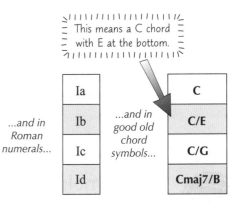

C
C/E
C/G
Cmaj7/B

> These numbers are used in figured bass — see page 57.

Inversions

*So now you know what inversions **are**. Now get to grips with what to **do** with them too...*

Inversions are Handy for **Moving Between Chords**

When you play chords one after another, it sounds nicer if the notes move smoothly from one chord to the next. Inversions help to smooth out any rough patches...

1) Moving from a C chord in root position to a G chord in root position means all the notes have to jump a long way. It sounds clumsy and not all that nice.

● = fifth
● = third
● = root

2) If you move from a C chord in root position to a G chord in first inversion instead, the transition is much, much smoother.

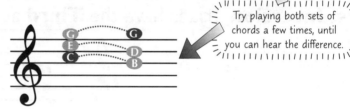

Try playing both sets of chords a few times, until you can hear the difference.

3) You can use second and third inversions too — whatever sounds best.

Unscramble the **Inversion** to Work Out the **Root Note**

This isn't exactly a life-saving skill. But it's dead useful...

If you come across an inverted chord you can work out which is the root note. Once you know that, and you know what key you're in, you can tell whether it's chord IV, VII, II or whatever.

1) Basically you have to turn the chord back into a root position triad.
2) Shuffle the order of the notes around until there's a third interval between each one.
3) When the notes are arranged in thirds, the root will always be at the bottom.

B to D is a THIRD, but D to G is a FOURTH. You need to move the G to find the root chord.

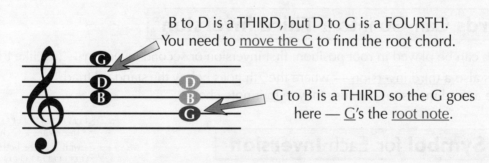

G to B is a THIRD so the G goes here — G's the root note.

4) There are no sharps or flats in the key signature, so the piece is in C major. G's the fifth note of C major, so this is chord V.

REVISION TIP

Unscramble inversions — go back to your roots...

There's a lot to take in when it comes to inversions. Don't go racing through this page — go over it one bit at a time, letting all the facts sink in. Playing the chords for yourself will help.

Different Ways of Playing Chords

*So far, the chords in this section have all been written as three notes. It sounds dull if you do it all the time. To liven things up there are **chord figurations** — different ways of playing the chords.*

Block Chords are the Most Basic

This is probably the <u>easiest</u> way to play chords. The notes of each chord are played <u>all together</u> and then <u>held</u> until the next chord.

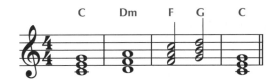

Rhythmic Chords Give You Harmony and Rhythm

1) Rhythmic chords are <u>chords</u> played to a <u>funky rhythm</u>.
2) You play all the notes of each chord at the same time, like you do for block chords.
3) You don't <u>hold</u> the notes though — you play them to a <u>rhythm</u> that <u>repeats</u> in each bar.
4) <u>Rhythm guitar</u> and <u>keyboards</u> often play rhythmic chords.

In Broken and Arpeggiated Chords the Notes are Separate

Accompanying chords don't <u>have</u> to have to be played at all once. You can play the notes <u>separately</u>.

1) Here's one way of doing it — it goes <u>root</u>, <u>fifth</u>, <u>third</u>, <u>root</u>.

2) This pattern was really popular around the time <u>Mozart</u> was alive (last half of the 1700s). It's called <u>Alberti bass</u> after the composer Domenico Alberti — it usually goes <u>root</u>, <u>fifth</u>, <u>third</u>, <u>fifth</u>.

3) The <u>notes of a chord</u> are sometimes <u>played in order</u> (e.g. root, third, fifth, root) <u>going up</u> or <u>coming down</u>. This is called an <u>arpeggio</u> (are-pedge-ee-o).

4) In an <u>arpeggiated chord</u>, you play the notes <u>one at a time</u>, but in <u>quick succession</u> (imagine strumming a harp). On a piano, you <u>hold down</u> each key as you build up the chord. They're usually written with a <u>wiggly line</u>, like this:

5) A <u>walking bass</u> usually moves in <u>crotchets</u>, often either in <u>steps</u> (see p.28) or <u>arpeggios</u>.
6) A <u>drone</u> is a <u>long</u>, <u>held-on note</u>, usually in the <u>bass</u>, that adds harmonic interest.
7) <u>Pedal notes</u> are a bit different — they're <u>repeated</u> notes, again usually in the <u>bass part</u>. However, the <u>harmony</u> on top of a pedal note <u>changes</u> (whereas a drone sets up the harmony for the whole piece).

Think about using an Alberti bass in your composition...

When you get chord symbols over the music you can play the chords <u>any way you like</u>. Try all these ways of playing chords and think about <u>using them</u> in your compositions.

Examples and Practice

Read on for some more examples of the different kinds of chords.

Examples

Track 15 These are some of the most <u>common</u> chords — learn to recognise them.

- a) <u>major</u> triad
- b) <u>minor</u> triad
- c) <u>diminished</u> triad
- d) <u>augmented</u> triad
- e) <u>major</u> triad with a <u>major</u> 7th
- f) <u>major</u> triad with a <u>minor</u> 7th
- g) <u>minor</u> triad with a <u>major</u> 7th
- h) <u>minor</u> triad with a <u>minor</u> 7th

Track 16 A <u>sequence</u> of chords, showing different <u>inversions</u>:

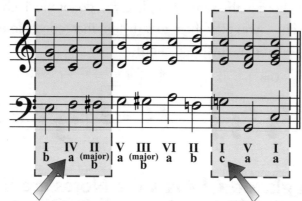

> What inversion a chord is depends on which note is on the bottom — it doesn't matter how the other notes of the triad are arranged on top.

In these first <u>three</u> chords, chords in the <u>first inversion</u> lead nicely on to <u>root chords</u> a <u>perfect 4th</u> up. The <u>semitone</u> steps in the bass make these progressions sound smooth and logical.

At the <u>end</u> of the sequence, listen out for the <u>third from last</u> note (<u>second inversion</u> of <u>chord I</u>), which leads into the <u>cadence</u> that ends the phrase (see p.42-43 for more on cadences).

How well do you know your chords... Find out by answering these practice questions.

Practice Questions

Track 17 Describe each of the eight chords on the track, using one of the following words:

major	minor	diminished	augmented

> You can play these tracks more than once.

a) ....

b) ....

c) ....

d) ....

e) ....

f) ....

g) ....

h) ....

Track 18 For each of the following you'll hear a root note, and then an inversion. Which inversions are they?

a) ....

b) ....

c) ....

d) ....

e) ....

f) ....

g) ....

h) ....

Using Decorations to Vary the Harmony

*If you want to **liven things up** in a harmony you can add a sprinkle of **melodic decoration**.*

Melodic Decoration **Adds Notes** to the Tune

1) <u>Decorative notes</u> are <u>short notes</u> that move between notes or create <u>fleeting clashes</u> (<u>dissonance</u>) with the accompanying chord. They make things sound <u>less bland</u>.

2) Decoration that belongs to the key of the melody (e.g. B in C major) is called <u>diatonic</u>.

3) Decoration that <u>doesn't</u> belong to the key (e.g. F♯ in C major) is called <u>chromatic</u>.

4) There are <u>four</u> main ways of adding melodic decoration.

1) **Auxiliary** Notes are **Higher** or **Lower** than the Notes **Either Side**

1) An auxiliary note is either a <u>semitone</u> or <u>tone</u> <u>above</u> or <u>below</u> the notes either side.

2) The two notes before and after the auxiliary are always the <u>same pitch</u>, and always belong to the accompanying chord.

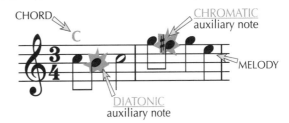

2) **Passing** Notes **Link** the Notes **Before** and **After**

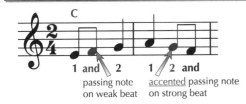

1) A passing note <u>links</u> the notes before and after. They either belong to the same chord or link one chord with another.

2) They're usually put on <u>weak beats</u>. When they <u>are</u> on the strong beat they're called '<u>accented passing notes</u>'.

3) **Appoggiaturas** **Clash** with the Chord

1) An appoggiatura <u>clashes</u> with the accompanying chord. It's written as a <u>little note</u> tied to the note of the chord, and takes <u>half the value</u> of the note it's tied to.

2) The note <u>before</u> it is usually quite a <u>leap</u> away (jumps between notes of more than a <u>2nd</u> are called <u>leaps</u>).

3) The note after the appoggiatura is always <u>just above</u> or <u>below</u>. It's called the <u>resolution</u>. The <u>resolution</u> has to be from the <u>accompanying chord</u>.

4) Appoggiaturas usually fall on a <u>strong beat</u>, so the resolution note falls on a <u>weaker beat</u>.

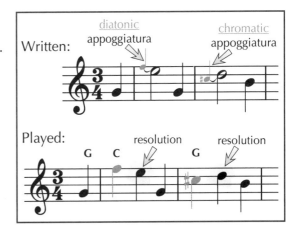

4) **Suspensions** **Clash** then Go Back to **Harmonising**

A suspension is a series of three notes called the <u>preparation</u>, <u>suspension</u> and <u>resolution</u>.

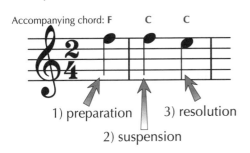

1) The <u>preparation</u> note belongs to the accompanying chord. It's usually on a weak beat.

2) The <u>suspension</u> is the <u>same pitch</u> as the preparation note. It's played at the same time as a <u>chord change</u>. It <u>doesn't</u> <u>go</u> with the new chord, so you get <u>dissonance</u>.

3) The <u>resolution</u> note moves up or down (usually down) from the suspension to a note in the accompanying chord. This <u>resolves</u> the dissonance — everything sounds lovely again.

Section Three — Keys, Scales and Chords

Phrases and Cadences

Notes in a melody fall into 'phrases' just like the words in a story are made up of sentences.
A cadence is the movement from the second-to-last to the last chord of a phrase — it finishes it off.

A **Phrase** is Like a Musical '**Sentence**'

There should be clear <u>phrases</u> in any melody. A tune <u>without</u> phrases would sound odd — just like a story with no sentences wouldn't make much sense.

1) Phrases are usually <u>two</u> or <u>four</u> bars long.

2) Phrases are sometimes marked with a <u>curved line</u> called a <u>phrase mark</u>, that goes <u>above</u> the stave. Not all music has phrase marks but the phrases are <u>always</u> there. Don't confuse phrase marks and slurs. A phrase mark <u>doesn't</u> change how you play the notes.

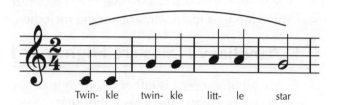

Cadences Emphasise the **End of a Phrase**

1) A <u>cadence</u> is the <u>shift</u> between the <u>second-to-last chord</u> and the <u>last chord</u> in a phrase.

2) The <u>effect</u> you get from shifting between the two chords works like a <u>comma</u> or a <u>full stop</u>. It <u>underlines</u> the end of the phrase and <u>gets you ready</u> for the next one.

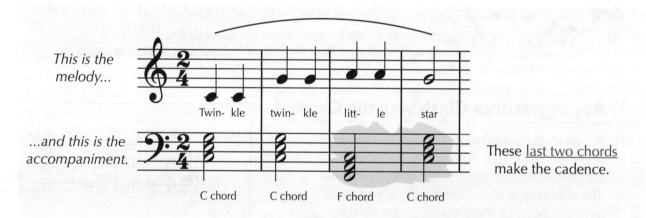

This is the melody...

...and this is the accompaniment.

These <u>last two chords</u> make the cadence.

There are **Four Main Types** of Cadence

These pairs of chords are <u>only</u> cadences when they come at the end of a phrase. Anywhere else in a phrase, they're <u>just chords</u>.

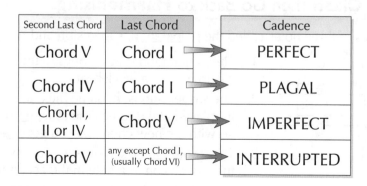

Second Last Chord	Last Chord	Cadence
Chord V	Chord I	PERFECT
Chord IV	Chord I	PLAGAL
Chord I, II or IV	Chord V	IMPERFECT
Chord V	any except Chord I, (usually Chord VI)	INTERRUPTED

More on these on the next page...

Cadences

*Learning the **names** of the different cadences is no use unless you also learn what they're **for**.*

Perfect and Plagal Cadences Work Like Full Stops

1) A perfect cadence makes a piece of music feel finished or complete.

2) It goes from Chord V to Chord I — in C major that's a G chord to a C chord.

3) This is how a perfect cadence goes at the end of 'Twinkle, Twinkle, Little Star':

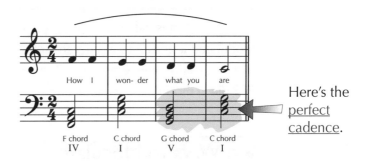

Here's the perfect cadence.

4) A plagal cadence sounds really different from a perfect cadence but it has a similar effect — it makes a piece of music sound finished.

5) A plagal cadence in C major is an F chord (IV) to a C chord (I). Play it and see what it sounds like. The plagal cadence gets used at the end of lots of hymns — it's sometimes called the 'Amen' cadence.

Imperfect and Interrupted Cadences are Like Commas

Imperfect and interrupted cadences are used to end phrases but not at the end of a piece. They work like commas — they feel like a resting point but not an ending.

An imperfect cadence most commonly goes from chord I, II or IV to V. Here's one going from chord I to chord V at the end of the third line of 'Twinkle, Twinkle':

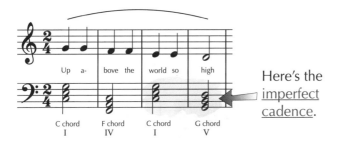

Here's the imperfect cadence.

In an interrupted cadence chord V can go to any chord except I, but it usually goes to chord VI. You expect it to go to chord I — so it sounds "interrupted". In C major an interrupted cadence may go from a G chord (V) to an Am chord (VI).

Some Minor pieces Finish with a Tierce de Picardie

1) If a piece of music is in a minor key, you'd expect it to finish with a minor chord.

2) However, some composers (especially Baroque composers) finish a minor piece with a major chord, by using a major third in the last chord. This is known as a Tierce de Picardie (or Picardy third).

This excerpt is from Scarlatti's Piano Sonata in G Minor (Cat's Fugue). Even though the piece is in G minor, it finishes with a G major chord.

You need to listen to cadences to understand them...

Cadences probably won't make much sense unless you try playing them. Play the cadences for yourself (or listen to Track 19 — see p.48) until you can hear the differences between them.

Modulation

*Most of the notes in a piece of music come from one key — but to vary the melody or harmony you can **modulate** (change key). It can happen just once, or a few times. It's up to the composer.*

The **Starting Key** is Called '**Home**'

1) The key a piece <u>starts out in</u> is called the <u>home key</u> or <u>tonic key</u>.

2) If the music's modulated it goes into a <u>different key</u>.

3) The change of key is usually only <u>temporary</u>. The key <u>goes back</u> to the home key after a while.

4) However much a piece modulates, it usually <u>ends</u> in the home key.

There are **Two** Ways to Modulate

1) Modulation by **Pivot Chord**

1) A pivot chord is a chord that's in the home key <u>and</u> the key the music modulates to.

2) <u>Chord V</u> (G, B, D) in <u>C major</u> is exactly the same as <u>chord I</u> in <u>G major</u> — so it can be used to <u>pivot</u> between C major and G major.

3) Sometimes, the <u>key signature</u> changes to show the new key. More often, <u>accidentals</u> are written in the music where they're needed.

The home key here is <u>C</u>. At the end of the <u>first bar</u> the accompaniment uses the chord <u>G, B, D</u> to pivot into G major:

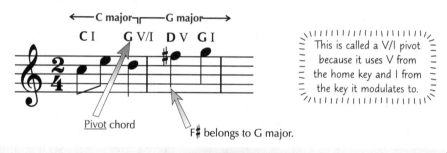

<u>Pivot</u> chord

F♯ belongs to G major.

This is called a V/I pivot because it uses V from the home key and I from the key it modulates to.

Related keys...

1) It sounds best if you modulate to <u>related keys</u>.

2) The <u>closest</u> keys are (major) keys <u>IV</u> and <u>V</u> and the <u>relative minor</u>.

3) The <u>next closest</u> are the relative minors of keys IV and V.

Relative minor of **IV** D minor	**IV** F major	Home key **I** C major	**V** G major	Relative minor of **V** E minor

Relative minor
 A minor

2) **Abrupt** Modulation

1) In abrupt modulation there's <u>no pivot chord</u>, and no other preparation either. It just happens.

2) Often the modulation is between two keys just <u>one semitone apart</u>, e.g. from <u>C major</u> to <u>C♯ major</u>.

3) <u>Pop songs</u> often modulate <u>up</u> one semitone. It creates a <u>sudden</u>, <u>dramatic effect</u> — it's meant to give the music an <u>excited</u>, <u>uplifting</u> feeling.

You can choose related keys but you can't choose your family...

If you see <u>accidentals</u> it often means the music's modulated, but <u>not always</u>. The accidental could also be there because: 1) the music's written in a <u>minor key</u> — harmonic or melodic (see p.25); or 2) the composer fancied a spot of <u>chromatic</u> decoration (see p.41). That's composers for you...

Texture

*Here's one last way composers vary the harmony — by changing the **texture**. Texture's an odd word to use about music — what it means is how the different parts (e.g. chords and melody) are **woven together**.*

Texture is **How** the parts **Fit Together**

1) An important part of music is how the <u>different parts</u> are <u>woven together</u>.
   This is known as <u>texture</u> — it describes how the <u>melody</u> and <u>accompaniment</u> parts <u>fit together</u>.
2) <u>Monophonic</u>, <u>homophonic</u> and <u>polyphonic</u> are all different types of texture.
3) Some textures are made up of the <u>same</u> melodic line that's passed round <u>different parts</u>.
   <u>Imitation</u> and <u>canons</u> are good examples of this.

Monophonic Music is the **Simplest**

1) In <u>monophonic</u> music there's <u>no harmony</u> — just one line of tune (e.g. a <u>solo</u> with <u>no accompaniment</u>).
2) Parts playing in <u>unison</u> or <u>doubling</u> each other (i.e. the same notes at the same time) are also monophonic.
3) Monophonic music has a <u>thin texture</u>.

Polyphonic Music **Weaves Tunes Together**

1) <u>Polyphonic</u> music gives quite a complex effect because there's <u>more than one tune</u> being played at once.

2) It's sometimes called <u>contrapuntal</u> music.
3) Parts that move in <u>contrary motion</u> (one goes <u>up</u> and another goes <u>down</u>) are polyphonic.
4) <u>Two-part music</u> (with two separate melodic lines) is also polyphonic.

In **Homophonic** Music, the Parts Move **Together**

1) If the lines of music move at more or less the <u>same time</u>, it's <u>homophonic</u> music.
2) <u>Parallel motion</u> (when parts move with the <u>same interval</u> between them, e.g. parallel 5ths) is also homophonic.
3) If the melody line is <u>independent</u> and plays a <u>different rhythm</u> to the accompaniment, this texture is known as <u>melody with accompaniment</u> (it's <u>different</u> to homophony).

In **Heterophonic** Music the Instruments **Share** the Tune

In heterophonic music there's <u>one tune</u>. <u>All</u> the instruments play it, but with <u>variations</u>, and often at <u>different times</u>.

Polyphonic, homophonic and heterophonic music all have quite a thick texture.

You might have to write about texture in the exam...

Make sure you know all the proper words to describe texture, and that you can tell the difference between the different types — examiners love asking about it so it'll come in handy...

Texture

*When there's **one** part, the music's **pure** and **simple**, but put **more parts in** and it's much more **complex**.*

Imitation — Repeat a Phrase With **Slight Changes**

1) In imitation a phrase is repeated with slight changes each time.

2) It works particularly well if one instrument or voice imitates another and then overlaps.

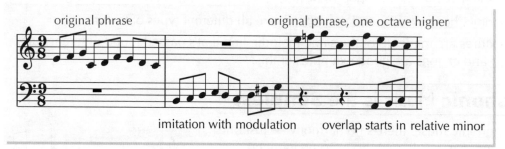

original phrase

original phrase, one octave higher

imitation with modulation

overlap starts in relative minor

Canon — **Same Melody** Different Parts

1) In a canon, each part plays the same melody, but they come in separately and at regular intervals. The parts overlap.

2) A canon is also known as a round. There are some really well-known rounds, e.g. 'London's Burning'.

3) Canons are an example of contrapuntal (or polyphonic) music (see previous page).

4) Composers from the Baroque period (1600-1750) like Bach and Vivaldi used lots of canons.

This excerpt comes from 'Spring' from Vivaldi's Four Seasons. The solo violin and first violin often play in canon.

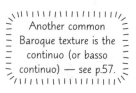

Another common Baroque texture is the continuo (or basso continuo) — see p.57.

Solo Violin

First Violin

Solo Violin

First Violin

Looping and Layering are Modern Techniques

1) In the 1960s and 70s, composers like Steve Reich started developing new techniques in their music.

2) They took recordings of sections of music, words, rhythms and other sounds and repeated them over and over again. These are called loops.

3) The loops were often created by cutting pieces of tape and sticking the ends together so they could be played over and over again — this is looping.

4) If there are lots of different loops being played at the same time it's called layering.

A layer of fruit, a layer of sponge, a layer of custard...

There are a few more words on this page that'll be useful if you need to write about musical texture in the listening exam — imitation, canon, looped and layered. Make sure you know what they mean.

Texture

*Composers use **different textures** to **vary** their music. They can change the **number** of instruments and whether they play the **same notes** or in **harmony**. They can also **split** tunes between **different instruments**.*

More Than One Part Can Play the Same Melody

1) If there's just <u>one part</u> playing with <u>no accompaniment</u>, there's just a <u>single melody line</u>.

2) If there's <u>more than one</u> instrument playing the <u>same melody</u> at the <u>same pitch</u>, they're playing in <u>unison</u>.

3) If there's <u>more than one</u> instrument playing the <u>same notes</u> but in <u>different ranges</u>, they're playing in <u>octaves</u>.

All of these are examples of monophonic textures.

Some Instruments Play Accompanying Parts

1) The instruments that <u>aren't</u> playing the tune play the <u>accompaniment</u>. Different <u>types</u> of accompaniment give different <u>textures</u>.

2) If the accompaniment is playing <u>chords</u> underneath the melody with the <u>same rhythm</u> as the melody but <u>different notes</u>, the texture is <u>homophonic</u>. It sounds <u>richer</u> than a single melody line, unison or octaves.

3) If there are <u>two choirs</u> singing at <u>different times</u>, the music is <u>antiphonal</u>. The two choirs will often sing <u>alternate phrases</u> — like <u>question and answer</u> or <u>call and response</u>. A lot of <u>early religious vocal music</u> was antiphonal. You can also get the same effect with two groups of <u>instruments</u>.

Group 1
Group 2

4) If there's <u>more than one</u> part playing <u>different melodies</u> at the <u>same time</u>, the music is <u>contrapuntal</u> (or <u>polyphonic</u>). Contrapuntal parts <u>fit together</u> harmonically.

The examples on this page use the melody from Handel's 'Water Music'.

Would you care to accompany me to the cinema...

There are quite a few tricky <u>textures</u> to learn on this page. Listen to the different types, and try and <u>recognise</u> what they sound like so that you can describe them if they come up in the <u>exam</u>.

Examples

Track 19 should help you get a better idea about cadences, and Track 20 gives you some different examples of modulation. Listen to them lots of times until you can recognise them straight away.

Examples

Track 19 You'll hear this bar played **four** times, followed by a different cadence each time.

a) The <u>perfect</u> cadence sounds totally <u>complete</u> — perfect, in fact. You can't imagine it moving on to any other chord.

b) The <u>plagal</u> cadence is sometimes called the "amen cadence" — it sounds <u>peaceful</u> and reassuring.

c) The <u>imperfect</u> cadence is the <u>opposite</u> of the perfect cadence. Instead of bringing things to a close, it seems to open up loads of possibilities.

d) The <u>interrupted</u> cadence starts off like a perfect cadence but ends with a more open, <u>melancholy</u> feel.

Track 20 Listen to these **three** short excerpts. Each one is a different example of a <u>modulation</u> from one key to another. In each excerpt the pattern goes like this:

Note 1 <u>Original</u> key

Note 2 <u>Original</u> key

Note 3 <u>Pivot chord</u> (in the original key and the new key)

Note 4 <u>New</u> key

Practice Questions

Practise your hard-won knowledge of chords, modulation and texture with the questions on this page and the next. Listen to each track a few times to make sure you've heard it properly.

 Practice Questions

Track 21 This question is about identifying cadences.
You will hear eight phrases, a)-h), all starting like this:

Write down whether the final cadence is perfect, plagal, imperfect or interrupted.

a) ....

b) ....

c) ....

d) ....

e) ....

f) ....

g) ....

h) ....

Track 22 *For each of the following tracks, fill in the missing notes in the melody, then answer the questions.*

a)

b) The chord in the fourth bar has an A in the bass.
What inversion of chord I is this?

....

c) What type of cadence does the passage end with?

....

Track 23 a)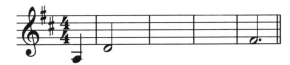

b) In this passage, the harmony tends to move in time with the melody.
What is the name of this type of musical texture?

....

c) What type of cadence does the passage end with?

....

d) Which note is sustained in the bass in the second-to-last bar?

....

Section Three — Keys, Scales and Chords

Practice Questions

Practice Questions

 a)

b) In the first chord in bar 2, the left hand plays the major of chord II. Which note in this chord is not in the scale of the home key?

....

c) What type of cadence does the passage end with?

....

b) Circle each auxiliary note in the passage, and say whether each is diatonic or chromatic.

c) Which one of the following best describes the chord in bar 4? Ring your answer.

       1st inversion   **harmonic**   **relative minor**   **suspension**

 a)

b) What key does this passage start in?

....

c) What key does it finish in?

....

d) The B flat chord at the start of bar 3 comes before the dominant chord of the new key. Give the name of a chord in this position in a modulation.

....

e) Fill in the blanks in the following sentence with the appropriate Roman numerals:

    The B flat chord is chord .... in the home key

    and chord .... in the final key.

Warm-up and Exam Questions

Warm-up Questions

1) Name **two** instruments that are frequently used to play chords.

2) Which **three** chords in a major key produce major triads?

3) If the *root* of a chord is on the top, and the *third* of the chord is on the bottom, which inversion is the chord in?

4) Name **three** different ways of playing chords.

5) What do you call a melodic decoration that belongs to the same key as the main melody?

6) List **three** ways melodies can be decorated to help vary the harmony within a piece of music.

7) At what point in a piece of music would you expect to find an imperfect or interrupted cadence?

8) What's another name for the texture known as polyphonic?

Exam Question

Now practise your exam technique with the question below and over the page.

Track 27

Play the excerpt **four times** then answer the questions on the next page.

Leave a short pause for writing time before each playing.

Here is the complete score for the excerpt:

Exam Question

a)   What instrument is playing this piece?

....
[1 mark]

b)   How would you describe the way the left hand is playing at **1**?

....
[1 mark]

c)   Which of the following best describes the cadence at **2**?
     Circle your choice from the options below.

                        perfect   **plagal**   **imperfect**

[1 mark]

d)   Which key is this excerpt in?

....
[1 mark]

e)   Look at the key of the piece. How would you explain the sharpened note at **3**?

....
[1 mark]

f)   What term is used to describe the dots above the notes at **4**?

....
[1 mark]

g)   Which of these options best describes the texture of this music?
     Circle your choice.

        monophonic   **melody with accompaniment**   **heterophonic**

[1 mark]

Revision Summary for Section Three

You've reached the end of Section Three — it's time to find out what you've taken in.
- Try these questions and tick off each one when you get it right.
- When you've done all the questions for a topic and are completely happy with it, tick off the topic.

Major and Minor Scales (p.24-26) ☑

1) How many notes are there in a major scale? How many notes are there in a minor scale?
2) Write out the names of the notes of a scale in words, numbers and Roman numerals.
3) Write down the tone-semitone pattern for a major scale.
4) What does a key signature tell you?
5) How do you find the 'relative minor' of a major scale?
6) D major has two sharps — F and C. What's the key signature of the relative minor?
7) Write out A minor in each of the three types of minor scale and label the tone and semitone gaps.
8) How many major scales are there altogether?
9) How many minor scales are there altogether?
10) Write down all the major scales in order around the circle of fifths, starting with C major.

Modes, Other Scales and Intervals (p.27-29) ☐

11) Write out two common modes.
12) What's a pentatonic scale? What types of music often use pentatonic scales?
13) What are the notes in a G major pentatonic scale?
14) What's a chromatic scale? How many notes are there in a chromatic scale?
15) What's the difference between a melodic and a harmonic interval?
16) Give the name and number of each of these intervals: a) A to C   b) B to F   c) C to B   d) D to A
17) What's a tritone?

Chords, Triads and Inversions (p.34-39) ☑

18) What do you call chords with: a) clashing notes   b) notes that sound good together?
19) What are the two most common types of triad? Describe how you make each one.
20) What makes a 7th chord different from a triad?
21) Write down the letter symbols for these chords: a) A minor   b) D diminished triad
22) Draw the scale of G major on a stave, then build a triad on each note. *(Don't forget the F sharps.)*
23) Which three chords of any major or minor scale are known as the 'primary' chords?
24) Where do the root, third and fifth go in: a) a first inversion chord   b) a second inversion chord?
25) Name and describe four different chord figurations.

Decorations, Cadences, Modulation and Texture (p.41-47) ☑

26) What's the difference between a 'diatonic' decoration and a 'chromatic' decoration?
27) Explain the following terms: a) auxiliary note   b) passing note   c) appoggiatura
28) What is a musical phrase and what job does a cadence do in a phrase?
29) How many chords make up a cadence?
30) Write down the four different types of cadence and which chords you can use to make each one.
31) What do you call it when a piece in a minor key ends on a major chord?
32) What do people mean when they talk about the 'texture' of music?
33) Explain the difference between monophonic music, homophonic music and polyphonic music.

Common Melodic Devices

Melodic devices are methods that composers use to construct **melodies**.
You need a few good **technical** words to describe them — like **conjunct**, **disjunct**, **triadic** and **scalic**.

Melodies can be Conjunct or Disjunct

1) <u>Conjunct</u> (or <u>stepwise</u>) melodies move mainly by <u>step</u> — notes that are a <u>tone</u> or a <u>semitone</u> apart.

2) The melody <u>doesn't</u> jump around, so it sounds quite <u>smooth</u>.
   This example shows a conjunct melody:

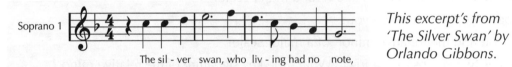

This excerpt's from 'The Silver Swan' by Orlando Gibbons.

3) <u>Disjunct</u> melodies move using a lot of <u>jumps</u> — notes that are more than a <u>major 2nd</u> (a <u>tone</u>) apart.

4) The melody sounds quite <u>spiky</u> as it jumps around a lot.

5) Disjunct melodies are <u>harder</u> to sing or play than conjunct ones.
   This example shows a disjunct melody:

This one's from 'Nessun Dorma' by Puccini.

6) The <u>distance</u> between the lowest and highest notes in any melody is called the <u>range</u> (or <u>compass</u>).

Triadic Melodies Use the Notes of a Triad

1) Triads are chords made up of <u>two intervals</u> of a third on top of each other — so triadic melodies usually move between the notes of a triad. (There's more on triads on page 35.)

2) For example, a <u>C major</u> triad is made up of the notes <u>C</u>, <u>E</u> and <u>G</u>. There's a <u>major third</u> between C and E, a <u>minor third</u> between E and G and a <u>perfect fifth</u> between <u>C</u> and <u>G</u>. There's more on intervals on pages 28-29.

3) This example shows a triadic melody:

This excerpt is from the first movement of Haydn's Trumpet Concerto.

Scalic Melodies Use the Notes of a Scale

1) A <u>scalic</u> melody moves up and down using the notes of a <u>scale</u>.

2) Scalic melodies are <u>similar</u> to conjunct melodies, but they can only move to the <u>next note</u> in the <u>scale</u>. Conjunct melodies can have a few <u>little jumps</u> in them.

3) Like conjunct melodies, scalic melodies sound quite <u>smooth</u>. Here's an example of a scalic melody (it's also from the first movement of Haydn's Trumpet Concerto):

Some melodies contain all of these melodic devices...

These different types of melody are pretty <u>easy</u> to spot if you have the <u>music</u> in front of you, but it's a bit <u>harder</u> if you're <u>listening</u> to them. Listen out for them in all types of music and practise <u>identifying</u> them.

Common Melodic Devices

*Call and response is used a lot in **blues**, **rock** and **pop**, as well as **African** and **Indian** music — so it's important that you know what it is. It's used in both **instrumental** and **vocal** music.*

Call and Response is Like a **Musical Conversation**

1) Call and response is a bit like question and answer. It takes place either between two groups of musicians, or between a leader and the rest of the group.

2) One group (or the leader) plays or sings a short phrase. This is the call. It's then answered by the other group. This is the response.

3) The call ends in a way that makes you feel a response is coming — e.g. it might finish with an imperfect cadence (see page 43).

4) Call and response is very popular in pop and blues music. Often the lead singer will sing the call and the backing singers will sing the response.

In a 12-bar blues structure (see p.130), the usual pattern of a call and response would be A, A1, B:

A is the call (4 bars)

A1 is the call repeated with slight variations (4 bars)

B is the response (4 bars).

To make things more complicated, sections A and B can have a 2-bar call and response of their own:

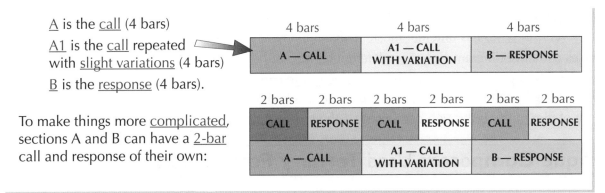

Indian and African Music Use Call and Response

1) In Indian music, call and response is usually used in instrumental music. One musician will play a phrase and it'll either be repeated or improvised upon by another musician.

2) African music uses call and response in religious ceremonies and community events. The leader will sing first and the congregation will respond.

3) Call and response is also used in African drumming music (see p.133). The master drummer plays a call and the rest of the drummers play an answering phrase.

Some Melodies Form an Arch Shape

1) If a melody finishes in the same way it started, then the tune has an arch shape.

2) The simplest example of this is ABA — where the first section is the same as the last section of the piece. This is extended in some pieces to ABCBA, or even ABCDCBA.

3) This gives a symmetrical melody because the sections are mirrored. It makes the whole piece feel more balanced.

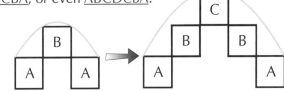

Call and response is used in a lot of music...

... so make sure you can spot it if it comes up in the exam — remember to listen out for it in both instrumental and vocal music. Keep your ears pricked for arch-shaped melodies too.

Common Forms

Form or *structure* is the way a piece of music is organised as a whole. **Strophic** form, **through-composed** form and **da capo arias** are all **song structures**. **Cyclic** form is found in **large** works like **symphonies**.

In **Strophic Form** Each **Verse** has the **Same Tune**

1) In strophic form, the same section of music is repeated over and over again with virtually no changes.
2) Strophic form is used in Classical, folk, blues and pop music.
3) In strophic songs, the music for each verse is the same, but the lyrics change in every verse. Hymns are a good example of this.
4) Strophic form can be thought of like this: A, A1, A2, A3, etc. — the same section is repeated but with a small change (the lyrics).
5) The first part of Led Zeppelin's 'Stairway to Heaven' is in strophic form.

In **Through-Composed Form** Each **Verse** is **Different**

1) Through-composed form is the opposite of strophic form — the music changes in every verse.
2) Every verse of lyrics has different music to accompany it, so there's no repetition.
3) Verses can have different melodies, different chords, or both.
4) This form is popular in opera, as the changing music can be used to tell stories. Verses sung by different characters can be completely different.
5) A lot of film music is through-composed — the music changes to reflect what's happening on-screen.

'Bohemian Rhapsody' by Queen is a through-composed pop song.

Baroque Composers Used **Ternary Form** in **Arias**

1) An aria is a solo in an opera or oratorio (see p.86).
2) Arias from the Baroque period (1600-1750) are often in ternary form (see p.81). Arias like this are called 'da capo arias'. Handel wrote lots of these.

After repeating Section A and Section B you come to the instruction da capo al fine. It means "go back to the beginning and play to where it says fine". The fine is at the end of Section A. That's where the piece finishes.

Works in **Cyclic Form** Have a **Common Theme**

1) Pieces in cyclic form have common themes in all the movements. These themes link the movements together.
2) Big works like sonatas, symphonies and concertos are sometimes in cyclic form.
3) The linking themes vary in different ways, e.g. they might be played on different instruments, played faster or slower, or played in a different key in different movements. You'll still be able to recognise them though.
4) An example of a common theme in a piece in cyclic form is the four-note theme of Beethoven's Fifth Symphony. It appears in all the movements of the symphony.
5) Film music often has a theme — a bit of melody that keeps popping up throughout the film. The main theme from 'Star Wars®' by John Williams is really easy to recognise.

Don't mind me — I'm just passing through...

Make sure you're completely sorted with the definitions and proper names of all these forms. Have a listen to the suggested pieces, and check you can spot the features of the forms they're written in.

Common Forms

Continuo and **ground bass** are both types of **bass part**. A *cadenza* is played by a **soloist**.

A **Continuo** is a **Bass Part**

1) A <u>continuo</u> (or <u>basso continuo</u>) is a <u>continuous bass part</u>. Most music written in the <u>Baroque period</u> has a continuo that the <u>harmony</u> of the whole piece is based on (see p.80).

2) The continuo can be played by <u>more than one</u> instrument, but at least one of the <u>continuo group</u> must be able to play <u>chords</u> (e.g. a <u>harpsichord</u>, <u>organ</u>, <u>lute</u>, <u>harp</u>, etc.). A <u>cello</u>, <u>double bass</u> or <u>bassoon</u> could also be used. The most common combination was a <u>harpsichord</u> and a <u>cello</u>.

3) Continuo parts were usually written using a type of <u>notation</u> called <u>figured bass</u>. Only the <u>bass notes</u> were written on the stave, but <u>numbers</u> underneath the notes told the performers which <u>chords</u> to play. The continuo players would then <u>improvise</u> using the <u>notes</u> of the <u>chord</u>.

4) If there <u>weren't</u> any numbers written, the chord would be a <u>normal triad</u> (the <u>root</u>, the <u>third</u> and the <u>fifth</u>). A <u>4</u> meant play a <u>fourth</u> instead of the <u>third</u>, and a <u>6</u> meant play a <u>sixth</u> instead of the <u>fifth</u>. A <u>7</u> meant that a <u>7th</u> should be added to the chord.

5) The improvisation is called a <u>realization</u> — the performer would 'realize' a continuo part.

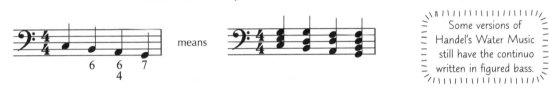

Some versions of Handel's Water Music still have the continuo written in figured bass.

Ground Bass Pieces Have **Repetition AND Variety**

1) A <u>ground bass</u> is a <u>repeated bass part</u> that's usually <u>four</u> or <u>eight</u> bars long. It can be played by the left hand on a <u>harpsichord</u> or <u>piano</u>, or by the <u>cello</u> and <u>double bass</u> in a chamber orchestra. A ground bass is a type of <u>ostinato</u> — a short <u>pattern</u> of notes <u>repeated</u> throughout a piece of music.

2) The <u>tune</u> is played over the ground bass part. First you hear the main tune, then a load of <u>variations</u>. The variations are played as one <u>continuous</u> piece — there are <u>no gaps</u> between them.

3) The ground bass part can be varied too. You change the <u>starting note</u> but keep the <u>pattern</u> the same.

First time round, the ground bass tune starts on C.   *Later on you get the same tune starting on G.*

4) The ground bass piece gets more and more <u>complex</u> as it goes on. It can be <u>developed</u> by adding extra, <u>decorative</u> notes to the melody, using more <u>advanced harmonies</u> and <u>adding</u> more <u>instruments</u> to give a <u>richer texture</u>.

A **Cadenza** is Where a **Soloist** can **Show Off**

1) A <u>cadenza</u> is a bit of music that's played by a <u>soloist</u>, usually in the middle of a <u>concerto</u> (see p.91).

2) Almost all <u>concertos</u> have a cadenza — it allows the soloist to <u>show off</u> their <u>technique</u>.

3) Cadenzas started out as <u>improvisations</u> on the <u>main themes</u> of a piece, but now most of them are <u>written out</u> by the <u>composer</u>. However, <u>different musicians</u> will interpret the cadenza in their own way.

Right, that's this page done — better continuo onto the next one...

Listen to a couple of different musicians' performances of Haydn's <u>Trumpet Concerto in E♭ major</u> — the <u>cadenzas</u> will sound <u>different</u> in each one, even though the soloists are playing the <u>same notes</u>.

Popular Song Forms

*It's not just **Classical** music that follows set **structures** — **pop songs** do as well.*

Pop Songs Usually Have an **Intro**

Pop tunes almost always start with an <u>intro</u>. It does <u>two jobs</u>:

- It often uses the best bit from the rest of the song to <u>set the mood</u>.
- It grabs people's <u>attention</u> and makes them <u>sit up and listen</u>.

Most Pop Songs Have a **Verse-Chorus Structure**

<u>After</u> the intro, the structure of most pop songs goes <u>verse-chorus-verse-chorus</u>.

- All the verses usually have the <u>same tune</u>, but the <u>lyrics change</u> for each verse.
- The chorus has a <u>different tune</u> from the verses, usually quite a catchy one. The lyrics and tune of the chorus <u>don't change</u>.
- In a lot of songs the verse and chorus are both <u>8 or 16 bars long</u>.

'Be My Baby' by 60s girl group The Ronettes has a verse-chorus structure.

The old verse-chorus thing can get repetitive. To avoid this most songs have a <u>middle 8</u>, or <u>bridge</u>, that sounds different. It's an <u>8-bar section</u> in the <u>middle</u> of the song with <u>new chords</u>, <u>new lyrics</u> and a whole <u>new feel</u>.

The song ends with a <u>coda</u> or <u>outro</u> that's <u>different</u> to the verse and the chorus. You can use the coda for a <u>big finish</u> or to <u>fade out gradually</u>.

Pop Songs Can Have **Other Structures** Too

For example:

CALL AND RESPONSE

This has <u>two bits</u> to it. <u>Part 1</u> is the call — it asks a musical <u>question</u>. <u>Part 2</u>, the response, responds with an <u>answer</u> (p.55).

RIFF

A <u>riff</u> is a <u>short section</u> of music that's <u>repeated</u> over and over again (a bit like an <u>ostinato</u> — see p.83). Riffs can be used to build up a <u>whole song</u>. <u>Each part</u>, e.g. the drums or bass guitar, has its own riff. All the riffs <u>fit together</u> to make one section of the music. They often <u>change</u> for the <u>chorus</u>.

'All of Me' by John Legend is an R&B ballad.

BALLADS

These are songs that tell <u>stories</u>. Each verse usually has the <u>same rhythm</u> and <u>same tune</u>.

32-BAR SONG FORM

This breaks down into <u>four 8-bar sections</u>. Sections 1, 2 and 4 all have the <u>same melody</u>, but may have different lyrics. Section 3 has a <u>contrasting melody</u>, making an AABA structure. The 32 bars may be repeated. The song 'Somewhere Over the Rainbow' from the film 'The Wizard of Oz' has this form.

SUGGESTED LISTENING

Verse — chorus — verse — chorus — tea break — chorus...

Songs from <u>musicals</u> follow these structures too. Have a listen to '<u>Any Dream Will Do</u>' from '<u>Joseph and the Amazing Technicolour Dreamcoat</u>', '<u>Bui Doi</u>' from '<u>Miss Saigon</u>' and '<u>Somewhere That's Green</u>' from '<u>Little Shop of Horrors</u>', and look for the structures.

Warm-up and Exam Questions

1) Describe each of the following melody structures:

   Conjunct **Disjunct** **Triadic** **Scalic**

2) What is through-composed form?

3) What is a ground bass, and what instruments often play these parts?

Exam Question

If there are bits you get stuck on in this question, reread the last few pages, then try again.

Play the excerpt **four** times, leaving a short pause between each playing.

Track 28

a) i) The key signature of the excerpt is shown below.
   What key is the excerpt in?

   ....
   [1 mark]

   ii) What is the interval between the notes shown on the right?
   Circle your answer.

   Diminished fifth   **Perfect fifth**   **Augmented fifth**

   [1 mark]

b) In the first half of the excerpt, the piano's lines are answered by
   the violin. What is this back-and-forth movement called?

   ....
   [1 mark]

c) Describe how the violin melody changes throughout the excerpt.

   ....

   ....

   ....

   ....
   [3 marks]

Exam Question

Play the excerpt **four** times, leaving a short pause between each playing.

Track 29

a) What musical period was this piece composed in?

....

[1 mark]

b) Name two instruments that play in the excerpt.

....

....

[2 marks]

c) The melody at the start of the excerpt is shown below.

i) Fill in the missing notes in bars 3 and 4.
The rhythm is given above the stave.

[7 marks]

ii) Which word best describes the melodic style in this excerpt?
Circle your choice from the options below.

Conjunct   **Disjunct**   **Triadic**

[1 mark]

d) What type of bass part is used in this piece?

....

[1 mark]

e) Give one instrument that plays the bass part.

....

[1 mark]

Revision Summary for Section Four

You're done and dusted with <u>Section Four</u> — do a quick stretch and get ready to <u>test your knowledge</u>.

- Try these questions and <u>tick off each one</u> when you <u>get it right</u>.
- When you've done <u>all the questions</u> for a topic and are <u>completely happy</u> with it, tick off the topic.

Common Melodic Devices (p.54-55) ☑

1) Explain what is meant by each of the following words that are used to describe melodies:
   - a) conjunct,
   - b) disjunct,
   - c) triadic,
   - d) scalic. ☑
2) What is call and response? ☑
3) Name two types of music that use call and response. ☑
4) Explain what is meant by an arch-shaped melody. ☑

Common Forms (p.56-57) ☑

5) What's the difference between strophic and through-composed form? ☑
6) Give an example of a type of music that's often written in through-composed form, and explain why this form is used. ☑
7) What's a da capo aria? ☑
8) What is cyclic form? ☑
9) What is basso continuo? ☑
10) Explain how figured bass works. ☑
11) Describe the structure of a ground bass piece. ☑
12) What's a cadenza? ☑

Popular Song Forms (p.58) ☑

13) Why do pop songs have an introduction? ☑
14) Describe verse-chorus structure. ☑
15) What is a bridge? ☑
16) What is a riff? ☑
17) What is the structure of a song in 32-bar form? ☑
18) Name two structures (other than 32-bar form) often used in pop songs. ☑

Brass Instruments

*You probably know a lot about **your** instrument. It's also a good idea to know about the instruments other people play so you can understand what they're up to. **Brass** first.*

Brass Instruments are All Made of Metal

1) Brass instruments include <u>horns</u>, <u>trumpets</u>, <u>cornets</u>, <u>trombones</u> and <u>tubas</u>.

2) They're all basically a length of <u>hollow metal tubing</u> with a <u>mouthpiece</u> (the bit you blow into) at one end and a <u>funnel shape</u> (the <u>bell</u>) at the other.

3) The different <u>shapes</u> and <u>sizes</u> of these parts gives each brass instrument a different tone and character.

4) Brass instruments often play <u>fanfares</u> (short musical <u>flourishes</u>) in orchestral pieces. They're most commonly played on the <u>trumpet</u>, and can be accompanied by <u>percussion</u>. A fanfare might also be played as part of a <u>ceremony</u>.

French horn

trumpet

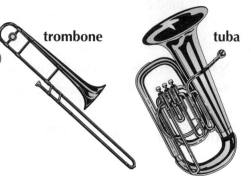

trombone

tuba

You Get a Noise by 'Buzzing' Your Lips

1) To <u>make a sound</u> on a brass instrument, you have to make the air <u>vibrate</u> down the tube.

2) You do it by '<u>buzzing</u>' your lips into the <u>mouthpiece</u>. You <u>squeeze</u> your lips together, then <u>blow</u> through a tiny gap so you get a <u>buzzing noise</u>.

3) You have to squeeze your lips together <u>tighter</u> to get <u>higher notes</u>.

4) Notes can be <u>slurred</u> (played together <u>smoothly</u>) or <u>tongued</u> (you use your tongue to <u>separate</u> the notes).

Brass Instruments Use Slides and Valves to Change Pitch

1) Squeezing your lips only gets a <u>limited range</u> of notes. To get a decent range, brass instruments use <u>slides</u> (like on a trombone) or <u>valves</u> (like on a trumpet).

2) The <u>slide</u> on a trombone is the <u>U-shaped tube</u> that moves in and out of the main tube. Moving it <u>out</u> makes the tube <u>longer</u> so you get a <u>lower</u> note. Moving it in makes the tube <u>shorter</u> so you get a <u>higher</u> note.

3) <u>Horns</u>, <u>trumpets</u> and <u>cornets</u> use three buttons connected to <u>valves</u>. The valves <u>open</u> and <u>close</u> different sections of the tube to make it <u>longer</u> or <u>shorter</u>. Pressing down the buttons in <u>different combinations</u> gives you all the notes you need.

Brass Players use Mutes to Change the Tone

1) A <u>mute</u> is a kind of <u>bung</u> that's put in the <u>bell</u> of a brass instrument. It's used to make the instrument play more <u>quietly</u> and change the <u>tone</u>. You wouldn't usually use one all the way through a piece — just for a <u>short section</u>.

2) <u>Different shapes</u> and <u>sizes</u> of mute change the tone in different ways, e.g. the <u>wah-wah</u> mute gives the instrument a wah-wah sound.

EXAM TIP

Brass instruments aren't always made of brass...

If you get brass in a listening test and need to say what instrument it is, remember that bigger instruments generally play lower notes and smaller instruments usually play higher notes.

Woodwind Instruments

*Some people get woodwind and brass muddled up. If you're one of them, **learn the difference**.*

Woodwind Instruments Used to be Made of Wood

Woodwind instruments got their name because they all use <u>air</u> — wind — to make a sound and once upon a time were all made of <u>wood</u>. Nowadays some are still made of <u>wood</u>. Others are made of <u>plastic</u> or <u>metal</u>. These are the main ones:

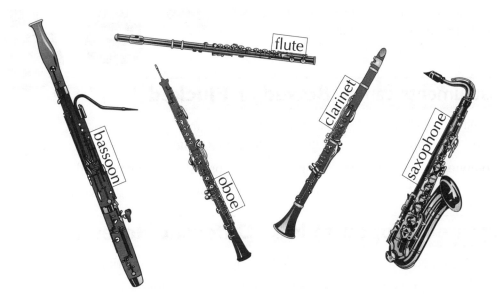

Woodwind Instruments Make Sound in Different Ways

To get a <u>sound</u> from a <u>woodwind</u> instrument, you have to make the <u>air</u> in its tube <u>vibrate</u>. There are <u>three different ways</u> woodwind instruments do this:

1) <u>Edge-tone instruments</u> — <u>flutes</u> and <u>piccolos</u>. Air is blown across an <u>oval-shaped hole</u>. The <u>edge</u> of the hole <u>splits</u> the air. This makes it <u>vibrate</u> down the instrument and make the sound.

2) <u>Single-reed instruments</u> — <u>clarinets</u> and <u>saxophones</u>. Air is blown down a <u>mouthpiece</u> which has a <u>reed</u> (a thin slice of wood/reed/plastic) clamped to it. The reed <u>vibrates</u>, making the air in the instrument <u>vibrate</u>, and creating the sound.

3) <u>Double-reed instruments</u> — <u>oboes</u> and <u>bassoons</u>. The air passes between <u>two reeds</u>, tightly bound together and squeezed between the lips. The reeds <u>vibrate</u> and you get a sound.

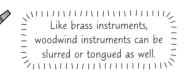

Like brass instruments, woodwind instruments can be slurred or tongued as well.

Different Notes are Made by Opening and Closing Holes

1) Woodwind instruments are covered in <u>keys</u>, <u>springs</u> and <u>levers</u> (or just holes for some instruments). These operate little <u>pads</u> that <u>close</u> and <u>open</u> holes down the instrument.

2) Opening and closing holes effectively makes the instrument longer or shorter. The <u>shorter</u> the tube, the <u>higher</u> the note. The <u>longer</u> the tube, the <u>lower</u> the note.

I can't see the woodwind for the clarinets...

Flutes and saxophones are made of metal but they're still woodwind instruments. The general term 'wind instruments' refers to both woodwind <u>and</u> brass instruments together, as they both use air to make a noise.

Orchestral Strings

*Orchestral strings are the **heart** of the orchestra — or so string players would have you believe.*

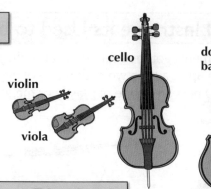

violin

viola

cello

double bass

Orchestral Strings are Very Alike

The double bass, cello, viola and violin are all made and played in a similar way. The main differences are the size and pitch.

The bigger the instrument is, the lower the sounds it makes. So the double bass plays the lowest notes and the violin plays the highest.

bow (made of wood and hair). The hair is drawn across the strings.

Stringed Instruments can be **Bowed** or **Plucked**

When the strings vibrate, the air inside the instrument vibrates and amplifies the sound. There are two ways to get the strings vibrating:

1) Bowing — drawing a bow across the string. *Con arco* (or just *arco*) means 'with bow'.

2) Plucking the string with the tip of your finger. The posh word for this is *pizzicato*.

The **Strings** are '**Stopped**' to Make **Different Notes**

1) You can get an "open note" just by plucking or bowing one of the four strings.

2) To get all the other notes, you have to change the length of the strings. You do this by pressing down with your finger. It's called stopping.

3) If you stop a string close to the bridge, the string's short and you get a high note.

4) If you stop a string further away from the bridge, the string's longer and you get a lower note.

5) Double-stopping is when two notes are played at the same time. Both strings are pressed (not open).

6) If you just touch a string lightly at certain points (instead of stopping), you can produce a series of higher, fainter-sounding notes called harmonics.

You Can Get **Very Varied** Effects with Stringed Instruments

mute

strings

bridge

1) **Tremolo**   The bow's moved back and forth really quickly. This makes the notes sort of trembly. It's a great effect for making music sound spooky and dramatic.

2) **Col legno**   The wood of the bow (instead of the hair) is tapped on the strings. This makes an eerie, tapping sound.

3) **Con sordino**   A mute is put over the bridge (the piece of wood that supports the strings). It makes the strings sound distant and soft. Mutes are made of wood, rubber or metal.

4) **Vibrato**   By wobbling the finger used to stop a string, a player varies the pitch slightly, creating a rich tone. This technique is also used on the guitar (see next page).

The **Harp** is Different...

1) The harp's always plucked — not bowed.

2) Most have 47 strings. Plucking each string in order on a concert harp is like playing up the white notes on a piano.

3) It has seven pedals. Pressing and releasing these lets you play sharp and flat notes.

4) You can play one note at a time, or play chords by plucking a few strings together.

EXAM TIP

Don't stop now, there are lots more instruments to come...

Make sure you learn the different string effects — you might need to identify them in the exam.

Guitars

*Guitars are **everywhere** so it's best to know a bit about how they work.*

An **Acoustic Guitar** has a **Hollow Body**

The acoustic guitar makes a sound the same way as the orchestral strings — by vibrating air in its belly. Slightly different types are used by pop, folk and classical guitarists, but the basic design is similar.

HOLLOW BODY makes the string vibrations resonate, giving a louder sound.

acoustic guitar

STRINGS tuned to the notes E(low)-A-D-G-B-E(high). Low E is the string nearest your head as you're playing. Played with fingers or a plectrum.

FRETS (the little metal strips on the fingerboard/neck) help the player find the correct finger position for different notes.

There are three different kinds of acoustic guitar:

1) The classical or Spanish guitar has nylon strings (the thickest three are covered in fine wire).
2) The acoustic guitar has steel strings and is used mainly in pop and folk music.
3) The 12-stringed guitar is often used in folk music. There are two of each string, giving a 'thicker' sound which works well for accompanying singing.

Some guitar music is written in tablature (tab for short) — the numbers tell guitarists which frets to place their fingers at for each string.

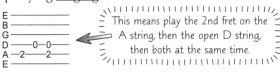

This means play the 2nd fret on the A string, then the open D string, then both at the same time.

Electric Guitars Use an **Amplifier** and a **Loudspeaker**

electric guitar

1) An electric guitar has six strings, just like an acoustic guitar, and is played in a similar way.
2) The main difference is that an electric guitar has a solid body. The sound's made louder electronically, using an amplifier and a loudspeaker.
3) A combo (short for combination) is an amplifier and loudspeaker 'all in one'.

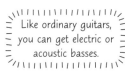

The **Bass Guitar** has **Four Strings**

1) The bass guitar works like a guitar except it usually has four strings, not six.
2) They're tuned to the notes E-A-D-G (from lowest note to highest).
3) It's lower pitched than other guitars because it has thicker and longer strings.
4) Most bass guitars have frets, but there are some (imaginatively named fretless basses) that don't.

Like ordinary guitars, you can get electric or acoustic basses.

Guitar Strings are **Picked** or **Strummed**

1) Plucking one string at a time is called picking. Classical and lead guitarists pick the notes of a melody. Bass guitarists almost always pick out the individual notes of a bass line. They hardly ever strum.
2) Playing two or more strings at a time in a sweeping movement is called strumming. It's how chords are usually played. Pop and folk guitarists tend to play accompaniments rather than tunes, so they do more strumming than picking.
3) A plectrum is a small, flat piece of plastic that guitarists can use to pluck or strum with.
4) 'Hammer-on' (ho) and 'pull-off' (po) are techniques that allow a guitarist to play notes in quick succession — they create a smoother, more legato sound than picking.
5) Another guitar technique is 'palm muting' (pm) — dampening the sound with your hand whilst plucking the strings. This can be done on bass guitars too.
6) To produce a different sound on the bass guitar, you can strike the strings with your thumb (instead of plucking with your fingers), which gives a more percussive sound. This is known as slap bass.
7) Guitarists can also press a tube (usually made of metal) called a slide or bottleneck against the strings. The player can move smoothly between notes by sliding this up or down the neck of the guitar.

Keyboard Instruments

*The actual **keyboard** looks much the same on most keyboard instruments, but the wires and mysterious levers **inside** vary quite a bit. That means the **sounds** they make vary too.*

Harpsichords, Virginals and Clavichords Came First

harpsichord

1) Harpsichords were invented long before pianos. They're still played today but they were most popular in the Baroque and early Classical periods.

2) Harpsichords have quite a tinny, string sound. When you press a key a string inside is plucked by a lever. You can't vary the strength of the pluck, so you can't vary the dynamics.

3) A virginal is a miniature table-top version of a harpsichord. In the sixteenth century, virginals were really popular in England.

4) The clavichord is another early keyboard instrument. Clavichords are small and have a soft sound. The strings are struck with hammers (called "blades"), not plucked, so you can vary the dynamics a little bit.

The Most Popular Keyboard Instrument Now is the Piano

1) The piano was invented around 1700. The technology is more sophisticated than it was in earlier keyboard instruments. When a key's pressed, a hammer hits the strings. The harder you hit the key, the harder the hammer hits the strings and the louder the note — there's a big range of dynamics.

2) Pianos have a wide range of notes — up to seven and a half octaves.

3) Pianos have pedals that let you change the sound in different ways.

The soft pedal on the left mutes the strings, making a softer sound.

The sustain pedal on the right lifts all the dampers. This lets the sound ring on until you release the pedal.

For more detail on the piano, have a look at page 100.

Grand pianos have a middle pedal too. This lets the player choose which notes to sustain. Modern pianos might have an extra mute pedal for very quiet practising.

Traditional Organs Use Pumped Air to Make Sound

1) The traditional organ (the massive instrument with hundreds of metal pipes that you see in churches and concert halls) is one of the most complicated instruments ever designed.

2) Sound is made by blowing air through sets of pipes called ranks. The air is pumped in by hand, foot or, on more recent organs, electric pumps.

3) The pipes are controlled by keyboards (called manuals) and lots of pedals which make a keyboard for the player's feet.

4) Pressing a key or pedal lets air pass through one of the pipes and play a note. Longer pipes make lower notes. Shorter pipes make higher notes.

5) Organs can play different types of sound by using differently designed pipes. Buttons called stops are used to select the different pipes. One stop might select pipes that make a trumpet sound, another might select a flute sound...

6) Modern electronic organs don't have pipes. Sound is produced electronically instead. These organs are much smaller and cheaper to build.

 REVISION TIP

You've got to learn it all...

Listen to music played on each of these instruments so that you know how they all sound — harpsichords have a more jangly tone than pianos, and organs are fairly easy to spot as well.

Percussion

*A percussion instrument is anything you have to **hit** or **shake** to get a sound out of it. There are **two types**: those that play tunes are called **tuned percussion**, and the ones you just hit are **untuned**.*

Tuned Percussion Can Play Different Notes

XYLOPHONES have wooden bars. The sound is 'woody'.

GLOCKENSPIEL — Looks a bit like a xylophone but the bars are made of metal. Sounds tinkly and bell-like.

CELESTA — a bit like a glockenspiel except that you use a keyboard instead of whacking it with a hammer.

TUBULAR BELLS — Each of the hollow steel tubes plays a different note. Sounds a bit like church bells.

TIMPANI — also called kettledrums. The handles on the side or the foot pedal can be used to tighten or relax the skin, giving different notes.

VIBRAPHONE — This is like a giant glockenspiel. There are long tubes called resonators below the bars to make the notes louder and richer. Electric fans can make the notes pulsate, giving a warm and gentle sound.

There are Hundreds of Untuned Percussion Instruments

Untuned percussion includes any instrument that'll make a noise — but can't play a tune. These are the instruments that are used for pure rhythm. It's pretty much impossible to learn every untuned percussion instrument, but try and remember the names of these.

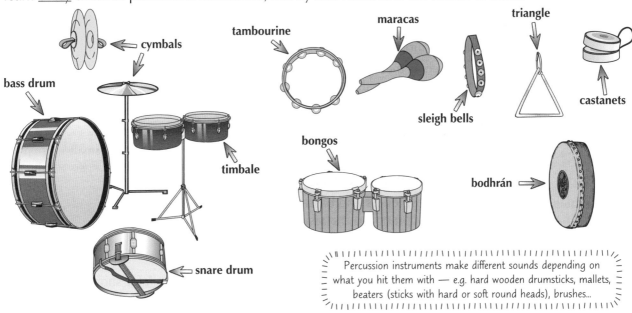

Percussion instruments make different sounds depending on what you hit them with — e.g. hard wooden drumsticks, mallets, beaters (sticks with hard or soft round heads), brushes...

Remember — xylophones are wooden, glockenspiels are metal...

In a band, the drummer's job is to make a song sound like it's going somewhere and keep everyone in time. In an orchestra, percussion emphasises the rhythm of the piece and also adds special effects — you can imitate thunder with a drum roll on the timpani, or the crashing of waves with clashes of the cymbals.

The Voice

*There are special names for male and female **voices** and **groups** of voices.*

Female Singers are Soprano, Alto or Mezzo-Soprano

1) A singer with a particular type of voice is expected to be able to sing a certain <u>range</u> of notes.

2) The range of notes where a particular singer is most <u>comfortable</u> is called the <u>tessitura</u>. This term can also describe the <u>most commonly used</u> range of notes within a vocal or instrumental part of a piece.

3) A <u>high</u> female voice is called a <u>soprano</u>. The main female parts in operas are sung by sopranos.

4) A <u>lower</u> female voice is called an <u>alto</u> — short for <u>contralto</u>.

5) <u>Mezzo-sopranos</u> sing in the <u>top</u> part of the <u>alto</u> range and the <u>bottom</u> part of the <u>soprano</u> range.

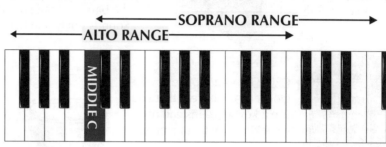

Male Voices are Tenor or Bass

1) <u>Higher</u> male voices are called <u>tenors</u>.

2) <u>Low</u> male voices are called <u>basses</u> (it's pronounced "bases").

3) <u>Baritones</u> sing the <u>top</u> part of the <u>bass</u> range and the <u>bottom</u> part of the <u>tenor</u> range.

4) Men who sing in the <u>female vocal range</u> are called <u>countertenors</u>.

5) Some tenors, baritones and basses can push their voices <u>higher</u> to sing some of the same notes as a <u>soprano</u>. This is called <u>falsetto</u> singing.

Children's Voices are Either Treble or Alto

1) A <u>high child's</u> voice in the <u>same range</u> as a <u>soprano</u> is called a <u>treble</u>.

2) A <u>low child's</u> voice is called an <u>alto</u>. They sing in exactly the <u>same range</u> as an adult alto.

3) <u>Girls'</u> voices <u>don't change much</u> as they get older. <u>Boys'</u> voices <u>drop</u> to a <u>lower range</u> when they hit puberty.

When Several Voices Sing Each Part It's a Choir

1) A <u>choir</u> is a group of singers. Each part is performed by <u>more than one</u> singer.

2) A <u>mixed voice choir</u> has sopranos, altos, tenors and basses (<u>SATB</u> for short).

3) An <u>all-male choir</u> has trebles, altos, tenors and basses — a treble has the same range as a soprano, so it's basically SATB.

4) A <u>male voice choir</u> is slightly different — it tends to have two groups of <u>tenors</u>, as well as <u>baritones</u> and <u>basses</u> (<u>TTBB</u> for short), with no higher parts.

5) An <u>all-female choir</u> has <u>two groups of sopranos</u> and <u>two groups of altos</u> (<u>SSAA</u> for short).

6) When a choir sings <u>without</u> an instrumental <u>accompaniment</u>, this is known as '<u>a cappella</u>'.

7) Music written for a choir is called <u>choral music</u> — see page 85.

These are the names for smaller groups:
2 singers = a **duet**
3 singers = a **trio**
4 singers = a **quartet**
5 singers = a **quintet**
6 singers = a **sextet**

No excuses — get on and learn all the voices...

The different voices don't just sound different in pitch — they've got different characters too, e.g. sopranos usually sound very clear and glassy, and basses sound more rich and booming.

Wind, Brass and Jazz Bands

*In your listening exam, you'll get marks for saying what type of **group** (or **ensemble**) is playing.*
***Wind**, **jazz** and **brass** bands can sound quite **similar**, so make sure you know the differences.*

Wind Bands have Woodwind, Brass and Percussion

1) Wind bands are <u>largish groups</u>, made up of 'wind' instruments —
   woodwind and brass — and percussion instruments.

2) There's <u>no string section</u>. If there was it would be an orchestra...

3) <u>Military bands</u> are wind bands. They tend to play <u>marches</u> — pieces with a
   <u>regular rhythm</u> (usually $\frac{4}{4}$ or $\frac{2}{4}$ time) that can be marched to.

Brass Bands have Brass and Percussion

1) A brass band is a group of <u>brass</u> and <u>percussion</u> instruments.

2) A typical brass band would have <u>cornets</u>, <u>flugelhorns</u>, <u>tenor</u> and <u>baritone horns</u>,
   <u>tenor</u> and <u>bass trombones</u>, <u>euphoniums</u> and <u>tubas</u>.

3) The exact <u>percussion instruments</u> depend on the piece being played.

4) Brass bands have been popular in <u>England</u> for <u>years</u>.

5) <u>Contests</u> are organised through the year to find out which bands are 'best'.
   There's a <u>league system</u> similar to football. The divisions are called <u>sections</u>.
   There are <u>five sections</u> and bands are <u>promoted</u> and <u>demoted</u> each year
   depending on how they do at the <u>regional</u> and <u>national</u> contests.

Jazz Bands are Quite Varied

1) Jazz bands have <u>no fixed set of instruments</u>.

2) Small jazz groups are known as <u>combos</u>. A typical combo
   might include a <u>trumpet</u>, <u>trombone</u>, <u>clarinet</u>, <u>saxophone</u>, <u>piano</u>,
   <u>banjo</u>, <u>double bass</u> and <u>drum kit</u> — but there's no fixed rule.
   Combos play in small venues like <u>clubs</u> and <u>bars</u>.

3) Larger jazz bands are known as <u>big bands</u> or <u>swing bands</u>. Instruments are doubled and tripled
   up so you get a <u>much bigger sound</u>. Big bands were really popular in the <u>1930s</u> and <u>1940s</u>.
   They played live at <u>dance halls</u>.

4) A large jazz band with a string section is called a <u>jazz orchestra</u> (though some jazz orchestras
   don't have a string section — they're just big jazz bands).

Jazz Bands have a Rhythm Section and a Front Line

In a jazz band, players are either in the <u>rhythm section</u> or the <u>front line</u>.

1) The <u>rhythm section</u> is the instruments responsible for <u>keeping the beat</u> and
   <u>adding the harmony parts</u>. The rhythm section's usually made up of the
   <u>drum kit</u> with a <u>double</u> or <u>electric bass</u>, <u>electric guitar</u> and <u>piano</u>.

2) The instruments that <u>play the melody</u> are the <u>front line</u>. This is usually
   <u>clarinets</u>, <u>saxophones</u> and <u>trumpets</u>, but could also be guitar or violin.

Keep at it — there are more groups to come...

You need to know the differences between wind, brass and jazz bands — if you reckon you've got it sorted,
test yourself by covering up the page and writing down the instruments that play in each type of band.

Chamber Music

*Chamber music is music composed for **small groups** and it's pretty formal stuff.*

Chamber Music was Originally 'Home Entertainment'

1) 'Chamber' is an old word for a room in a posh building like a palace or a mansion.

2) Rich people could afford to pay musicians to come and play in their 'chambers'. Musical families could play the music for themselves. The music written for these private performances is called chamber music.

3) Nowadays, you're more likely to hear chamber music in a concert hall or on a CD than live at someone's house. Let's face it — most people haven't got the cash to hire musicians for the evening, and they can download any music they want to listen to.

Chamber Music is Played by **Small Groups**

1) The rooms where musicians came to play were nice and big — but not enormous. Limited space meant that chamber music was written for a small number of musicians — between two and eight.

2) There's a name for each size of group:

Duet = two players
Trio = three players
Quartet = four players
Quintet = five players
Sextet = six players
Septet = seven players
Octet = eight players

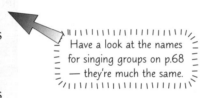
Have a look at the names for singing groups on p.68 — they're much the same.

3) With so few people in chamber groups, you don't need a conductor. Instead, one of the players leads. The others have to watch and listen carefully, to make sure the timing, dynamics and interpretation are right.

These instruments make up a 'piano trio' — see below.

4) Each part in the music is played by just one person.

Some **Chamber Groups** are **Extra-Popular** with Composers

Chamber music is written more often for some instrumental groups than others.

These are some of the most popular types of chamber group:

String trio	— violin, viola, cello
String quartet	— first violin, second violin, viola, cello
Piano trio	— piano, violin, cello (not three pianos)
Clarinet quintet	— clarinet, first violin, second violin, viola, cello (not five clarinets)
Wind quintet	— usually flute, oboe, clarinet, horn and bassoon

Chamber groups are small...

Learn the instruments that play in all the different chamber groups. Keep a special eye out for the piano trio and clarinet quintet — they're not what you'd expect. And finally, don't forget there's no conductor.

The Orchestra

*If you go to a classical concert, more often than not there'll be an **orchestra** up there on stage.*
Loads and loads of classical music has been written for orchestras.

A **Modern Orchestra** has **Four** Sections

If you go and see a <u>modern symphony orchestra</u>, it'll have <u>four sections</u> of instruments
— strings (p.64), woodwind (p.63), brass (p.62) and percussion (p.67).
The strings, woodwind, brass and percussion always sit in the <u>same places</u>.

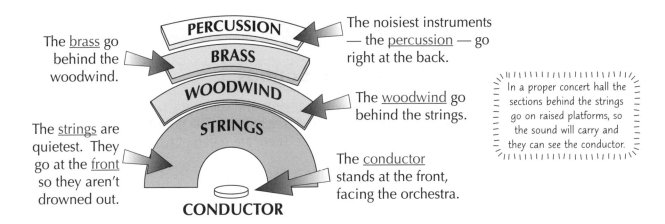

The <u>brass</u> go behind the woodwind.

PERCUSSION

BRASS

WOODWIND

STRINGS

The noisiest instruments — the <u>percussion</u> — go right at the back.

The <u>woodwind</u> go behind the strings.

The <u>strings</u> are quietest. They go at the <u>front</u> so they aren't drowned out.

The <u>conductor</u> stands at the front, facing the orchestra.

CONDUCTOR

In a proper concert hall the sections behind the strings go on raised platforms, so the sound will carry and they can see the conductor.

The **Conductor** has a **Complete Overview**

1) The conductor has a <u>score</u> — a version of the piece with <u>all the parts</u>. The <u>parts</u> are arranged in a <u>standard order</u>, one on top of the other, so that it's easy to see what any part is doing at any time. Woodwind parts are written at the <u>top</u>, followed by brass, percussion, and strings at the <u>bottom</u>.

2) The conductor <u>controls the tempo</u> by beating time with their hands, or a <u>baton</u> — a pointy white stick that's easy to see. There's a different way of beating time for each <u>time signature</u>.

3) The conductor '<u>cues in</u>' musicians — especially helpful for <u>brass</u> and <u>percussion</u>, who sometimes don't play anything for <u>hundreds of bars</u>, then suddenly have to play a <u>really loud, important bit</u>.

4) The conductor <u>interprets</u> the music. A conductor can decide whether to play one bit <u>louder</u> than another, whether to play a section in a <u>moody</u> or a <u>magical</u> way, and whether to make a piece sound very <u>smooth</u> or very <u>edgy</u>. They're a bit like a <u>film director</u> deciding the best way to <u>tell a story</u>.

An **Orchestra** is Any **Large Group with Strings**

<u>Symphony orchestras</u> (above) are the biggest type of orchestra. There are <u>other</u> smaller kinds too:

1) <u>String orchestra</u> — an orchestra with <u>stringed instruments</u> only.
2) <u>Chamber orchestra</u> — a <u>mini-orchestra</u>. It has a small string section, a wind and brass section with <u>one or two</u> of each instrument (but <u>no</u> tubas or trombones) and a small percussion section.

You have to do what the conductor tells you...

Copy out the diagram of the orchestra, but don't copy the labels. Close the book and see if you can fill in the different instrument sections in the right places. Then learn all about the conductor.

Music Technology

*Modern **technological** and 'virtual' instruments allow a huge variety of sounds to be created.*

MIDI lets you Connect Electronic Musical Instruments

1) MIDI was invented in 1983. It stands for Musical Instrument Digital Interface. It's a way of connecting different electronic instruments.

2) MIDI equipment is connected by MIDI cables.

3) MIDI data is digital information (i.e. in zeroes and ones). It's sent down the MIDI cables. MIDI instruments turn MIDI information into sound (or vice versa).

4) One important advantage of MIDI is that it allows musical equipment to be linked with computers, opening up a whole new world of music-making.

Synthesizers Let You Make New Sounds

Synthesizers come in different forms — some have keyboards and some don't. The most common ones today are virtual synthesizers, which are software-based (see below). The point of them is to let you create sounds, which often imitate musical instruments. There are different types of synthesizers:

1) Analogue synthesizers were mainly made in the 70s and early 80s. They've often got lots of knobs and sliders — you use these to change the sound.

2) Digital synthesizers started to be popular in the 80s. Most modern synthesizers are digital, though some of them try to mimic analogue synths. Digital synths usually have fewer knobs and sliders than analogue ones.

3) Software synths started to become popular in the late 90s. Software synths are computer programs (often linked to a sequencer — see below). They often have graphical sliders and knobs that you can move with a mouse. Some of them try to be like analogue and early digital synthesizers. They also try to recreate classic electric instruments like the Hammond organ.

Sequencers Let You Record, Edit and Replay Music

1) Sequencer is the posh word for equipment that can record, edit (mess about with) and replay music stored as MIDI or audio information. A "sequenced composition" is a musical piece produced mainly from synthesized sounds using a sequencer.

2) Modern sequencers are usually computer programs, which often include synthesizers and samplers.

3) Most sequencers can record audio (real sounds) as well as the MIDI stuff, so you can create synthesized music and then record your own voice or instruments along with it. If you're unhappy with part of a recording, it's easy to replace that section with a re-take.

4) Modern sequencers are multi-track recorders. This allows the various lines of music, such as those played by different instruments, to be recorded on separate tracks. The individual tracks can then be edited separately to achieve the perfect balance of sounds.

5) One of the big advantages of a sequencer is that it shows your music as actual notation or as representative boxes — this makes it much easier to change and try out new ideas.

6) Drum machines are special sequencers that play back rhythm patterns using built-in drum sounds.

This can all be a bit confusing...

Some of this stuff is quite technical — but don't panic. You don't need to have an in-depth understanding of how the different types of technology work — as long as you know what they do and what people use them for. You can even have a go at using them in your compositions.

Music Technology

*Sampling is a very popular way of putting **different sounds** into your music.*
*Samples can be **fiddled with** and **looped** to make long repeated sections.*

Samplers let you 'Pinch' Other People's Sounds

1) A <u>sampler</u> is a piece of equipment that can <u>record</u>, <u>process</u> (change) and <u>play back</u> bits of sound.
2) These sections of sound are called <u>samples</u>.
3) Samplers are often used to take a bit of a piece of music that's <u>already been recorded</u> to use in some new music.
4) You can sample anything from <u>instruments</u> to <u>birdsong</u> — even weird things like a <u>car horn</u>.
5) Today, samplers are most often used to <u>reproduce</u> the sound of <u>real instruments</u>, such as <u>strings</u> or <u>piano</u>. Most <u>pop music</u> is sampled.
6) <u>Pop stars</u> often use samples of <u>other people's</u> music in their own music — anything from <u>other pop songs</u> to bits from <u>Classical pieces</u>. For example:

   * <u>Madonna</u> used a sample of <u>ABBA's</u> '<u>Gimme! Gimme! Gimme! (A Man After Midnight)</u>' in her 2005 hit '<u>Hung Up</u>'.
   * <u>Take That</u> used a sample from <u>Verdi's *Requiem*</u> (see p.103) in '<u>Never Forget</u>' (1995).
   * <u>Fall Out Boy</u> used a sample of '<u>Tom's Diner</u>', originally by <u>Suzanne Vega</u>, in their song '<u>Centuries</u>' in 2014.

Samples Can be Added to Other Pieces

1) You don't have to create a piece made up <u>entirely</u> of samples — you can just add one or two, or use a whole range to create a <u>collage</u> of sound. The collage can then be put over the top of a repeating <u>drum and bass loop</u>.
2) <u>DJs</u> and <u>producers</u> often do this when they make a <u>dance remix</u> of a piece.

   > <u>REMIX</u> is a term used for a <u>different version</u> of a piece of music.
   > They're often used to turn <u>pop</u> or <u>rock</u> tunes into <u>dance</u> music
   > — e.g. by <u>speeding them up</u> and giving them a <u>fast drum beat</u>.

3) Samples can be added to a piece by <u>over-dubbing</u> — adding tracks <u>over the top</u> of other tracks. You can record a drum track, then <u>overlay</u> the guitar part, then the vocal part, etc.

DJs Choose, Play and Alter Music

1) <u>DJs</u> (<u>disc jockeys</u>) <u>choose</u> which tracks (lines of music) to play, and <u>change</u> bits of them (e.g. by adding <u>samples</u>). They choose <u>compatible tracks</u> — ones that work <u>well</u> together, e.g. tracks in the <u>same key</u>.
2) DJs play music in <u>clubs</u> and on the <u>radio</u>.
3) At a <u>live performance</u> in a club, the DJ sometimes adds <u>extra sounds</u> using <u>samples</u>, <u>keyboards</u> or a <u>drum machine</u> to build the piece up. Some DJs also <u>rap</u> over the top of the music.
4) DJs use a <u>mixing desk</u> to <u>combine</u> different tracks and <u>add extra sounds</u> to the music, and a set of <u>decks</u> to play their music.
5) The <u>amplification</u> is important — DJs need to make sure the right parts <u>stand out</u>, and that all parts can be <u>heard</u>. The amplification can be changed in <u>live performances</u>.

There's even a dance remix of Beethoven's 5th Symphony...

Again, there's lots of <u>technical bits</u> on this page. You might choose to use some samples in your own compositions, but even if you don't, you need to know how <u>other people</u> (like DJs) might use them.

Timbre

*When you're listening to music, you can pick out **individual instruments** because of their **unique sound** — e.g. a trumpet sounds nothing like a violin. This is all down to a little thing called **timbre**.*

Every Instrument Has its Own **Timbre**

1) <u>Timbre</u> is the <u>type of sound</u> that different instruments make. It's also known as <u>tone colour</u>.

2) <u>Musical notes</u> (and all sounds) are made by <u>vibrations</u>. Different instruments produce vibrations in <u>different ways</u>. For example, on a <u>string</u> instrument, the <u>bow</u> is drawn across the <u>string</u> to make it vibrate. On a <u>brass</u> instrument the vibrations are produced when the player '<u>buzzes</u>' their lips. The different <u>vibrations</u> make the <u>timbres</u> different.

3) The <u>size</u> and <u>material</u> of the instrument alter the timbre as well — e.g. a <u>cello</u> has a different timbre to a <u>violin</u> because it's <u>bigger</u>, and <u>wooden</u> flutes sound different from <u>metal</u> ones.

4) The same instrument can sound <u>different</u> depending on who's playing it. The <u>tone</u> (or quality) of the sound is affected by an individual's <u>playing style</u> and can be described as <u>rich</u>, <u>full</u>, <u>strong</u>, etc.

5) The overall nature of the sound produced by an instrument is called its <u>sonority</u>. <u>Timbre</u> and <u>tone</u> contribute to this, along with the <u>dynamics</u> and <u>articulation</u> of the music.

Instruments From the **Same Family** Have **Similar Timbres**

Even though each instrument has a <u>unique</u> timbre, it can still sometimes be <u>hard</u> to tell ones from the <u>same family</u> apart. Different families of instruments <u>change</u> the <u>timbre</u> in <u>different ways</u>:

STRING INSTRUMENTS

- String instruments (like the <u>violin</u>, <u>viola</u>, <u>cello</u> and <u>double bass</u>) have a <u>warm</u> sound. Notes are produced by making the <u>strings vibrate</u>, either using a <u>bow</u> or the <u>fingers</u>.
- All string instruments can be played *con arco* (with a bow), *pizzicato* (plucked), *con sordino* (muted) or *sul ponticello* (close to the bridge).
- <u>Double stopping</u> is when <u>two strings</u> are pressed at the <u>same time</u>, so <u>two notes</u> can be played at once.
- <u>Tremolo</u> sounds like <u>trembling</u> — the bow is moved <u>back and forth</u> very quickly.

PIANO

- When you press the <u>keys</u>, a <u>hammer</u> hits the strings inside the piano, making them <u>vibrate</u>.
- The timbre of the piano can be <u>changed</u> by using the <u>soft</u> or <u>sustain pedals</u>.

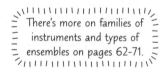

There's more on families of instruments and types of ensembles on pages 62-71.

WOODWIND INSTRUMENTS

- Wind instruments (e.g. <u>flute</u>, <u>clarinet</u>, <u>oboe</u> and <u>bassoon</u>) have a <u>soft</u>, <u>mellow</u> sound.
- <u>Edge-tone</u> instruments (e.g. flutes) make a <u>softer</u>, <u>breathier</u> sound than <u>reed</u> instruments (e.g. clarinets).
- Clarinets and oboes can <u>alter</u> their timbre by using a technique called '<u>bells up</u>', where the player <u>points</u> the end of the instrument <u>upwards</u>. This produces a <u>harsher</u> sound.

BRASS INSTRUMENTS

- Brass instruments (like the <u>trumpet</u>, <u>French horn</u>, <u>trombone</u> and <u>tuba</u>) have a <u>bright</u>, <u>metallic</u> sound.
- Playing <u>with a mute</u> (*con sordino*) can change the timbre.

PERCUSSION INSTRUMENTS

- Percussion instruments (e.g. <u>drums</u> and <u>xylophones</u>) make a sound when they're <u>struck</u>.
- What you hit them with can <u>change</u> the <u>timbre</u> — e.g. whether you use <u>sticks</u>, <u>brushes</u> or your <u>hands</u>.

SINGERS

- Singers produce notes when their <u>vocal cords</u> vibrate.
- The <u>speed</u> that they vibrate changes the <u>pitch</u> and the <u>timbre</u> — e.g. <u>bass</u> voices sound very <u>different</u> to <u>sopranos</u>.
- Techniques like <u>vibrato</u> (making the note <u>wobble</u>) can give a <u>richer</u> sound.
- <u>Falsetto</u> singing produces a much <u>thinner</u> sound.

I'm picking up good vibrations...

You may be asked to <u>describe</u> the timbre of different instruments that crop up in your exam.

Timbre

Electronic effects can be used to **alter** the timbre of an instrument or voice.

There are Lots of Different **Electronic Effects**

1) There are loads of <u>different ways</u> to <u>change</u> the sound of an instrument.

2) These effects are often used with electric guitars — they're really popular with <u>rock bands</u>, especially during <u>guitar solos</u>. Guitarists use <u>pedals</u> (e.g. a <u>wah-wah</u> pedal) to alter the <u>tone</u> or <u>pitch</u>.

3) The effects can also be used to change the sound of recorded music during <u>mixing</u> or <u>post-processing</u>.

4) <u>Electronic effects</u> (also called <u>studio effects</u>) include:

- **DISTORTION** <u>distorts</u> the sound.
- **REVERB** adds an <u>echo</u> to the sound.
- **CHORUS** makes it sound as if there's <u>more than one</u> player or singer — <u>copies</u> of the original sound are <u>mixed together</u>, with slight changes in <u>timing</u> and <u>pitch</u>.
- **PHASER** creates a '<u>whooshing</u>' effect (a bit like the noise an <u>aeroplane</u> flying overhead makes).
- **FLANGER** similar to a <u>phaser</u>, but makes a more <u>intense</u> sound. The effect is created by <u>combining</u> the <u>original sound</u> with a <u>copy</u>, and <u>varying the delay</u> between them. It's used a lot in <u>sci-fi programmes</u>.
- **PITCH SHIFTING** used to <u>bend</u> the natural note or <u>add</u> another <u>harmony</u>.
- **OCTAVE EFFECTS** creates <u>octaves</u> above or below the note being played.

Synthesized Sounds have **Different Timbres** to **Real Sounds**

1) The <u>natural</u> sound of an instrument can be digitally reproduced to create a <u>synthesized sound</u>.

2) <u>Electronic keyboards</u> have different <u>settings</u>, so they can be made to sound like pretty much any instrument, from violins to percussion.

One big <u>difference</u> between <u>real</u> and <u>synthesized sounds</u> is what happens to the <u>timbre</u> when the <u>volume</u> changes. When a <u>real</u> instrument is played <u>louder</u>, it has a <u>different timbre</u> to when it's played quietly. However, a <u>synthesized</u> sound has the <u>same timbre</u> at any volume — it's just the <u>loudness</u> that changes.

Sampling Uses **Recordings** of **Real Instruments**

1) The most effective way to <u>recreate</u> the sounds of real instruments is to use <u>sampling</u> (see p.73).

2) Sampling is where you <u>record</u> an instrument and use the recording (called a <u>sample</u>) in your music.

3) The samples can be <u>altered</u> to create different effects — there are lots of different <u>computer programs</u> that help you do this.

4) Samples can be <u>looped</u> (played over and over again), and other samples can be added <u>over the top</u>.

5) Most <u>electronic music</u> produced today uses looping, especially <u>drum patterns</u>.

6) It's <u>not</u> just instruments that can be sampled — you can take samples of anything you like, e.g. <u>traffic noises</u> or <u>doorbells</u>.

7) Lots of <u>pop songs</u> use samples — <u>Kanye West</u> sampled Ray Charles' '<u>I Got A Woman</u>' in his 2005 hit '<u>Gold Digger</u>'.

I'd like a sample of that cake please...

Have a listen to the 2005 hit '<u>Gold Digger</u>' by <u>Kanye West</u> — he uses a sample of '<u>I Got A Woman</u>' by <u>Ray Charles</u> (which was released more than 50 years earlier, in 1954).

Warm-up and Exam Questions

The questions on these pages are great for finding out what you know — don't ignore them.

Exam Question

Brush up on your exam technique with this question.

This question is about two excerpts, Track 30 and Track 31.

First play Track 30 **three** times, leaving a short pause for writing time between each playing.

 Track 30

a) Name the solo woodwind instrument that plays at the beginning.

....

[1 mark]

b) What is the other instrument that plays in the excerpt?

....

[1 mark]

Exam Question

c) Tick **one** box to indicate which shape best represents the opening of the melody played by the solo instrument.

Shape A ☐

Shape B ☐

Shape C ☐

[1 mark]

d) Describe the relationship of the two instruments heard here. Refer to the **texture** and any other interesting features.

....

....

[2 marks]

> Two marks available means you need to make two points. Don't forget to write about texture.

Track 31

Now play Track 31 **three** times, leaving a short pause for writing time between each playing.

e) Name the two solo woodwind instruments which play the melody at the beginning of this excerpt.

....

....

[2 marks]

> Make sure you write about the melody, not the accompaniment.

Turn over

Exam Question

f)   Name the family of instruments playing throughout this excerpt.

....

[1 mark]

g)   Ring the word that describes the scale used throughout the excerpt.

major   **minor**   **chromatic**

[1 mark]

h)   Tick one of the following to represent the backing melody played by the two wind instruments.

A   ☐

B   ☐

C   ☐

[1 mark]

i)   Ring **one** feature that you can hear in this excerpt.

accelerando   **crescendo**   **ritardando**

[1 mark]

Revision Summary for Section Five

That's a wrap on Section Five — have a go at these questions to see what you remember.
- Try these questions and tick off each one when you get it right.
- When you've done all the questions for a topic and are completely happy with it, tick off the topic.

Brass, Woodwind and Orchestral Strings (p.62-64) ☐

1) Name three brass instruments.
2) How do you vary the pitch on a brass instrument?
3) Name three woodwind instruments.
4) What are the three different mouthpieces used on woodwind instruments called? How do they work?
5) What are all those little keys, springs and levers for on a woodwind instrument?
6) What's the smallest orchestral string instrument?
7) What's the biggest string instrument that you play with a bow?
8) How do you make different notes on a string instrument?
9) What makes a harp different from the other string instruments? Give three differences.
10) Where would you put a mute on a bowed string instrument and what effect would it have?

Guitars, Keyboards, Percussion and Voices (p.65-68) ☐

11) How many strings are there on: a) an acoustic guitar   b) an electric guitar   c) a bass guitar?
12) What do you call those metal bits on the fingerboard of a guitar? Do you get them on a bass?
13) What's the proper word for twanging a guitar string with a plectrum?
14) Name three different keyboard instruments.
15) What's the biggest type of keyboard instrument?
16) What's the most popular keyboard instrument?
17) How could you tell you were listening to a church organ and not a harpsichord?
18) Name three tuned percussion instruments and six untuned percussion instruments.
19) What's the highest type of singing voice? What's the lowest type of singing voice?
20) What do you call a boy's voice when it's got the same range as a soprano?

Ensembles and Groups (p.69-71) ☐

21) How can you tell the difference between a wind band and a brass band?
22) What are the two sections of a jazz orchestra called, and what are their jobs?
23) Why's chamber music called chamber music?
24) How many people are there in: a) a trio   b) a sextet   c) a quartet   d) an octet?
25) How many clarinets are there in a clarinet quintet?
26) Sketch a plan of a standard symphony orchestra. Label the different sections and the conductor.
27) What sections are there in a string orchestra, chamber orchestra and jazz orchestra?

Music Technology and Timbre (p.72-75) ☐

28) How is MIDI information stored?
29) What do sequencers do?
30) What are samples? How can they be used in tracks?
31) Explain how sound is produced on: a) a string instrument   b) a piano   c) a brass instrument?
32) Name four different electronic effects.

The Baroque Style

*You need to know all about the **features** and **development** of **Western classical music** between 1650 and 1910. Let's start with the musical style from the start of that period — **Baroque music**.*

Baroque has a Recognisable Sound

The <u>Baroque</u> period was from about <u>1600-1750</u>. Key composers include <u>Bach</u>, <u>Handel</u>, <u>Vivaldi</u> and <u>Purcell</u>. Baroque music's pretty <u>easy to recognise</u>. These are the <u>main things</u> to look out for:

1) The <u>melodies</u> are built up from <u>short musical ideas</u> (called <u>motifs</u>), so you get quite a bit of <u>repetition</u>.

2) The <u>harmonies</u> are simple, with a fairly narrow range of chords — mainly <u>I</u> and <u>V</u>.

3) The <u>melody</u> is packed with <u>ornaments</u>, added in to make it sound more <u>interesting</u> (see p.84).

4) The <u>music</u> often involves <u>counterpoint</u> — where <u>two or more different lines of melody</u> are played at the same time. This <u>texture</u> is described as <u>contrapuntal</u> (or <u>polyphonic</u> — see p.45).

5) The <u>dynamics change suddenly</u>. Each bit is either <u>loud</u> or <u>soft</u> — this is called <u>terraced</u> or <u>stepped</u> dynamics. You <u>won't</u> hear any <u>gradual changes</u> in volume (no <u>crescendos</u> or <u>diminuendos</u>). This is mainly due to the prominence of the <u>harpsichord</u> in Baroque music — harpsichords could <u>either</u> play loud or soft, but couldn't change <u>gradually</u> between the two.

6) Baroque music is <u>tonal</u>:

> • From about 1600, Western composers used <u>major</u> and <u>minor keys</u> to write <u>tonal</u> music — this replaced <u>modal</u> music (see p.27).
>
> • Composers used <u>modulation</u> to switch between keys (see p.44) — this created <u>contrast</u> in their music.
>
> • Compositions were often made up of <u>sections</u> in <u>different keys</u>, with modulation between them. <u>New structures</u> were developed for organising pieces of music with a number of sections, e.g. <u>binary</u> and <u>ternary</u> forms (see next page).

String and Keyboard Instruments Played Key Roles

1) <u>String instruments</u> were dominant in a Baroque orchestra (just like today) — <u>violins</u>, <u>violas</u>, <u>cellos</u> and <u>double basses</u> were all used. (If you see '<u>violone</u>' in the score, it's played by a double bass today.)

2) <u>Keyboard</u> instruments such as the <u>harpsichord</u> and <u>organ</u> were also very important in Baroque music.

3) Woodwind instruments such as the <u>flute</u>, <u>recorder</u>, <u>oboe</u> and <u>bassoon</u> were also used.

4) The instruments available were much more <u>limited</u> than in the later musical periods. There were some early forms of <u>brass</u> instruments, such as <u>trumpets</u> and <u>horns</u>, but they didn't have any <u>valves</u> so could only play a <u>limited range</u> of notes.

5) <u>Orchestras</u> were generally <u>small</u> compared to modern orchestras. The size of an orchestra depended on the <u>resources</u> available, and the performance <u>space</u>. Music was often performed by <u>chamber groups</u> (see p.70) with a small number of musicians, but there were <u>larger orchestras</u> too.

Baroque Music Often Had a Basso Continuo

> 1) A <u>basso continuo</u> is a <u>continuous bass part</u> (see page 57). It's played throughout a piece, and is based on the <u>chords</u> of the piece.
>
> 2) It was often played on an <u>organ</u> or <u>harpsichord</u>, but could also feature additional instruments — e.g. <u>cellos</u>, <u>double basses</u> or <u>bassoons</u>.

'Baroque Around the Clock' was a huge hit...

You have to spot key features of Baroque music in the exam so make sure you learn them.

Baroque Structures

*Baroque composers used various **standard structures** to construct their music.*

The **Concerto Grosso** was a **Popular Form** of **Orchestral Music**

1) In a concerto grosso, a small group of soloists (called the concertino) is contrasted with the rest of the orchestra (the ripieno) and the basso continuo. The ripieno is usually a string orchestra. Handel wrote several concerto grossi (plural for grosso) — in his Concerto Grosso No. 5 (Op. 6), the concertino is made up of two violins and a cello, the ripieno is a string orchestra, and the continuo is played on the harpsichord. J.S. Bach's Brandenburg Concertos are concerto grossi.

2) Baroque composers also wrote solo concertos. Here a single solo instrument is 'showcased', allowing its performer to demonstrate the instrument's capabilities, accompanied by an orchestra. Vivaldi's 'Four Seasons' is a solo concerto for the violin. It was this type of concerto that was further developed by composers such as Mozart and Haydn in the Classical period — see p.91.

Binary and **Ternary Forms** are Made Up of **Different Sections**

1) Binary means something like 'in two parts' — binary form has two sections.
2) Binary form is usually used for Baroque dances, e.g. bourrée, minuet, gavotte, sarabande and gigue.
3) Each section is repeated. You play Section A twice, and then Section B twice, so it goes AABB.
4) Section B contrasts with Section A — the two bits should sound different.
5) The contrast is often made by modulating to related keys. Pieces in a minor key usually modulate to the relative major, e.g. A minor to C major. Pieces in a major key usually modulate to the dominant key (V), e.g. C major to G major.

1) Ternary form has three sections. The general structure is ABA, but the sections are often repeated, producing structures such as AABBAA.
2) Section A ends in the home key, normally with a perfect cadence (see pages 42-43). This makes it sound like a complete piece in itself.
3) In Section B the music often modulates to a related key, like the dominant or relative minor, and then goes back to the home key before it ends.
4) The last section can be exactly the same as Section A, or a slightly varied version. If it is varied, you call it A1 instead of A.

In a ritornello, the same musical idea or theme is repeated at various points in the piece. A more formal structure of this type is a rondo, where a main theme (A) is repeated, separated by a number of different sections, creating forms such as ABACA (see p.93).

Some **Works** Have an **Introduction** Called a **Prelude**

1) In the Baroque period, a prelude was a short, relatively simple piece of music. It usually served as an introduction to a longer piece or to a number of pieces of music.
2) The first movement of a suite (a set of dances) is often a prelude.
3) A prelude was often used as an introduction to a more complex piece such as a fugue. Bach wrote a prelude and fugue in each of the 24 keys in 'The Well-Tempered Clavier' — a collection of solo pieces for keyboard instruments.
4) In the Romantic period (see p.99-100), the term came to be used to describe a short, stand-alone piece.

This page is just a prelude to yet more fascinating structures...

You need to be able to spot these various structures, so make sure you learn all their features. If you're struggling to identify the different sections, listen out for a change of key — it'll probably be a new section.

Baroque Structures

Variations are pieces which start with **one pattern** or tune, and then **change it** in different ways.
There are **two** main structures for variations. They're called *'theme and variation'* and *'ground bass'*.

Theme and Variation Form Varies the Melody

1) In theme and variation form, the theme's usually a memorable melody.

2) The theme is played first. There's a short pause before the first variation is played, then another pause before the next variation. Each variation is a self-contained piece of music. There can be as many or as few variations as the composer wants.

3) Each variation should be a recognisable version of the main theme, but different from all the others.

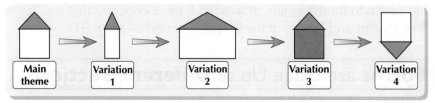

| Main theme | Variation 1 | Variation 2 | Variation 3 | Variation 4 |

'The Harmonious Blacksmith' by Handel is in theme and variation form.

You can vary a melody in loads of simple ways:

1) Start off with a basic theme...

2) Add notes to make the melody more complex.

3) Remove notes to simplify the melody.

4) Change the metre — e.g. from 2 beats in a bar to 3.

5) Add a countermelody — an extra melody over the top of the theme.

6) You can also change the tempo, change the key (from major to minor or vice versa), change some or all of the chords or add a different type of accompaniment instead of block chords.

A fantasia is a composition with an improvised feel — the composer uses their imagination and skill to compose a piece that doesn't follow a set structure. Fantasias often involve variations on a theme.

Ground Bass Form Varies Ideas Over a Fixed Bass Part

Ground bass is a continuous set of variations — there are no pauses. The main theme (called the ground) is a bass line which repeats throughout the piece — it is also known as basso ostinato. Varying melodies and harmonies which become gradually more complex are played over the ground. There are two types of Baroque dance that are in ground bass form — the chaconne and passacaglia. They're quite slow and stately.

Freshly ground bass — it goes all powdery...

Make sure you've learnt all the ins and outs of these structures. The examples of variations on this page are fairly simple, but they can become quite complex and require a lot of skill and practice to play well.

Baroque Melody Patterns

*Composers often create a melody by starting with a **key phrase**, then **adapting** it using different **techniques**.*

Melodic Inversion — Turning the Tune **Upside Down**

With <u>melodic inversion</u> you keep the <u>same intervals</u> between the notes, but they go in the <u>opposite direction</u>, i.e. down instead of up, and up instead of down. Basically you turn the tune on its head.

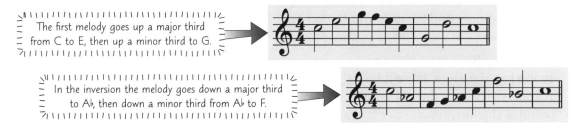

The first melody goes up a major third from C to E, then up a minor third to G.

In the inversion the melody goes down a major third to A♭, then down a minor third from A♭ to F.

Retrograde — Playing the Tune **Backwards**

Playing the notes <u>in reverse order</u> but with the same rhythm is called <u>retrograde</u>. This is the retrograde version of the first melody (above).

If you switch the notes so they're in reverse order <u>and</u> inverted, you get a <u>retrograde inversion</u>. This is the retrograde inversion of the first melody.

Sequencing — Repeat a **Pattern**, Vary the **Pitch**

1) Repeat the <u>pattern</u> of a phrase but start on a <u>different note</u>, higher or lower. This is called a <u>sequence</u>.

2) <u>Ascending</u> sequences go up in pitch. <u>Descending</u> sequences go down.

Imitation — Repeat a Phrase With **Slight Changes**

1) In <u>imitation</u>, a phrase is repeated with <u>slight changes</u> each time.

2) It works really well if one instrument or voice imitates <u>another</u> and then <u>overlaps</u>.

original phrase

original phrase, one octave higher

imitation with modulation

overlap starts in relative minor

Ostinato — Keep **One Pattern** the **Same**, Change the Rest

1) An ostinato is a pattern that's played <u>over and over</u> again.

2) The rest of the piece <u>changes around it</u>.

3) An ostinato is usually in the <u>bass</u> line, but it can be in other parts too.

4) <u>Ground bass form</u> (p.82) features ostinato <u>phrases</u> in the bass line — the repeated phrases can be quite <u>long</u>.

Here's the repeating pattern.

Section Six — Western Classical Tradition 1650-1910

Ornaments in Baroque Music

Ornaments are *short extra notes* that liven up the main melody — *Baroque composers used them a lot in their music.* There are a few *different types* of ornament...

A **Trill** is Lots of **Tiny Quick Notes**

1) In Baroque music, the trill starts one note <u>above</u> the written note then goes quickly <u>back and forth</u> between the <u>written note</u> and the note you <u>started</u> on.

2) Sometimes a trill ends with a <u>turn</u> (see below).

3) If the note above the written note <u>doesn't</u> belong to the <u>key signature</u>, there'll be a <u>sharp</u>, <u>flat</u> or <u>natural</u> sign above the trill symbol.

4) A trill is slightly different in <u>Classical</u> music — it starts <u>on</u> the written note and goes <u>up</u> to the note above.

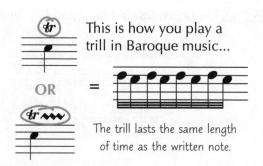

This is how you play a trill in Baroque music...

The trill lasts the same length of time as the written note.

An **Appoggiatura** is an **Extra Note** in a **Chord**

1) The appoggiatura starts on a note that <u>clashes</u> with the chord, then moves to a note that <u>belongs</u> in the chord (this is called the <u>resolution</u>).

2) The two notes are usually just one <u>tone</u> or <u>semitone</u> apart.

3) It normally takes <u>half the time value</u> of the note it 'leans' on.

Squeezing in a **Tiny Note** is Called **Acciaccatura**

"Acciaccatura" means <u>crushing in</u>. An acciaccatura is a note that's squeezed in before the main note and played <u>as fast as possible</u>.

Mordents and **Turns** are **Set Patterns** of Notes

MORDENTS

Mordents <u>start off</u> like trills.

The difference is they <u>end</u> on the written note, which is played a bit <u>longer</u> than the trilled notes. There are loads of different mordents but these two are the most common.

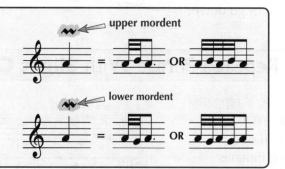

upper mordent

lower mordent

TURNS

Start on the note <u>above</u> the written note, then play the <u>written note</u>, followed by the note <u>below</u> the written note. End back on the <u>written note</u>.

For an <u>inverted turn</u> play the note <u>below</u> the written note, the written note, the note above that and finally the written note.

COMPOSING TIP

I've done my bit — now it's your turn...

Take a look at p.41 for more on decoration. You might even want to add some of these ornaments to your compositions to make them more exciting (don't go overboard though).

Choral Music

*Choirs have been around for ages. They vary in size from just a **few** singers to **hundreds**, and perform anywhere from **school halls** and **churches** to **concert halls**, **theatres** and **cathedrals**.*

Choral Music has Been Around for Over **600 Years**

1) The first choral pieces were sung in <u>churches</u> in the <u>14th century</u>. Before that, monks used to sing <u>plainsong</u> (a unison chant).

2) Most choral music in <u>Renaissance</u> and <u>Baroque</u> times was <u>sacred</u> (<u>church</u> music). Some was sung <u>a cappella</u> (without accompaniment) and some was accompanied by an <u>instrument</u>, such as an organ.

3) <u>Masses</u> were sung in Catholic churches. They were part of the church service. A <u>requiem</u> was a <u>mass</u> for the <u>dead</u>. There's more about masses and requiems on p.103.

4) <u>Oratorios</u> are <u>Bible stories</u> set to music (see next page). Masses, requiems and oratorios are all <u>sacred</u> music. They're made up of <u>choir</u> sections and <u>solo</u> sections.

5) <u>Secular</u> (<u>non-religious</u>) choral music is mainly made up of <u>choruses</u> in <u>operas</u> (see next page). Operas often tell <u>love stories</u> and are performed <u>on stage</u>. The chorus <u>emphasises</u> important bits.

> There's more on the different types of voice on p.68.

Choirs Were Originally **All Male**

1) <u>Baroque choirs</u> were fairly <u>small</u> — they'd sometimes have just <u>one singer</u> on each part. All parts were sung by <u>men</u> (women were <u>banned</u> from singing in church).

2) Most choir music was written for <u>4 different voices</u>: treble (a <u>boy soprano</u>), <u>countertenor</u> or <u>alto</u> (a <u>high-pitched</u> voice known as <u>falsetto</u>), <u>tenor</u> (a <u>high male</u> voice) and <u>bass</u> (a <u>low male</u> voice).

3) By the <u>Victorian era</u>, choirs were <u>huge</u> — they'd often have over 100 members (it was a <u>popular Victorian hobby</u>). The <u>Huddersfield Choral Society</u> was started in 1836 and still exists today.

4) Some choirs are <u>mixed-sex</u>, with music arranged for SATB voices: <u>soprano</u> (a <u>high female</u> voice), <u>alto</u> (a <u>lower female</u> voice), <u>tenor</u> (a <u>high male</u> voice) and <u>bass</u> (a <u>low male</u> voice).

5) <u>All-female</u> choirs are usually <u>SSAA</u> (2 soprano parts and 2 alto parts) or <u>SSA</u> (2 soprano parts and 1 alto part). <u>Male voice</u> choirs are often <u>TTBB</u> (2 tenor parts, 1 baritone part and 1 bass part).

Choral Singing is Still Popular Today

1) 20th and 21st century choirs are generally <u>smaller</u> than the large Victorian choirs — they'll often have around <u>80</u> members though. Some can have as many as <u>130</u> members.

2) Lots of 20th century <u>choral works</u> are written for <u>chamber choir</u> and <u>chamber orchestra</u>. These are just <u>small versions</u> of choirs and orchestras (they're called '<u>chamber</u>' because they used to perform in <u>rooms</u> or <u>chambers</u>, rather than a concert hall). Chamber choirs normally have <u>20-25</u> members.

3) Chamber choir pieces may have been a <u>reaction</u> against <u>19th century composers</u>, who often composed pieces for <u>massive</u> choirs.

Choirs Have **Soloists** Too

There are sometimes <u>solo sections</u> in choral works — the soloist might be <u>accompanied</u> by the rest of the choir, or just sing on their <u>own</u>, with or without <u>orchestral accompaniment</u>. The main <u>solo voices</u> are:

- <u>Soprano</u>, <u>alto</u>, <u>tenor</u> or <u>bass</u> (as described above).
- <u>Mezzo-sopranos</u> (a <u>female</u> voice that's lower than a soprano but higher than an alto), <u>baritones</u> (a <u>male</u> voice that's lower than a tenor but higher than a bass) or <u>contralto</u> (the lowest <u>female</u> voice that has a similar range to a countertenor).

Requiems, oratorios — there's Masses of stuff on this page...

J.S. Bach and Handel wrote a lot of choral music in the Baroque period — both sacred and secular. There's a whole page on Handel's oratorios and anthems on p.87 (but Bach doesn't get a page — sorry Bach).

Operas and Oratorios

Operas and oratorios are large vocal works, both made up of solo and chorus sections.

Operas are Like Plays Set to Music

1) An opera is a story set to music with singing and acting. Most operas are divided up into three parts (or 'Acts'). Operas are secular (non-religious).

2) The main characters are played by solo singers and are supported by a chorus and an orchestra.

3) The story is acted out — usually with lavish sets, costumes and special effects.

4) In some operas every single word is sung (this is known as sung-through) — in others there's a bit of talking from time to time.

5) Some operas have really serious, tragic themes. Others are more light-hearted and comic. These are the names for the main types:

6) The words of an opera are called the 'libretto'. This is often written by a 'librettist' working alongside the composer.

Grand opera	serious, set entirely to music (sung-through)
Opera seria	formal, serious opera, often mythological themes
Opera buffa	comic opera with lighter, more everyday themes
Opéra comique	like opera buffa but with some spoken dialogue
Operetta	shorter than a proper opera, lighter themes

In Opera There are Three Types of Song

ARIA

1) An aria is a solo vocal piece, backed by the orchestra.

2) Arias are used to show the thoughts and emotions of the main characters.

3) The arias have the memorable, exciting tunes. They're challenging for the performers and let them show their vocal tone and agility.

In England and France, arias are sometimes known as 'airs'.

RECITATIVE

1) A recitative is a song for a soloist that tells the story and moves it along. The rhythm of the words tends to imitate the rhythm of normal speech.

2) A recitativo secco is a recitative that's unaccompanied or backed by simple chords.

3) A recitativo stromentato or accompagnato is a recitative with orchestral backing. The accompaniment is used to increase the dramatic tension of the words.

CHORUS — A bit where the whole chorus (or choir) sings together. Choruses are usually written for SATB choirs (see previous page), but in Baroque operas the soprano parts would be sung by trebles (boy sopranos).

Oratorios are Religious Versions of Operas

1) Oratorios often tell Bible stories, or tales with a religious or moral theme — they're a type of sacred music.

2) They're not usually acted out with scenery and costumes (unlike operas).

3) They normally have an instrumental accompaniment.

4) Oratorios have arias, recitatives and choruses just like operas.

COMPOSER	LIVED	FAMOUS ORATORIO
Carissimi	1605-1674	Jephte
Handel	1685-1759	Messiah
Haydn	1732-1809	The Creation
Berlioz	1803-1869	L'Enfance du Christ
Mendelssohn	1809-1847	Elijah
Elgar	1857-1934	The Dream of Gerontius
Tippett	1905-1998	A Child of Our Time

5) The table above gives some composers and their most famous oratorios. Have a listen to them and try to spot the different types of song, as well as listening out for the different musical styles.

Handel

Handel was one of the most important composers in the Baroque period.

Handel was a German Composer

1) George Frideric Handel was born in Germany in 1685. From about 1710, he lived in England. He died in London in 1759 and is buried in Westminster Abbey.

2) He was popular with Queen Anne, George I and George II — he composed 'Zadok the Priest' for the coronation of George II (see below), and it's been played at every coronation since then. He also wrote music for the Calvinist church in Germany and the Church of England.

3) Handel wrote loads of music, including lots of oratorios and operas (see p.86). As well as choral music, he also wrote many orchestral pieces — one of the most famous is the 'Water Music'.

Messiah is a Famous Oratorio by Handel

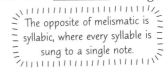
He also wrote lots of other oratorios — including Solomon, Israel in Egypt and Judas Maccabaeus (which has the famous 'See the Conquering Hero').

1) Messiah tells the story of Jesus' life.

2) It's written for SATB soloists, SATB choir and a full orchestra. At the time Handel wrote it, all the parts would have been sung by men.

3) Handel wrote it for a small choir, but it has since been performed by choirs with hundreds of singers.

4) Much of the Messiah is melismatic (a single syllable of text is sung over a succession of notes). In the chorus 'For Unto Us a Child is Born', the soprano part has a run of 57 notes for the word 'born'.

Tenor

Crook - ed

The opposite of melismatic is syllabic, where every syllable is sung to a single note.

5) Handel also uses word-painting — where the music matches the words. E.g. the word 'crooked' is split over four notes each time it is sung, making it sound crooked.

6) The most famous bit of the Messiah is probably the 'Hallelujah Chorus', but there are lots of other choruses, recitatives and arias (as well as some duets and instrumental sections).

Handel Wrote the Coronation Anthems for George II

1) Handel wrote four anthems (choral pieces performed in Protestant churches) for the coronation of George II and Queen Caroline in October 1727.

2) The anthems are 'Zadok the Priest', 'Let Thy Hand Be Strengthened', 'The King Shall Rejoice' and 'My Heart is Inditing'. Each one is divided into different sections. The lyrics are taken from the Bible.

3) As they were written for a grand occasion, the anthems need a large choir and massive orchestra to perform them, which emphasised the importance of the event.

4) Although the strings are used for most of the accompaniment, Handel frequently uses trumpet fanfares in the most triumphant sections (e.g. when the choir sings 'rejoic'd' in 'Zadok the Priest'), which adds to the ceremonial feel. He also uses oboes, bassoons, timpani and organ (which plays a basso continuo in some sections).

5) Much of the music is in a major key as it was written for a celebration, but there are a couple of sections in a minor key for the more solemn aspects of the coronation.

6) Handel uses a variety of textures to different effects. For example, the repeated line 'God Save the King' in 'Zadok the Priest' is sung homophonically in rich chords to give it more impact. In contrast, the 'Alleluja' section of 'Let Thy Hand Be Strengthened' is polyphonic, with parts weaving in and out of each other in imitation to give it a bright, celebratory feel. There's also parallel harmony (see p.45), with parts moving together in thirds (e.g. in the 'Glory and Worship' section of 'The King Shall Rejoice').

SUGGESTED LISTENING

Hallelujah — it's the end of the page...

Have a listen to 'Zadok the Priest' — it's in D major and sounds very triumphant. The last section ends with a plagal cadence (a plagal cadence is chord IV then chord I — see p.43).

From Baroque to Classical

*Classical music came from Baroque, so it's **similar but not the same**...*

Tastes Moved Towards a Simpler Sound

Classical
1750–1820

1) The <u>Classical</u> period of music was from around <u>1750 to 1820</u>. <u>Mozart</u>, <u>Haydn</u> and <u>Beethoven</u> were key composers during this time.

2) The style of music <u>didn't just change overnight</u> — the Classical style <u>developed</u> from the Baroque style as <u>tastes changed</u> and <u>instruments</u> became more <u>versatile</u>.

3) Towards the <u>end</u> of the Baroque era, many composers <u>moved away</u> from the <u>polyphonic</u> sound (see p.45) that had been a key feature of the period. They began to write more <u>homophonic music</u> with a <u>clear melody line</u> and <u>fewer ornaments</u> (see p.84).

4) This development can be seen in the compositions of J.S. Bach's sons, <u>C.P.E. Bach</u> and <u>J.C. Bach</u>. They were influenced by <u>new styles</u> as well as their <u>father's compositions</u>, and they composed much more <u>homophonic</u> music than their father.

5) There was also a move towards more <u>subtle dynamics</u>. Composers began to use <u>crescendos</u> and <u>diminuendos</u> rather than sudden changes in volume — this was partly due to the invention of the <u>piano</u> (see below).

Forms and Structures Developed Too

1) Baroque forms and structures <u>changed over time</u>, and grew into popular Classical <u>structures</u>:

- The <u>solo concerto</u> became <u>more popular</u> than the <u>concerto grosso</u> (see p.81) — it became an <u>important form</u> in the <u>Classical period</u>.

- The <u>Baroque trio sonata</u> consisted of a number of movements played by <u>three instruments</u> plus a <u>harpsichord continuo</u>. This developed into the <u>Classical sonata</u>, a form consisting of three or four movements, usually composed for a <u>solo instrument</u> (see p.91).

- In the <u>Baroque</u> period, operas often began with an '<u>Italian overture</u>' — an <u>orchestral</u> piece consisting of <u>three sections</u> — a <u>fast</u> section followed by a <u>slow</u> section, followed by another <u>fast</u> section. These pieces were often performed <u>independently</u> of the opera. The <u>Classical symphony</u> (see p.92) developed from this (although Classical symphonies tended to have <u>four</u> movements).

2) Other forms that were popular in the Baroque period continued to be used — <u>binary form</u>, <u>ternary form</u> and <u>theme and variation form</u> (see p.81-82) were still <u>important</u> in the <u>Classical era</u>. <u>New structures</u> such as <u>sonata form</u> (p.92) were also developed.

The Invention of the Piano had a Big Impact

1) The <u>piano</u> was invented in about <u>1700</u>. It became more popular than the harpsichord because it was able to create a much <u>greater variety</u> of tones — the notes could be played in a <u>legato</u> or <u>staccato</u> style and the <u>dynamics</u> could be <u>varied</u> depending on how hard the keys were pressed. The full name of the piano is actually '<u>pianoforte</u>', which means '<u>soft-loud</u>'.

2) <u>C.P.E. Bach</u> and <u>J.C. Bach</u> both composed for the <u>piano</u> and were <u>influential</u> in increasing its <u>popularity</u>. The piano became <u>very widely used</u> in Classical music.

3) <u>Other instruments</u> (such as the <u>clarinet</u>) were <u>developed</u>, and this led to important changes in the structure of the <u>orchestra</u> — see the next page.

Souvenir shops suffered terribly as the use of ornaments declined...

Remember, Classical music developed from Baroque music, so many of the features you've come across in Baroque music still make an appearance. But there's lots of new stuff to get to grips with too...

The Classical Orchestra

*Orchestras **got bigger** during the Classical period as new instruments were developed.*
*The **set-up** of an orchestra (i.e. what instruments were included) became more **standardised**.*

Orchestral Music was Written for **Wealthy Audiences**

1) At the start of the Classical period, composers worked for royalty and aristocrats.
   They were paid to write music for official events, church services and plain old entertainment.
   Composers had to write music that their patrons (employers) would approve of.

2) Later in the Classical period, society changed. Middle-class people had more money and
   wanted entertainment. Public concert halls were built, where people could go to listen to music.

3) Famous Classical composers like Haydn and Mozart worked for patrons,
   but they also put on concerts in the new concert halls.

4) By the 1800s, composers could earn quite a bit of money from ticket sales
   at concert halls. This gave them more freedom — they could write for the
   tastes of concert-goers instead of just pleasing their patrons.

Orchestras **Grew** During the **Classical Period**

1) At the start of the Classical period, composers wrote for smallish orchestras — mainly strings,
   with horns, flutes and oboes. There'd be two horns and one or two woodwind.

2) Later on, the woodwind section grew — clarinets were developed during the Classical period and
   were included in the orchestra. Mozart was the first composer to use the clarinet in a symphony.

3) Brass instruments were used more widely. Horns were developed so
   they could produce more notes and play in a greater variety of keys.

4) The percussion section grew too — timpani became a
   standard fixture, and some orchestras used bass drums,
   snare drums, triangles and cymbals as well.

5) In some early Classical music, there'd be a harpsichord (see p.66),
   but after a while composers stopped using it. The harpsichord was
   there to fill in the harmonies, but it wasn't really needed once the
   extra woodwind had been added.

6) This is a fairly typical layout for a later Classical orchestra:

PERCUSSION		
FRENCH HORNS		TRUMPETS
FLUTES		CLARINETS
	OBOES	BASSOONS
SECOND VIOLINS	VIOLAS	DOUBLE BASSES
FIRST VIOLINS		CELLOS

Classical Orchestras Mostly Use **String Instruments**

1) The most important section in a Classical orchestra is the strings.
   They're the dominant sound in most Classical music.
   The violins generally play most of the melodies.

2) The wind instruments play extra notes to fill out the harmony.
   When they do get the tune, they mostly double the string parts.

3) You do hear the occasional wind solo. Orchestral pieces called concertos (see p.91)
   feature one or two solo instruments accompanied by an orchestra.

4) In later Classical music, the woodwind section started to have a more independent role.
   They'd sometimes play the melody alone, and there'd be more solos.
   The strings were still really important though.

You need to know what instruments were used in the Classical era...

Orchestras grew in size because composers in the Classical period began to include more parts
for different instruments. This gave rise to a greater variety of music later in the Classical period.

The Classical Style

A whole page about the features of Classical music... enjoy.

Classical Melodies Have a **Clear, Simple Structure**

Classical music sounds <u>clearer</u> and <u>simpler</u> than music from other periods. This is partly because the melodies are structured in a very straightforward way, with <u>short</u>, <u>balanced</u> 2- or 4-bar phrases.

Here's an excerpt from Haydn's *Clock Symphony* (see p.94):

And here's the opening of Mozart's *Piano Sonata No. 16 in C major* with two-bar phrases:

Classical **Textures** are Mainly **Melody** and **Chords**

1) Most Classical music has just <u>one melody</u> with <u>accompanying chords</u>. This makes the tune really stand out (see page 45).

2) These accompanying chords can be played in <u>different ways</u>:

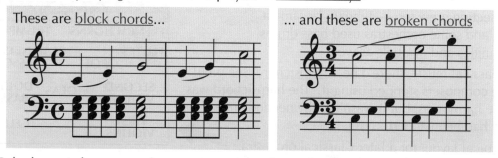

These are <u>block chords</u>...   ... and these are <u>broken chords</u>

3) <u>Polyphony</u> (where <u>several tunes</u> weave in and out of each other) is used too, but not as often.

Classical Music Uses **Major** and **Minor Keys**

1) Classical music is always in either a major or minor key — the <u>tonality</u> is major or minor.

2) <u>Bright</u>, <u>cheery</u> bits are in major keys and <u>gloomy</u>, <u>sad</u> bits are in minor keys.

3) Classical harmony is what's known as <u>diatonic</u> — nearly <u>all</u> the notes belong to the <u>main key</u>.

The **Beat** is Obvious and **Easy to Follow**

1) The <u>metre</u> in Classical music is very regular. You can happily <u>tap your foot</u> in time to the music.

2) The <u>tempo</u> stays <u>constant</u> — the speed of the beat stays pretty much the same all the way through, <u>without</u> massively <u>speeding up</u> or <u>slowing down</u>.

Classical style — a wig, tailcoat and breeches...

This is important stuff, so make sure you're happy with the key features of the Classical period. Make a list of them all, then learn it. Keep going over it to check you know them off by heart.

Classical Structures

Concertos, sonatas and symphonies were very popular in the Classical period.
Take your time and make sure that you're familiar with each one of these structures.

Concertos are Played by a Soloist and Orchestra

1) A concerto is a piece for a soloist and orchestra. The soloist has most of the melody, and can really show off. The orchestra does get the melody too — they're not just an accompaniment.

2) A concerto usually has three movements — quick, slow and quick.

3) They often have a bit called a cadenza (p.57), where the orchestra stops and the soloist can show everyone how brilliant they are. A cadenza is sometimes improvised — it's often just indicated by a pause above the music.

4) Piano and violin concertos were the most popular in the Classical period, but some concertos were written for other solo instruments too. Composers used concertos to showcase the new instruments (like the clarinet and the keyed trumpet) and show off their capabilities.

5) Famous examples of Classical concertos include Haydn's Trumpet Concerto in E♭ major (listen out for the cadenza in the first movement) and Mozart's Horn Concerto No. 4 in E♭ major.

A Symphony is Played by a Full Orchestra

1) A symphony is a massive piece. They can last more than an hour and have real impact because they use the full orchestra.

2) Symphonies usually have four movements (but some have three, and they can have more than four). The contrast between the movements is important.

3) At least one of the movements is in sonata form (see next page) — usually the first, and sometimes the last.

4) Examples include Haydn's Surprise Symphony and Beethoven's Eroica Symphony.

Overtures and Suites were also Written for Orchestras

1) An overture is a one-movement piece for orchestra.

2) Overtures are written as introductions to larger works like operas and ballets.

3) They use ideas, moods and musical themes from the main work to prepare the audience. For an example, have a listen to Mozart's overture to his opera *The Magic Flute*.

4) Classical orchestral suites are another offshoot of ballets and operas.

5) In music from this period, a 'suite' is an orchestral arrangement of the music used to accompany the action on stage. It would be put together as a separate piece of music and played at concerts.

Sonatas are for One or Two Instruments

1) Sonatas are mostly written for one instrument, but there are some sonatas for two instruments and a few for two different instruments, with each one playing a different part.

2) A sonata usually has three or four movements, with breaks in between them.

3) A sonata has a similar structure to a symphony — it has one or more movements in sonata form (see next page).

4) Piano sonatas were very popular in the Classical era — Haydn alone wrote 62. Have a listen to Mozart's Piano Sonata in C Major, Haydn's Piano Sonata in C Major and Beethoven's Sonata Pathétique.

Classical Structures

*The **movements** of compositions were usually written in **standard forms** and arranged in a certain order. **Symphonies**, **sonatas** and **concertos** all follow a **similar pattern** — now there's a stroke of luck...*

Symphonies, Sonatas and Concertos have a Standard Structure

1) The <u>four movements</u> of a <u>symphony</u> have the forms shown in the <u>table</u> below.

2) <u>Sonatas</u> with <u>four movements</u> also follow this structure. If the <u>sonata</u> only has <u>three movements</u>, the <u>minuet</u> (third movement in the table) is <u>left out</u>.

3) <u>Concertos</u> usually have <u>three movements</u> — they have the <u>first</u>, <u>second</u> and <u>fourth</u> movements from the table.

FIRST MOVEMENT	sonata form	brisk and purposeful
SECOND MOVEMENT	ternary or variation form	slower and songlike
THIRD MOVEMENT	minuet or scherzo	fairly fast and dance-like
FOURTH MOVEMENT	rondo, variation or sonata form	fast and cheerful

See page 81 for ternary form and page 82 for variation form. The other forms are explained over the next couple of pages.

Sonata Form has Three Main Sections

The <u>movements</u> of a sonata or symphony are themselves made up of a number of <u>different sections</u>. <u>Sonata form</u> has the following sections:

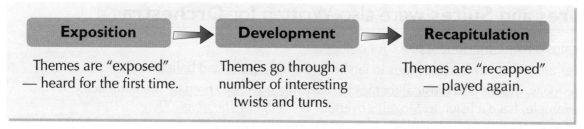

Exposition	Development	Recapitulation
Themes are "exposed" — heard for the first time.	Themes go through a number of interesting twists and turns.	Themes are "recapped" — played again.

1) The <u>exposition</u> has a number of <u>contrasting themes</u>. It ends in a <u>different</u> (but related) key to the one it started in.

2) The <u>development</u> keeps the piece <u>interesting</u>. It takes <u>extracts</u> from the exposition <u>themes</u>, explores <u>variations</u> on them, and presents them in <u>different keys</u> — the development often <u>modulates</u> through a number of keys. Completely <u>new</u> material might be introduced too.

3) The <u>recapitulation</u> pulls it all <u>together</u> again — the exposition themes are <u>repeated</u>, generally in the <u>same order</u> as in the exposition. They're usually <u>changed</u> a bit — the composer might add <u>ornaments</u> (see p.84) or <u>shorten</u> them. Some themes are heard in a <u>different key</u> — a theme that was in the <u>relative key</u> in the exposition usually moves to the <u>tonic key</u> in the recapitulation.

4) Composers sometimes use <u>bridge sections</u> between the themes and <u>links</u> between the main sections. They usually add a <u>coda</u> to finish off the piece <u>neatly</u> as well.

Fear not, there are more forms to come...

Make sure you've got <u>sonata form</u> clear in your head — it comes up in sonatas, symphonies and concertos. And don't get confused... sonata form is the structure of the <u>first movement</u> of a sonata, not the whole thing.

Classical Structures

*Here's some more detail on the **forms** that make up the **movements** of a **concerto**, **sonata** or **symphony**.*

Minuets and Scherzos are in Ternary Form

1) In a sonata or symphony, 'minuet' is short for 'minuet and trio' and scherzo is short for 'scherzo and trio'. The third movement of a four-movement work is either a minuet or a scherzo.

2) A minuet is a French dance with three beats in a bar.

3) The trio is another minuet in a contrasting but related key — often the dominant or relative minor. It's often written for three instruments (which is why it's called a trio).

4) The minuet is played first, followed by the trio section, and then the minuet is played again — this gives the movement ternary form (see p.81).

5) The individual minuet and trio sections often have their own ternary form. A common structure for a minuet and trio is shown below.

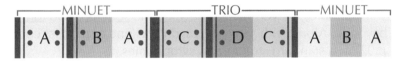

6) A scherzo and trio is very similar, but a scherzo is faster and more light-hearted than a minuet — scherzo means 'joke' in Italian. Beethoven was one of the first composers to use a scherzo like this.

Rondo Form Can Have Any Number of Sections

1) The final movement of a concerto, sonata or symphony is often a rondo.

2) Rondo means going round. A rondo starts with a main idea in Section A, moves into a new section, goes round again to A, moves into another new section, goes round again to A, etc., etc. The new section after each Section A always contrasts with A.

3) Section A is known as the main theme or refrain. The contrasting sections are called episodes.

4) The main theme is always in the home key. Each episode tends to modulate to a related key for contrast.

Musical Signposts Tell You What's Coming Next

1) You've seen that the movements of a work are themselves made up of a number of sections. The most obvious clue that a new section is starting in Classical music is a change of key.

2) Classical composers were also keen on dropping hints that a new section was about to start. These hints are known as musical signposts. They're not all that easy to spot at first, but with a bit of practice you should get the hang of it:

- Bridge passages lead smoothly into the new theme and also help prepare the new key.
- Cadences (p.42-43) clearly mark the end of a phrase or section, and they come at the end of a piece too. When they do, the chords used in the cadence are repeated several times, to let the audience know it's all over.

ABACADAEAFAGAHA — my rondo got a bit out of hand...

These structures might come in handy for your compositions (OK, writing a full symphony might be a bit over the top, but rondo form or minuet and trio form are a bit more manageable).

Orchestral Music of Haydn

Haydn was one of the most important composers of the Classical period.

Haydn was an Austrian Classical Composer

1) <u>Franz Joseph Haydn</u> (known just as <u>Joseph Haydn</u>) was born in <u>Austria</u> in <u>1732</u>. He died in <u>1809</u>.

2) He composed over 100 <u>symphonies</u> and many other works, including a number of <u>concertos</u>, <u>string quartets</u>, <u>piano trios</u>, <u>oratorios</u> and <u>operas</u>.

3) For most of his career, Haydn was employed as the <u>Kapellmeister</u> (musical director) for the noble <u>Esterházy family</u> — he <u>composed</u>, <u>conducted</u> and <u>performed</u> music for Prince Esterházy, who was his <u>patron</u>. Haydn worked for <u>four different princes</u> during his employment.

Haydn Wrote 12 Symphonies to be Performed in London

1) Over the course of his many symphonies, Haydn helped <u>develop</u> the <u>structure</u> and <u>form</u> used in Classical symphonies (and beyond). Along with <u>Mozart</u>, Haydn was one of the first composers to introduce <u>sonata form</u> (see p.92) as a <u>standard structure</u> in symphonies.

2) His symphonies display a sense of <u>balance</u> through his use of <u>dynamics</u>, <u>phrasing</u>, <u>sequences</u> and <u>harmony</u>. He was also known for his <u>intelligence</u> and <u>wit</u> in his compositions.

3) During the early 1790s, Haydn travelled to <u>London</u> twice. He wrote <u>six symphonies</u> for <u>each visit</u> — Nos. 93-104 (these 12 symphonies are known as the <u>London symphonies</u>).

4) These symphonies were written for a <u>later Classical orchestra</u> (see p.89). There'd be a <u>string section</u> (first and second <u>violins</u>, <u>violas</u>, <u>cellos</u> and <u>double basses</u>) and usually <u>2 each</u> of <u>woodwind</u> (<u>flutes</u>, <u>oboes</u> and <u>bassoons</u> — and <u>clarinets</u> in the later symphonies), <u>brass</u> (<u>trumpets</u> and <u>horns</u>) and <u>timpani</u>.

5) Some of the London symphonies have <u>names</u> which describe a particular <u>feature</u> of the music:

- <u>Symphony No. 101 in D Major</u> is known as the <u>Clock Symphony</u>. It gets its name from a '<u>ticking</u>' pattern in the <u>second movement</u>. The ticking is usually played <u>pizzicato</u> (plucked) on the <u>strings</u> and <u>staccato</u> on the <u>woodwind</u>.

- Haydn's <u>sense of humour</u> is demonstrated in the second movement of his '<u>Surprise</u>' symphony (No. 94) with a <u>sudden loud chord</u> in the middle of a <u>quiet section</u>.

- <u>Symphony No. 103 in E♭ Major</u> is known as the <u>Drumroll Symphony</u> because the first movement opens with a long dramatic drumroll on the <u>timpani</u>.

He Also Wrote Concertos for Lots of Different Instruments

Haydn wrote many concertos, for a <u>range</u> of instruments — including <u>violin</u>, <u>cello</u>, <u>double bass</u>, <u>horn</u>, <u>flute</u> and <u>oboe</u>. He only wrote one concerto for <u>trumpet</u>, but this is one of his <u>best-known</u> concertos.

- Haydn's <u>Trumpet Concerto in E♭ Major</u> was written for his friend <u>Anton Weidinger</u>, who'd just invented a '<u>keyed trumpet</u>', which was capable of playing many <u>more notes</u> than the earlier 'natural trumpet'.

  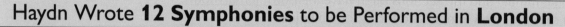 *The keyed trumpet was a precursor to today's valved trumpet.*

- Haydn used the concerto to show off the <u>versatility</u> of the new instrument — the <u>first three notes</u> of the trumpet's main melody were something it wouldn't have been capable of playing before. This <u>immediately</u> told the original audience that they were hearing something <u>new</u> and <u>exciting</u>.

- The concerto has <u>three movements</u> — the first (<u>Allegro</u>) is in <u>sonata form</u>, the second (<u>Andante</u>) is a slower, more lyrical movement in <u>ternary</u> (ABA) form, and the third (<u>Allegro</u>) is in <u>rondo</u> form.

SUGGESTED LISTENING

What a surprise — you need to learn about Haydn...

Listen to the movements of the three London symphonies mentioned above, and try to spot the different features that give each one its name. Watch out for the surprise — it made me jump.

Mozart — Clarinet Concerto in A Major

The study piece for this Area of Study is the third movement of Mozart's Clarinet Concerto in A Major.

Mozart was a **Child Prodigy**

1) <u>Wolfgang Amadeus Mozart</u> was born in <u>Salzburg</u> in <u>1756</u> and died in <u>Vienna</u> in <u>1791</u>. He was taught <u>performance</u> and <u>composition</u> by his father, <u>Leopold Mozart</u>, who was also a composer.

2) Wolfgang showed his <u>musical talent</u> at a very <u>young</u> age — he composed his first piece of music when he was just <u>5 years old</u>. By the time he was <u>10</u> he had <u>toured Europe</u>, performed for <u>kings</u> and <u>queens</u> and written his first <u>symphonies</u>.

3) He went on to write over <u>600</u> pieces of music, including <u>operas</u>, <u>masses</u>, <u>symphonies</u> and <u>concertos</u>. He also wrote smaller works, like <u>chamber music</u> and <u>string quartets</u>.

4) Mozart wrote over <u>40</u> symphonies in his life. Along with <u>Hadyn</u>, Mozart was one of the first composers to introduce <u>sonata form</u> (see p.92) as a <u>standard structure</u> in symphonies.

5) He wrote most of his symphonies before he was <u>27</u>, then <u>returned</u> to them later in his life — e.g. <u>Symphony No. 40</u> was written in <u>1788</u>. In the time between, he wrote <u>concertos</u> for a <u>variety</u> of instruments, including <u>piano</u>, <u>violin</u>, <u>horn</u> and <u>clarinet</u>, and <u>operas</u> such as *The Marriage of Figaro*.

The **Clarinet Concerto** was Mozart's **Last Significant Work**

1) Mozart had originally planned to write it as a concerto for the <u>basset horn</u> — a type of clarinet that can reach notes <u>four semitones lower</u> than a standard clarinet. He had <u>already written</u> some of the music several years before he completed the <u>clarinet concerto</u>.

2) This concerto was written in 1791, in the middle of the <u>Classical</u> period. Like many of Mozart's later works, the concerto is <u>expressive</u> and <u>lyrical</u>, with a close relationship between the <u>solo clarinet</u> and the <u>orchestra</u>. It was the <u>last significant work</u> that Mozart completed in his life — his <u>Requiem</u>, which he started after the clarinet concerto, was <u>never finished</u>.

3) Mozart wrote the concerto (and his <u>clarinet quintet</u>) for <u>Anton Stadler</u>, a well-known clarinetist of the period. The clarinet was a <u>relatively new</u> instrument at the time — Mozart was one of the <u>first composers</u> to use it a lot in his compositions.

It Follows **Traditional Concerto Form**

1) The piece has <u>three movements</u>, which is the <u>traditional</u> form for a concerto (see p.92). The first movement (<u>Allegro</u>) is in <u>A major</u> and the second (<u>Adagio</u>) is in <u>D major</u>, the <u>subdominant key</u> (see p.24). The third movement (<u>Rondo Allegro</u>) returns to <u>A major</u> — this is your study piece.

2) As well as the solo <u>clarinet in A</u>, the concerto features two <u>flutes</u>, two <u>bassoons</u>, two <u>horns</u>, and <u>strings</u> (two groups of <u>violins</u>, <u>violas</u>, <u>cellos</u> and <u>double basses</u>) in the orchestra.

3) The clarinet and the horn are both <u>transposing instruments</u>. This means that the notes they play <u>sound different</u> to the written notes. Both of these instruments are in A — when a <u>C</u> is played on the clarinet or horn, it sounds like the <u>A below</u> the written note. When the rest of the orchestra's parts are written in <u>A major</u> (with three sharps), the <u>clarinet</u> and <u>horn</u> parts are written in <u>C major</u>.

4) As with all Classical concertos, Mozart's concertos gave the <u>soloist</u> an opportunity to <u>show off</u>. While there isn't a traditional <u>cadenza</u> (see p.57), the first movement has <u>tricky technical</u> passages with <u>light accompaniment</u>, where the soloist can provide <u>short improvisations</u> throughout the music.

5) The soloist doesn't always have a <u>starring role</u> though — at times in the first movement, the clarinet <u>accompanies</u> the orchestra with an <u>Alberti bass</u> (see p.39).

Mozart's full name was Johannes Chrysostomus Wolfgangus Theophilus Mozart...

This concerto was written for a clarinet in A. Clarinets also come in B♭ — these are more common nowadays.

Mozart — Clarinet Concerto in A Major

*In case you were wondering, the bar numbers start from the first **full** bar, not the upbeat.*

The **Rondo Movement** has a **Theme** and **Three Episodes**

1) The third movement of the clarinet concerto is a <u>rondo</u> (see p.93), with a <u>main theme</u> (A) and three <u>episodes</u> — two of them (B) are based on the <u>same material</u>, and the other (C) is different. The <u>time signature</u> of the third movement is $\frac{6}{8}$.

The key changes (modulates) in some of the sections — this table shows the starting and finishing keys.

2) The <u>structure</u> of the movement is <u>ABACABA</u>:

Section	A	B	A	C	A	B	A	Coda
Bars	1*-56	57-113	114-137	138*-177	178-187	188-246	247-300	301-353
Starting Key	A major	A major	A major	F♯ minor	D major	A major	A major	A major
Finishing Key	A major	E major	F♯ minor	D major	A major	A major	A major	A major

The sections marked with * in the table start on the <u>anacrusis</u> (the <u>upbeat</u>). The bar number in the table gives the first <u>full bar</u> of the section, but it starts on the <u>last quaver</u> of the <u>previous</u> bar.

3) There are <u>distinct</u> 2- and 4-bar phrases <u>throughout</u> the movement — this is typical of the <u>Classical</u> period.

4) The <u>main theme</u> is based around runs of <u>semiquavers</u>. It's mainly <u>conjunct</u> (see p.54) with lots of <u>staccato</u>, which makes it feel fast, light and playful. There is a contrast in the <u>dynamics</u> — the clarinet part is mainly ***p***, but some sections of the orchestra accompaniment <u>crescendo</u> to ***f***. The main theme has a definite ending with three <u>A major</u> chords, unlike the episodes which <u>flow smoothly</u> back into the main theme.

5) When the movement <u>returns</u> to the <u>main theme</u> in bars 114 and 178, it <u>isn't</u> played in full. There are also differences such as changes in <u>articulation</u> — for example, <u>staccato</u> phrases from the main theme are <u>not always</u> staccato when the theme returns.

The **'B' Episode** feels **Slower** than the **Main Theme**

1) The <u>B episode</u> of the third movement is heard for the <u>first time</u> in bar 57. In contrast to the <u>main theme</u>, this episode starts with longer notes (e.g. <u>dotted crotchets</u> instead of <u>semiquavers</u> — though there are semiquavers <u>later</u> in the episode), which makes the <u>tempo</u> of the music seem <u>slower</u>, even though it hasn't actually changed.

2) The <u>dynamics</u> are generally quiet (***p***), and the <u>texture</u> in this episode is <u>thinner</u> than the main theme — at the beginning, the clarinet solo is <u>only accompanied</u> by the <u>violins</u>. The <u>other strings</u> are added <u>later</u> in the episode, and the <u>wind instruments</u> are only heard briefly.

3) Episode B <u>returns</u> at bar 188, but there are some <u>differences</u> between the two episodes, for example:

   - There are some differences in <u>orchestration</u>, e.g. a slight variation on the <u>second violin</u> phrase in bars 73-76 appears in the <u>cello</u> part in bars 214-217.

   - There is a series of <u>modulations</u> starting in bar 196, including to <u>minor keys</u>, which means the <u>mood</u> changes to a more <u>sombre</u> feel.

   - There are <u>pauses</u> in bars 219 and 221, where the music has a <u>short rest</u> before it continues. This creates moments of <u>silence</u>, where everything <u>stops</u>.

The **'C' Episode** Contains **Wide Leaps** in **Pitch**

1) The C episode starts at <u>bar 138</u>, and starts in a <u>minor key</u>. The <u>broken chords</u> (see p.39) and the alternating <u>crotchet-quaver</u> rhythm in the clarinet part provide contrast to the runs of <u>semiquavers</u> in the main theme and Episode B.

2) The clarinet part features <u>wide leaps</u> in pitch, including jumps of more than <u>two octaves</u> in bars 161-163.

3) The dynamics are mainly ***p*** but with bursts of ***f*** in the orchestra in bars 158-159.

4) Episode C is followed by the <u>main theme</u>. It isn't played again in full — a short, 10-bar <u>reprise</u> is used as a <u>linking passage</u> to lead into the <u>third episode</u> (the repeat of episode B).

Mozart — Clarinet Concerto in A Major

There are lots of differences between the episodes and the main theme, but they have plenty in common too...

The **Movement** Features Different **Musical Devices**

1) This concerto has a lot of examples of <u>chromaticism</u> (where a piece <u>frequently</u> uses <u>notes</u> that are not in the <u>key</u> that the piece is <u>written in</u>) — e.g. the <u>first violin</u> part in bars 76-77 moves from B to A♯ to A to G. Short <u>chromatic passages</u> are often used to move from one section into the next — e.g. the <u>viola</u> and <u>bass</u> parts move <u>chromatically</u> from the end of episode B into the first repeat of the main theme.

2) Throughout the movement, musical <u>ideas</u> are repeated — sometimes they appear unchanged, but often they are <u>adapted</u> by changing the <u>rhythm</u>, <u>articulation</u> or <u>pitch</u>. For example, the first bar of episode B (bar 57) reappears with a slightly <u>different rhythm</u> and at a <u>different pitch</u> in bar 233. This <u>altered</u> rhythm is also heard in the <u>first violin</u> part through bars 73-79. This repetition of ideas helps to create a sense of <u>unity</u> in the movement. The coda also <u>recaps</u> ideas from the main theme to bring the piece to a close.

3) There are a variety of other <u>musical devices</u> used in this movement:

   • <u>Sequences</u> (see p.83) are used throughout — for example, bars 31-34 in the violin parts.

   • In bar 131, <u>hemiola</u> (see p.14) is used — the music feels like it has <u>moved</u> from $\frac{6}{8}$ into $\frac{3}{4}$. Both <u>time signatures</u> have <u>six quavers</u> per bar.

   • There are examples of <u>ornamentation</u> (see p.84) throughout the movement, for example the <u>trills</u> in bars 315-317 and <u>acciaccaturas</u> in bars 214-220.

   • <u>Pedal notes</u> (see p.39) are used in the <u>cello</u> and <u>double bass</u> parts in bars 301-306.

The **Orchestra** Supports the **Soloist**

1) When the <u>solo clarinet</u> is playing, the orchestra is generally <u>light</u> and <u>thin in texture</u>. This is to make sure that the <u>soloist</u> can be heard <u>above</u> the orchestra. An example of this can be heard in the <u>first eight bars</u>, where the clarinet is only accompanied by the <u>strings</u>. Sometimes, the clarinet plays <u>unaccompanied</u> too — generally, the <u>full orchestra</u> is only used when the clarinet isn't playing.

2) The texture is <u>melody with accompaniment</u> when the orchestra supports the soloist, but it's often <u>homophonic</u> when the soloist isn't playing.

3) There is some <u>call and response</u> between the orchestra and the soloist, where the clarinet <u>starts</u> a phrase and the orchestra <u>completes</u> it (or the other way around), such as in bars 97-109.

4) The orchestra also <u>echoes</u> the soloist by repeating phrases with <u>small variations</u> — for example, the <u>first eight bars</u> of the <u>clarinet solo</u> is copied by the orchestra in bars 9-16. There are some <u>rhythmic differences</u> — for example, compare the clarinet in bar 3 to the first violin in bar 11:

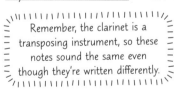
Remember, the clarinet is a transposing instrument, so these notes sound the same even though they're written differently.

5) The clarinet part requires a lot of <u>technical skill</u> — it involves lots of <u>semiquavers</u> and <u>difficult runs</u>, such as the ones in bars 84-88 and 225-229. It's also <u>very fast</u>, with a wide range of <u>pitch</u>. It is <u>virtuosic</u>, designed to <u>show off</u> the skill of the soloist and, when it was <u>originally written</u>, to show off a <u>new instrument</u> as well.

I'll start revising again soon — just three more episodes...

Listen to the piece a couple of times while following along with the score. Listen out for where the piece moves into a new episode — it'll help you understand how the episodes link with the main theme. Make sure you check out some of the specific examples on these pages, too.

Orchestral Music of Beethoven

Beethoven was a very influential composer whose career bridged the Classical and Romantic periods.

Beethoven was a German Composer

1) Ludwig van Beethoven was born in Germany in 1770 and died in Vienna in 1827.

2) His hearing deteriorated over the course of his life, resulting in almost complete deafness for his last ten years. However, he continued to compose, and produced some of his best pieces despite this (e.g. Symphony No. 9 premiered in 1824).

3) He wrote lots of orchestral music (including symphonies and concertos), as well as sonatas and string quartets.

4) He was a very significant composer in Western classical music — his music is famous for its drama, intensity and emotion. Beethoven was important in developing musical styles — he moved from the stricter forms and harmonies of the Classical period to the freer forms and richer harmonies of the Romantic era. There's more on Romantic music on the next couple of pages.

Some of Beethoven's Nine Symphonies Have Names

1) Symphony No. 3 is known as the *Eroica* symphony — 'eroica' means 'heroic', and it certainly sounds heroic (listen out for the horn fanfares in third movement).

2) No. 5 is the *Fate* symphony — the famous four-note motif (see p.80) that opens the symphony (and appears throughout it) is thought to represent fate knocking at the door.

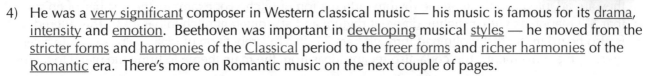

3) No. 6 is the *Pastoral* symphony:

- The *Pastoral* symphony is an example of programme music (music that sets a scene or tells a story). It represents a visit to the countryside (which is where the name comes from).
- Each movement has a description of the scene it portrays — for example, the second movement is 'scene by the brook'. Unusually, this symphony has five movements (there's an additional quick movement after the third movement scherzo).
- The music is very descriptive — in the second movement, the woodwind imitate bird calls, the third movement represents a folk dance and the fourth movement portrays a violent storm.

4) Symphony No. 9 is the *Choral* symphony — it uses a choir, which sings in the final movement. The words come from a poem called 'Ode to Joy'. Beethoven swapped the order of the second and third movements in this symphony (so the scherzo comes before the slow movement).

Beethoven Pushed the Boundaries of Classical Music

1) Whilst most of his symphonies have the standard four-movement structure (see p.92), Beethoven's early symphonies were already moving away from the strict forms of Classical music. For example, the *Eroica* symphony (No. 3) is nearly twice as long as typical Classical symphonies, and is very emotional (especially the second movement, which is a funeral march).

2) Beethoven made full use of the developments in instruments. His symphonies often used large orchestras, with lots of woodwind instruments (that played an independent role). He was one of the first composers to regularly use trombones, and the first to use a choir in a symphony (No. 9).

3) Beethoven used lots of variation in dynamics — in his Piano Concerto No. 1 in C Minor they range from *pp* to *ff*, with sudden *fp* changes and *sf* accents, plus more gradual crescendos and diminuendos. Dynamics like these are more common in Romantic music than Classical.

I'm going to call my symphony Trevor...

Have a listen to the *Pastoral* symphony and try to pick out the features described above.

The Romantic Period

*The Romantic period was about how **passionate emotions** can be **expressed** through **art** and **music**.*

The **Romantic Period** was in the **19th Century**

1) The Romantic period was from about 1820-1910 (though there's always a bit of an overlap between different musical periods).
2) Writers, artists and composers at this time were portraying contrasting emotions and ideas, such as love and hate, happiness and grief, and life and death.
3) They were inspired by the natural world too, and were fascinated by supernatural ideas.
4) Composers wrote programme music — music based on a poem or painting, or that tells a story.
5) Tchaikovsky, Wagner and Chopin were all Romantic composers. Some of Beethoven's later pieces also fitted into the Romantic period.

Romantic Music is More **Dramatic** Than Classical

1) Romantic music used a wide range of dynamics. Sudden changes made the music very dramatic — it could go from ***ppp*** to ***fff*** and back again within a bar. Sforzandos and accents added to the drama.
2) To make the music more expressive, composers gave extra instructions — as well as tempo markings, they would include instructions like *dolce* (sweetly), *amoroso* (lovingly) or *agitato* (agitated).
3) There were more tempo changes — a piece might change speeds lots of times within the same section. Musicians in this period used *rubato* as well — it means 'robbed time' and it's when performers speed up a little in one phrase and slow down in another to make up for it. It gives them the freedom to be more expressive.
4) Composers added extra notes to chords to make the harmonies more interesting — they used 7ths, 9ths, 11ths and 13ths (9ths, 11ths and 13ths are just 2nds, 4ths and 6ths but an octave higher). They helped create dissonance (clashing notes), which let them show emotions like pain and misery.
5) There was a lot of virtuoso playing — composers wrote technically difficult music to give performers the chance to show off. It was very exciting to watch and listen to. Rachmaninov and Liszt wrote solo piano music that had to be written on four staves as there were so many notes to play.
6) Lots of Romantic composers were very proud of the countries they came from — they used folk tunes and dance rhythms from their homelands to show their national pride. Tchaikovsky used the French and Russian national anthems in his 1812 Overture.

The Orchestra **Developed** in the **Romantic Period**

1) Orchestras got much bigger — extra instruments were added.
2) The piccolo, bass clarinet and contrabassoon (which plays an octave lower than the bassoon) were added to the woodwind section.
3) Percussion sections grew to include xylophones, glockenspiels, drums, cymbals, bells and triangles as standard. Celestes (keyboard instruments that sound like glockenspiels) and harps were used too.
4) Brass instruments now had valves so were able to play more notes. Trombones and tubas were added.
5) The changes allowed composers to write music with a larger range of texture, timbre and dynamics.
6) The development of the piano (see next page) meant that it became a much more popular and important instrument. Lots of piano music was written in the Romantic period.

If music be the food of love — play on...

Make sure you know all the key features of Romantic music — you might well need to spot them in the exam. You'll need to listen out for dynamic contrasts, variations in tempo and interesting harmonies.

The Romantic Period

*The **piano** was definitely one of the most **important** instruments in the **Romantic period**.*

The **Piano Developed** in the **Romantic Period**

The piano's been around since the <u>18th century</u>, but the <u>developments</u> in the <u>19th century</u> made it really popular with <u>Romantic</u> composers.

SIZE: the piano <u>changed shape</u> a bit and got <u>bigger</u> (and <u>louder</u>). This meant it had a <u>bigger dynamic range</u>.

KEYS: the number of <u>keys</u> (and <u>notes</u>) <u>increased</u> to just over <u>7 octaves</u>. Composers now had a larger range in <u>pitch</u> to compose for.

PEDALS: both <u>pedals</u> (the <u>sustain</u> pedal that <u>holds notes on</u> and the <u>soft</u> pedal) became more <u>effective</u>. Some <u>modern</u> pianos have <u>three</u> pedals — the third pedal allows some notes to be held on while others are not.

STRINGS: the strings inside were both <u>thicker</u> and <u>longer</u>, making a <u>fuller tone</u>. They were also pulled <u>tighter</u>, so they were more <u>tense</u>.

FRAME: the frame used to be made of <u>wood</u>, but was now made of <u>metal</u> (to cope with the new strings). This made it easier to <u>transport</u> them.

HAMMERS: the hammers were given a <u>felt</u> covering (instead of a <u>leather</u> one). This made the <u>tone softer</u> and more <u>rounded</u>.

Melodies Were the **Focus** of Piano Pieces

1) In Romantic piano pieces, the <u>melody</u> was the most important part. Melodies were often marked *<u>cantabile</u>* — to be played in a <u>singing style</u>.

2) There were lots of <u>virtuosic sections</u> and <u>cadenzas</u> (see p.57) to give the pianist chance to <u>show off</u>.

3) The music had a <u>large range</u> of <u>dynamics</u>, <u>articulation</u> and <u>tone</u>. Pianists had to use the <u>pedals</u> a lot to get the <u>right sounds</u>.

4) The <u>accompaniment</u> was often <u>broken chords</u> (see p.39), but unlike many <u>Classical</u> pieces, the broken chords would be spread across <u>several octaves</u>.

Concertos, Sonatas and **Preludes** Were Written for the **Piano**

1) The piano was popular as the <u>solo</u> instrument in <u>concertos</u> — the pianist was able to really <u>show off</u> in the <u>cadenza</u>. <u>Rachmaninov</u> wrote famous piano concertos.

2) Lots of <u>sonatas</u> (see p.91) were written for the piano — <u>Chopin</u> (see next page), <u>Liszt</u>, <u>Mendelssohn</u> and <u>Schumann</u> (see p.102) all composed piano sonatas.

3) <u>Preludes</u> were originally the bit of music that came <u>before</u> the <u>main piece</u>. During the Romantic period, they became popular as <u>stand-alone pieces</u>. <u>Debussy</u>, <u>Liszt</u>, <u>Rachmaninov</u> and <u>Chopin</u> all wrote preludes for the piano.

I'll have soup as a prelude to my dinner...

Pianos were popular because they were so versatile — with a range of over seven octaves, composers had fewer limitations when they were composing. The newly-developed piano could play a range of dynamics, and the pedals could be used to change the tone of the instrument too. Perfect for Romantics.

Piano Music of Chopin

As you saw on the previous page, the piano was very popular in the Romantic period.
Some composers (like Chopin) just couldn't get enough of it.

Chopin was a **Polish Composer**

1) Frédéric Chopin was born in Poland in 1810 — lots of his music uses Polish folk tunes and dance rhythms. He died in Paris in 1849.
2) He made a name for himself in Vienna before moving to Paris.
3) As well as composing, he also performed and taught music.
4) He composed a lot of piano music, and had a reputation as a 'tragic' Romantic composer, because he was ill a lot, and died young.

Chopin Mainly Wrote **Piano Music**

This doesn't cover every single type of Chopin's piano compositions — he wrote loads of others too.

1) The vast majority of Chopin's compositions were solo piano pieces — even his main orchestral works were piano concertos. He also wrote a number of songs for voice and piano.
2) His music was characterised by its expressive melodies and unique treatment of the piano. He came up with new ways of fingering (such as playing the black keys with the thumb) and made extensive use of the pedals to explore the full potential of the piano.
3) Chopin wrote many piano solos based on dances — including mazurkas, polonaises (both types of Polish dance) and waltzes, as well as a few others, such as a bolero and a tarantella.
4) He composed four piano impromptus — compositions with no strict form and an improvised feel that were popular with Romantic composers.
5) Chopin wrote twenty-seven piano études (studies) that developed the style from a set of exercises to concert pieces that had an imaginative melody while still being technically demanding. Most have been given nicknames (e.g. 'Revolutionary' or 'Waterfall'), though Chopin didn't use these names.
6) A nocturne is a piece meant to represent the night. Chopin wrote twenty-one nocturnes, developing a style established earlier in the Romantic period. Key features of the nocturnes include a melody in the right-hand part above broken chords (see p.39) in the left, a generally sad feel and a slow tempo.

Chopin Wrote a **Prelude** in **Every Key**

He also wrote three other preludes that don't form part of this set.

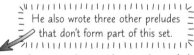

1) Chopin wrote a set of twenty-four preludes — one in each major and minor key. The order of the preludes alternates between major and minor keys and follows the circle of fifths (see p.26) — No. 1 is in C major, No. 2 is in A minor, No. 3 is in G major, etc. Each prelude is fairly short (the longest is only 90 bars), so they're often performed as a set — but each works as a stand-alone piece.
2) Like the études, many of the preludes have been given nicknames that represent features of the piece — e.g. the 'Raindrop' prelude (see below). Each prelude has different characteristics (e.g. particular rhythms or distinctive bass parts). They cover a wide range of tempos, from *lento* to *presto*.
3) The preludes demonstrate many key features of Romantic music. For example:

- Prelude No. 15 in D♭ Major is known as the 'Raindrop' prelude because of repeated quavers played throughout the piece, in either the right hand (an inverted pedal) or left-hand part (a pedal note — see p.39). The 'raindrops' are occasionally doubled in octaves.
- The piece is marked *sostenuto* ('sustained'), which means it should have a slow, held-back tempo. Chopin uses augmentation (see p.18) to make parts of the prelude feel slow and heavy.
- Chopin also includes many other musical directions — such as *sotto voce* ('in an undertone'), *smorzando* ('dying away'), a range of dynamics and marks to show when to press the pedals.
- The piece is in ternary form (ABA) — section A is in D♭ major, and section B is in C♯ minor (D♭ and C♯ are enharmonic equivalents — see p.11), but both sections explore different keys as well.

Piano Music of Schumann

Schumann mainly wrote piano music and music for voice and piano —
but he did branch out into other genres, including symphonies and an opera.

Schumann was a German Composer

1) <u>Robert Schumann</u> was born in <u>1810</u> and died in <u>1856</u>. He spent most of his life in <u>Germany</u>.

2) He gave up a degree in <u>law</u> with the aim of becoming a <u>concert pianist</u>, but an <u>injury</u> to his <u>hand</u> meant he had to <u>abandon</u> that dream. Instead, he focused on <u>composition</u>.

3) Most of his <u>early</u> work was <u>piano music</u>, but <u>later</u> in his career he composed other works, such as <u>symphonies</u>, <u>Lieder</u> (see below) and an <u>opera</u>.

4) He married <u>Clara Wieck</u>, the daughter of his piano teacher — she was also a talented <u>pianist</u> and <u>composer</u>. Many of Schumann's pieces were <u>written for</u>, or <u>inspired by</u>, his <u>wife</u>.

5) Schumann was an important composer in the <u>Romantic period</u> — he was <u>highly regarded</u> for his ability to combine <u>poetry</u> and <u>music</u>.

Schumann's Piano Pieces Have Descriptive Titles

1) Many of Schumann's <u>piano pieces</u> are examples of <u>programme music</u> (see p.99). Their titles <u>describe</u> what the music <u>represents</u> — examples include *Papillons* ('<u>Butterflies</u>'), *Nachtstücke* ('<u>Night Pieces</u>'), *Waldszenen* ('<u>Forest Scenes</u>') and *Kinderszenen* ('<u>Scenes from Childhood</u>').

> *Kinderszenen* is made up of <u>thirteen pieces</u>, most of which are fairly <u>short</u> (some of them last for less than a minute). Each piece has a <u>name</u> (such as '<u>Blindman's Buff</u>' and '<u>The Poet Speaks</u>'). Some of the pieces are <u>light</u> and <u>playful</u>, while others are more <u>gentle</u> and <u>reflective</u>. Nine are in <u>major keys</u> and the other four are in <u>minor keys</u>. The <u>first</u> and <u>last</u> are in the same key (<u>G major</u>), which provides a sense of <u>unity</u> for the whole set.

2) *Carnaval* is a solo piano piece composed in 1834-35 — it depicts a <u>masked ball</u> at a <u>carnival</u>. It has twenty-two movements — most of which represent <u>characters</u> at the carnival (e.g. a <u>pierrot</u> and a <u>harlequin</u>) or <u>friends</u> of Schumann (including <u>Clara</u> and <u>Chopin</u>).

3) He also wrote a number of <u>variations</u> (see p.82). He based his variations on <u>themes</u> written by composers he <u>admired</u>, such as <u>Beethoven</u>, <u>Paganini</u> and his wife <u>Clara</u>.

Other composers of Lieder include Schubert, Beethoven and Brahms.

Schumann Wrote Lots of Lieder

A <u>Lied</u> (pronounced 'leed') is a <u>song</u> for <u>one singer</u> and a <u>piano</u> (the plural of Lied is <u>Lieder</u>). Lieder were really popular in the <u>Romantic period</u>, especially with <u>German</u> composers.

- Lieder are usually based on <u>German poems</u>. They tell <u>stories</u> — they're often very <u>dramatic</u>.
- The <u>piano part</u> in a Lied is <u>more</u> than just a background accompaniment. It helps with the <u>story-telling</u> and sets the <u>mood</u>.
- Lieder are usually either <u>through-composed</u> or have a <u>strophic</u> structure (see p.56). They often have <u>motifs</u> — little bits of repeated music that represent an <u>idea</u>, <u>character</u> or <u>place</u>.
- A <u>collection</u> of Lieder could be put together in a <u>song cycle</u> (a set of songs with the same <u>theme</u>).

Schumann wrote many of his Lieder in <u>1840</u> (the year he married Clara), including two of his famous <u>song cycles</u>, *Frauenliebe und -leben* and *Dichterliebe*. The first (which means '<u>woman's love and life</u>') is a set of eight Lieder, based on poems by <u>Adelbert von Chamisso</u>. The second (meaning '<u>a poet's love</u>') is a set of sixteen, based on poems by <u>Heinrich Heine</u>. This cycle has themes of <u>love</u>, <u>nature</u> and <u>fairy tales</u>.

Robert Schumann — Lieder of the pack...

When you're listening to piano music by Chopin and Schumann, see if you can pick out the features of the piece that are typical of the Romantic period (see p.99-100 for a reminder).

Requiems

After many pages of orchestral or piano music, I'm going to finish this section with a return to choral music.

A **Mass** is a Type of **Sacred Music**

1) A mass is a Roman Catholic church service. Parts of it are often set to music, and sung by a choir and soloists. These parts include:

2) The words of a mass were traditionally in Latin.

3) Masses were originally written to be used in church, but they're now often performed in concerts too.

4) Famous settings of the mass include J.S. Bach's Mass in B Minor and Beethoven's Mass in C Major. There are also modern masses, such as The Armed Man: A Mass for Peace by Karl Jenkins.

> The term 'mass' can be used in the Church of England too.

- *Kyrie* ('Lord have mercy...')
- *Gloria* ('Glory be to God...')
- *Credo* ('I believe in one God...')
- *Sanctus* ('Holy, holy, holy...')
- *Benedictus* ('Blessed is He...')
- *Agnus Dei* ('O Lamb of God...')

A **Requiem** is a **Mass** for the **Dead**

1) A mass for the dead is called a requiem. Requiems use some parts of the normal mass (such as the *Kyrie*, *Sanctus* and *Agnus Dei*), but miss out the happier sections (e.g. the *Gloria* and the *Credo*).

2) These sections are replaced by more solemn bits. These include the *Introit*, which begins 'Requiem aeternam' ('Grant them eternal rest'), the *Dies Irae* (which means 'Day of Wrath') and the *Pie Jesu* (which is taken from the last couple of lines of the *Dies Irae* and means 'Merciful Jesus').

Requiems were **Popular** with **Romantic Composers**

1) Although there had been earlier requiems (such as the well-known Requiem Mass in D Minor by Mozart), it was during the Romantic period that requiems became popular as a form of large-scale composition for performance in concert rather than a church service.

2) The text of the requiem is very dramatic and emotional (especially the *Dies Irae*), so it's easy to see why Romantic composers chose to set it to music.

3) Requiems are usually in a minor key to match the grave nature of the lyrics. Romantic requiems were often written for a large choir and massive orchestra to add drama and tension to the music.

> Verdi's Requiem was written in 1873-74 in memory of the writer Alessandro Manzoni. It was sung by four soloists (soprano, mezzo-soprano, tenor and bass) and a full choir. The singers are accompanied by a huge orchestra — including 2 flutes, a piccolo, 4 bassoons and a large brass section with a whopping 8 trumpets. There's also a prominent percussion section, which has timpani, a bass drum and crash cymbals. This made it very dramatic — the *Dies Irae* in particular, which starts with loud orchestral chords (with bass drum off-beats) and a wide range of pitch from the choir. The trumpet fanfare after the *Dies Irae* starts with one trumpet and builds up to all eight before the choir enters, creating a rich polyphonic texture. There are gentler sections to provide contrast (such as the *Agnus Dei*), where the soloists sing above a light orchestral accompaniment.

> In contrast to Verdi's operatic style, Fauré's Requiem (which he started in 1887 and revised several times before the final version was completed in 1900) is gentle and serene. The vocal parts are for a choir and just two soloists (a soprano and a baritone). The orchestra is joined by an organ. Instead of the exciting *Dies Irae*, Fauré includes a tranquil *Pie Jesu*, sung by the soprano soloist with a quiet orchestral accompaniment. Some sections are in a major key and sound calm and peaceful, though there are more emotional sections with rich harmonies and dramatic crescendos.

Be prepared for a dies irae if you don't revise...

There are later requiems too — a famous 20th century example is the War Requiem by Benjamin Britten (see p.153), which uses Latin words from the Requiem Mass and war poems by Wilfred Owen.

Warm-up and Exam Questions

Before you have a go at the exam questions, give these warm-up questions a whirl — they'll get your brain in gear and give you a fighting chance when you get onto the harder ones.

Warm-up Questions

1) Describe how dynamics were used in the Baroque period.

2) In a concerto grosso, what is: a)   the concertino?   b)   the ripieno?

3) Describe ground bass form.

4) What is an appoggiatura?

5) What were the four different types of voice in a Baroque choir?

6) What is an aria?

7) Who wrote Messiah?

8) Name an instrument that was included in the Classical orchestra but was not used in orchestras of the Baroque period.

9) What is the standard structure of a Classical concerto?

10) How is a basset horn different to a regular clarinet?

11) What is the form of the third movement of Mozart's Clarinet Concerto in A Major?

12) Name two other Classical composers.

13) Give the approximate dates of the Romantic period.

14) What does *sotto voce* mean?

15) What is a Lied?

16) Name one section of a requiem that doesn't appear in a mass.

Exam Questions

Have a go at these exam-style questions.

Track 32 is an excerpt from the third movement of Mozart's Clarinet Concerto.
Play the excerpt four times, leaving a short pause between each playing.

Track 32

a)   Other than the clarinet, name one wind instrument that can be heard in this excerpt.

....

[1 mark]

Exam Questions

b) Which two of the examples of ornamentation below are used in this excerpt?
Circle your answers.

trill   **turn**   **appoggiatura**   **acciaccatura**   **mordent**

[1 mark]

c) About halfway through the excerpt, the music moves from the main theme into the
first episode. Describe the similarities and differences between the two sections.

....

....

....

....

....

[4 marks]

d) Which musical device is used towards the end of the excerpt? Circle your answer.

pedal note   **ostinato**   **ground bass**   **sequence**   **word painting**

[1 mark]

e) Identify two features of the excerpt that indicate it was composed in the Classical period.

....

....

....

....

[2 marks]

f) Describe the melody in the clarinet part in the last four bars of the excerpt.

....

....

....

....

[2 marks]

Exam Questions

Track 33 is an excerpt from 'Dies Irae' by Verdi.
Play the excerpt **four** times. Leave a short pause between each playing.

Track 33

a) i) What larger work does this movement come from?

....
[1 mark]

ii) What does 'Dies Irae' mean? Circle your answer.

Lord have mercy　　**Eternal rest**　　**Day of wrath**　　**Merciful Jesus**
[1 mark]

b) Tick one box for each statement below to indicate whether it is true or false.

	True	False
The excerpt opens with homophonic chords.	☐	☐
The bass drum plays on the off-beats.	☐	☐
The choir sing in unison.	☐	☐
The strings play ascending runs between the choral sections.	☐	☐

[4 marks]

c) Describe the texture of this excerpt.

....

....

....

....

....
[3 marks]

Exam Questions

d)   This piece is marked *allegro agitato*. Explain what this means.

....

....

[1 mark]

e)   i) During which period of Western classical music history was this piece composed?

....

[1 mark]

ii) Identify the features of this piece that are typical of that period and explain why they
were used. You might want to comment on musical elements such as instrumentation,
dynamics and harmony, as well as any other elements you think appropriate.

....

....

....

....

....

....

....

....

....

....

....

[8 marks]

Revision Summary for Section Six

That's the end of Section Six — test yourself to see how much you've picked up.
- Try these questions and tick off each one when you get it right.
- When you've done all the questions for a topic and are completely happy with it, tick off the topic.

The Baroque Period (p.80-84) ☑

1) Give the approximate dates of the Baroque period. ☑
2) What is a basso continuo and what instruments would normally play it? ☑
3) What is a concerto grosso? ☑
4) Which Baroque structure can be described as ABA? ☑
5) What was the function of a prelude in the Baroque period? ☑
6) In theme and variation form, what is the theme? ☑
7) What is the main difference between theme and variation form and ground bass form? ☑
8) Explain what each of these terms means: a) melodic inversion   b) retrograde   c) ostinato. ☑
9) Name three different ornaments used by Baroque composers and explain what they are. ☑

Choral Music (p.85-87) ☑

10) What is a falsetto voice? ☑
11) What are the four different voices in an SATB choir? ☑
12) What is a baritone voice? ☑
13) Name the three types of song in an opera. ☑
14) What is an oratorio? ☑
15) Give a brief definition of word-painting. ☑
16) Name two of Handel's coronation anthems. ☐

The Classical Period (p.88-98) ☑

17) Give the approximate dates of the Classical period. ☑
18) Why did the piano become increasingly popular in the Classical period? ☑
19) What was the most important section in a Classical orchestra? ☑
20) What is a symphony? ☑
21) What is the structure of a symphony with 4 movements? ☑
22) Briefly describe rondo form. ☑
23) Name two of Haydn's 'London symphonies'. ☑
24) Which two transposing instruments are used in Mozart's Clarinet Concerto in A Major? ☑
25) How many episodes does the third movement of this concerto have? ☑
26) What is meant by 'chromaticism'? ☑
27) What is programme music? ☐
28) Name a symphony by Beethoven that is an example of programme music. ☑

The Romantic Period (p.99-103) ☑

29) Name three techniques that Romantic composers used to show drama and emotion in their work. ☑
30) What instrument was most of Chopin's music written for? ☑
31) Describe Schumann's *Carnaval*. ☑
32) What is a song cycle? ☐
33) What is a requiem? ☑
34) What instruments and voices are needed to perform Verdi's Requiem? ☑

Section Six — Western Classical Tradition 1650-1910

Voices in Pop

This section starts by looking at some general things that are relevant to most pop music — first up, vocals.

The **Lead Singer** Sings the **Main Melody**

The lead singer (or <u>vocalist</u>) sings the main melody of a song. They're the <u>soloist</u>, and if they're part of a <u>band</u>, they're often the most <u>famous</u> member (e.g. <u>Freddie Mercury</u> in <u>Queen</u>, <u>Jon Bon Jovi</u> in <u>Bon Jovi</u> and <u>Axl Rose</u> in <u>Guns N' Roses</u>). If you get a pop song in the Listening Exam, say something about the lead vocalist's <u>style</u>. It's even worth mentioning obvious stuff like whether the singer's <u>male</u> or <u>female</u>.

Backing Singers Sing the **Harmonies**

The backing vocalists are the ones who sing the <u>harmonies</u>. These are the main ways backing singers do their thing:

Listen out for the backing vocals in 'Surfin' USA' by The Beach Boys.

IN HARMONY	**IN UNISON**	**DESCANT**	**CALL AND RESPONSE**
all singing <u>different notes</u>	all singing the <u>same notes</u>	singing a <u>higher</u> part in time with the main tune	<u>repeating</u> whatever the lead vocalist sings or <u>answering</u> the lead with another tune

Singers Can Do All Sorts of **Fancy Stuff**

There are different ways to sing. Make sure you can <u>describe</u> exactly what you're hearing. Listen out for:

1) **A CAPPELLA** — singing with <u>no instrumental backing</u>.

2) **VIBRATO** — when singers <u>quiver up and down</u> slightly in pitch. It makes the voice sound <u>warmer</u> and <u>more expressive</u>.

Vocal parts can be syllabic (one note per syllable) or melismatic (multiple notes per syllable).

3) **FALSETTO** — when men (or occasionally women) make their voices go <u>really high</u>. <u>Sam Smith</u>, <u>The Bee Gees</u> and <u>Michael Jackson</u> are all famous for their falsetto voices.

4) **PORTAMENTO** — when a singer <u>slides</u> from one note to another.

5) **SCAT** — <u>improvising</u> using syllables like '<u>doo</u>' and '<u>dat</u>'. Scat comes from <u>jazz music</u>.

6) **RIFFING** — when singers <u>decorate</u> and add bits to the tune. They often go up and down a scale before coming to rest on one note. Riffing usually comes at the <u>end of a phrase</u>, <u>between sections</u> or to <u>finish the song</u>. <u>Whitney Houston</u>, <u>Mariah Carey</u> and <u>Celine Dion</u> are famous for riffing.

7) **BELTING** — when a singer sings notes from their <u>higher register</u> at a <u>louder volume</u> than normal. It's often used for the <u>emotional climax</u> in <u>musical theatre</u> songs (see p.117-118).

8) **RAPPING** — when <u>rhyming lyrics</u> are <u>spoken</u> or <u>chanted</u> to a <u>rhythmic beat</u>.

9) **BEATBOXING** — using the <u>voice</u> to make <u>percussive sounds</u>, imitating a <u>drum kit</u> or <u>DJ equipment</u>.

Electronic Effects Can Be Added to Vocal Parts

There's more on these effects on p.72-73 and p.75.

Another way to make the vocals on a pop song sound interesting is to add <u>electronic effects</u>.

1) **REVERB** (short for <u>reverberation</u>) adds an <u>echo</u> to a sound.

2) **MULTI-TRACKING** (or <u>layering</u>) is when <u>each part</u> is recorded on its own <u>track</u>, and all the tracks are played back together. It means <u>one singer</u> can record <u>all</u> the parts in a song — for example, in some <u>Queen</u> songs, <u>Freddie Mercury</u> sings the <u>solo part</u> and the <u>backing vocals</u> at the <u>same time</u>.

3) **SAMPLING** is when you use a <u>short recording</u> (a <u>sample</u>) of someone else's voice in your song.

4) A **VOCODER** (a type of <u>synthesizer</u>) <u>electronically alters</u> a voice recording and creates <u>weird effects</u>. Similar technology is used with <u>auto-tuning</u> — adjusting notes on a recording so that they're in tune.

He swore he could hit the high notes, but that was falsetto...

Next time you're listening to pop music, pay close attention to the techniques the singers use.

Instruments of Pop

Pop songs can use any instruments at all — but there are some common instruments that are often used.

Most Pop Songs Use **Electric Guitars**

The **Lead Guitar** Plays **Tunes**, the **Rhythm Guitar** Plays **Chords**

The lead guitar plays the melody, as well as improvised solos in the instrumental sections
(Brian May from Queen and Slash from Guns N' Roses are famous for their guitar solos).
The lead guitar also adds in fancy bits all the way through to decorate the tune.

The rhythm guitar fills in the harmony all the way through. They either strum the chords
or pick out broken (arpeggiated) chords (see p.39) and often play rhythmic riffs (see p.58).
Some artists (e.g. Bob Dylan and Ed Sheeran) play rhythms on acoustic guitars instead.

The **Bass Guitar** Plays the **Bass Lines**

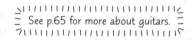
See p.65 for more about guitars.

The bass guitar plays the lowest notes. The bass guitarist picks out individual notes
(not chords) to form the bass line. As well as picking, bass guitarists sometimes play
glissandos by sliding their finger up and down the string (this is easier on a fretless bass).

Electric Guitars Can Play **Effects**

By plugging an electric guitar into an effects box or using different pedals you can get all sorts of effects:
1) **DISTORTION** — a grungy, dirty sound.
2) **FUZZ** — fuzzy-sounding distortion.
3) **CHORUS** — makes it sound like more than one instrument is playing.
4) **FLANGER** and **PHASER** — create a 'whooshing' noise.
5) **WAH WAH** — makes the guitar go, er... "wah wah".
6) **COMPRESSION** — evens out variations in volume.
7) **PANNING** — sends different sounds through different speakers. If you've got two guitarists
trading solos, one could be panned left and one right to separate the sounds.

You can also produce reverb (echo) on a guitar as well. There's more about guitar effects on p.75.

The **Drums** Add the **Rhythm**

1) The drummer sets the tempo and plays rhythms to fit the style of the song (like the rhythm guitar).
2) The main instruments of a drum kit are snare drum, bass drum, hi-hat, tom-toms and cymbals. There
are different playing techniques — e.g. for a rim shot, you hit both the rim and head of the snare drum.
3) Drum pads and drum machines can replace acoustic drums, or sometimes play alongside them.

The **Piano** or **Keyboard** Provides **Melody** and **Harmony**

The piano or keyboard can play the melody (and instrumental solos) or chords to fill out the harmony.
Not all pop songs will have a piano, but some only have a piano accompaniment (e.g. Bob Dylan's 'Make
You Feel My Love' and Adele's 'Someone Like You'). These songs tend to be gentler than other pop songs.

Synthesizers Can Do Lots of Jobs

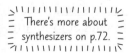
There's more about synthesizers on p.72.

Synthesizers (synths) can play any part — they can make the sound of virtually any instrument
you want, e.g. a full string section or brass section (although some bands have live strings
or brass). They can play rhythmic chords, solos or hooks (short, catchy, memorable bits).

Rock 'n' Roll

Rock 'n' roll is sometimes used to mean rock music in general — but for these two pages, it means the particular style of music that developed in the USA in the 1950s and '60s and spread across the world.

Rock 'n' Roll Came from the United States in the 1950s

1) Rock 'n' roll developed in the southern states of America in the late 1940s and early 1950s. African Americans moved to urban areas, which meant that black and white people were living closer together than ever before. Their styles of music mixed and evolved, creating new genres of music.

2) Rock 'n' roll was a mix of rhythm 'n' blues (which itself came from blues — see p.129-130) and country and western music, but also had influences of gospel, folk and jazz. Typical songs were a faster version of the 12-bar blues with the distinctive twang of country and western singing.

3) It might seem pretty tame today, but rock 'n' roll caused a massive uproar in the 1950s. Teenagers loved it, but their parents' generation hated it — they thought it was tasteless and immoral, and some even went as far as to say it was evil. Teenagers could afford to buy their own records though, so rock 'n' roll was extremely successful, and made superstars out of its biggest artists (e.g. Elvis Presley). It was used in films and TV programmes, which made it even more popular.

Cleveland DJ Alan Freed made the term 'rock 'n' roll' popular.

4) Rock 'n' roll continued to develop throughout the '50s and '60s, leading to rock music itself from the mid 1960s (see p.112-113).

Rock 'n' Roll Songs Were Lively With a Strong Beat

1) Rock 'n' roll songs were generally up-tempo, with a clear beat (most of them were in $\frac{4}{4}$). This made them ideal for dancing — dances in high school gyms were popular (like in *Grease*), and popular TV shows featured teenagers dancing to current hits.

2) The general line-up for a rock 'n' roll band was a lead singer, electric guitars, a bass guitar, a drum kit and sometimes a piano. In earlier bands, the piano played more of a lead role and some had a saxophone as well. A double bass was used before the bass guitar became more common.

3) The lyrics appealed to teenagers because they were about teenage issues, such as love, school, cars and summer holidays. Key lines were repeated throughout the song, which made them memorable.

4) The structure of the songs was fairly simple — most were either strophic (all verses had the same tune — see p.56) or had a verse-chorus structure (see p.58). Some had an AABA structure (four sections, three with the same melody and one that contrasts). A lot of hits featured at least one instrumental section, where a soloist (usually the lead guitarist) would improvise.

5) The verses and choruses themselves were often based on a 12-bar blues. There was a lot of call and response between the lead singer and the band, and most songs had a catchy hook.

Early Rock 'n' Roll Stars Included Bill Haley and Elvis Presley

- One of the first rock 'n' roll hits was 'Rock Around the Clock' by Bill Haley & His Comets.
- Elvis Presley was a huge star — his early hits included 'Hound Dog', 'Heartbreak Hotel' and 'Jailhouse Rock'. Elvis also acted and sang in films, which made him even more popular. He was adored by teenage girls — at his concerts, his gyrating hips caused a commotion.
- Bill Haley, Elvis Presley, Jerry Lee Lewis (who sang 'Great Balls of Fire') and Buddy Holly ('That'll Be The Day') were all rockabilly singers (a sub-genre of rock 'n' roll).
- Britain produced some rock 'n' roll stars as well, who were heavily influenced by American rock 'n' roll. The Beatles started out in rock 'n' roll (there's more about them on p.114).

Rock 'n' roll was more controversial than pineapple on pizza...

In a nutshell, rock 'n' roll took the African American rhythm 'n' blues and made it accessible to young people of all backgrounds. Rock 'n' roll was more than just a type of music — it was an entire culture.

Rock Music

*Rock music is **developing** all the time — but you need to know about rock music from the '60s and '70s.*

Rock Music Developed in the 1960s

1) During the <u>1960s</u>, rock 'n' roll <u>evolved</u> into more <u>guitar-dominated</u> music known simply as <u>rock</u>.

2) Like the <u>12-bar blues</u> (see p.130), rock songs tend to be based around the chords <u>I</u>, <u>IV</u> and <u>V</u> (and sometimes <u>VI</u>). Songs are often in $\frac{4}{4}$ with a <u>steady drum rhythm</u> and follow a <u>verse-chorus structure</u>.

3) Rock music often uses <u>power chords</u> (chords made up of the <u>tonic</u> and <u>fifth</u>).

4) Many rock bands were <u>formed</u> in the 1960s — though most <u>continued</u> into the following decades.

- <u>The Rolling Stones</u> had hits in the '60s including '<u>(I Can't Get No) Satisfaction</u>' and '<u>Get Off Of My Cloud</u>'.

- <u>Led Zeppelin's</u> most famous song, '<u>Stairway to Heaven</u>' (see p.114), was released in <u>1971</u>, but the band was formed in the late '60s.

- Other <u>rock bands</u> from the '60s and '70s include <u>The Beatles</u> (see p.114), <u>The Kinks</u> (who had a hit in the UK and the USA with '<u>You Really Got Me</u>'), <u>The Who</u> (who sang '<u>My Generation</u>' and '<u>Pinball Wizard</u>') and <u>The Doors</u> (who had US No.1 singles with '<u>Light My Fire</u>' and '<u>Hello, I Love You</u>'.)

The Instrumentation Varies

1) A <u>rock band</u> was originally made up of a <u>lead electric guitar</u>, a <u>rhythm electric guitar</u>, a <u>lead singer</u>, a <u>bass guitar</u> and a <u>drummer</u>.

2) As rock developed, <u>more instruments</u> were added. In some songs, bands might use a <u>string section</u> (with <u>violins</u> and <u>cellos</u>), a <u>brass section</u> (<u>trumpets</u> and <u>trombones</u>) or a <u>wind section</u> (<u>flutes</u>, <u>clarinets</u>, <u>saxophones</u> and <u>oboes</u>). They also brought in <u>pianos</u> or <u>keyboards</u> and <u>synthesizers</u>.

3) Musicians used the <u>effects</u> on <u>electric guitars</u> to produce new sounds — like <u>distortion</u>, <u>feedback</u> (the noise you get when a guitar or microphone is too close to a speaker) and <u>reverberation</u> (echo).

Developments in technology have played an important part in rock music.

4) Rock bands use lots of other <u>techniques</u> to get <u>unusual sounds</u> — <u>Led Zeppelin</u> often used a <u>pounding beat</u> turned up really loud as their main rhythm. They sometimes used <u>violin bows</u> on their <u>guitar strings</u> to get a <u>sustained note</u>.

Rock Songs Are a Way of Expressing Yourself

1) Lots of rock bands write their <u>own lyrics</u> to songs (as well as the music). They use things like <u>religious themes</u>, <u>political causes</u> and <u>personal experiences of love</u> and some told <u>stories</u>.

2) <u>Led Zeppelin</u>, <u>David Bowie</u> and <u>Bob Dylan</u> all use the influences of <u>folk music</u> — they've written whole albums in a folky style (often described as <u>folk rock</u>).

3) <u>Costumes</u> were used to help the music along — David Bowie's <u>jumpsuits</u> and <u>make-up</u> (such as his famous <u>lightning bolt</u> make-up) really helped to <u>set the scene</u> for the <u>characters</u> that appeared in Bowie's songs (e.g. <u>Major Tom</u> and <u>Ziggy Stardust</u>).

Don't forget the best rock instrument — the air guitar...

Listen to '<u>Stairway to Heaven</u>' from Led Zeppelin's *IV*. The structure is different to a 'typical' rock song, but still has plenty of the rock features covered on this page — see if you can pick some out.

Rock Music

Don't worry, you don't need to know masses of detail about the different types of rock music below.
Make sure you're happy with their common features though, such as the importance of the guitar.

There Are Lots of Types of Rock

Over time, rock has branched out into lots of different sub-genres. Here are some of the most popular:

HARD ROCK
- Loud and aggressive, dominated by a distorted electric guitar — solos and power chords were key features.
- Bands include Led Zeppelin and The Who.

HEAVY METAL
- Harder and more distorted than hard rock, with even longer guitar solos.
- Bands include Black Sabbath and Iron Maiden.

GLAM ROCK
- Theatrical and glitzy.
- Easier to listen to than hard rock, with a more rock 'n' roll feel and catchy hooks.
- Performers dressed up in spangly catsuits and wore lots of make-up.
- Artists include David Bowie and Kiss.

PUNK ROCK
- Harsh and angry music from the '70s — it's all about anarchy and rebellion. Lyrics were often shouted.
- Bands include The Sex Pistols and Blondie.

PROGRESSIVE (PROG) ROCK
- Songs were experimental and complicated, and albums often had a theme.
- Features long instrumentals, electronic effects and mythological or nonsensical lyrics.
- Bands include Yes and Pink Floyd.

PSYCHEDELIC ROCK
- From the '60s artistic movement psychedelia — it tried to recreate the surreal images and sounds experienced with hallucinogenic drugs like LSD.
- The music used lots of guitar effects and unusual electronic instruments and effects. It took inspiration from other cultures (including Eastern music). Lyrics were weird and dreamlike.
- Bands include The Beatles and The Doors.

Classic Rock Songs are Known as Anthems

1) Because of the powerful nature of the music and lyrics, a lot of rock songs can be described as anthems. They usually have memorable, singable (or shoutable) choruses. Here are a few examples:

   - 'Born to Be Wild' by Steppenwolf was released in 1968 — it was one of the first songs to be described as 'heavy metal' (see above), and even uses the words 'heavy metal thunder'. It has distorted electric guitars and the repeated line 'born to be wild' is simple and memorable.
   - 'We Will Rock You' by Queen was released in 1977. The only accompaniment to the vocals is the instantly-recognizable 'stamp stamp clap' rhythm that continues throughout the song (go on, you know you want to). The chorus is just one repeated line, almost like a chant. An electric guitar comes in right at the end and plays a solo.

Rock anthems were perfect for arena performances.

2) Arena rock (or stadium rock) came about in the middle of the 1970s — developments in technology meant that rock bands could be amplified more. This allowed them to perform in larger spaces, such as arenas and stadiums (hence the name).

3) Technology also meant that special effects (such as pyrotechnics and light shows) could be used. Arena performances were about the effects and experience as much as the music.

My heavy metal band has a lead singer and a mercury guitarist...

'We Will Rock You' features in the 2001 film *A Knight's Tale*, where it's played at a jousting tournament. Perhaps not the most historically-accurate choice of song, but you can't beat a classic rock anthem.

Rock Music

*I couldn't end these pages about rock music without talking more about a little band called **The Beatles**...*

The Beatles Were **Very Influential**

- The members of the band were John Lennon, Paul McCartney, George Harrison and Ringo Starr. They were all from Liverpool.

  Their producer George Martin was often known as 'the fifth Beatle'.

- Their standard line-up was Lennon on rhythm guitar, McCartney on bass guitar, Harrison on lead guitar and Starr on drums, although there was some variation. All four members provided vocals, and Lennon and McCartney were the main songwriters. In later songs, they used a variety of other instruments, including the piano and sitar.

- Their early songs (such as 'I Saw Her Standing There' and 'She Loves You') were influenced by Elvis Presley, Chuck Berry and other rock 'n' roll stars.

- Although they're usually classed as a rock band, their style changed so much over the years that it's almost impossible to put them into one category. As well as rock 'n' roll, they used musical ideas from rhythm 'n' blues, folk, classical music and non-Western cultures (such as Indian music). They also used pioneering recording techniques such as sampling.

- These different styles can be heard on their albums — for example, *Please Please Me* is rock 'n' roll, whereas *Help* has more of a rock sound.

- They had loads of hits — some of their most famous songs include 'Yesterday', 'Hey Jude', 'All You Need is Love', 'A Hard Day's Night' and 'I Want to Hold Your Hand'.

  In the mid '60s, the Beatles inspired a lot of excitement in the USA, which was known as 'Beatlemania'.

Sgt. Pepper's Lonely Hearts Club Band is a **Concept Album**

1) The Beatles' 1967 psychedelic rock album *Sgt. Pepper's Lonely Hearts Club Band* was one of the first rock concept albums — an album with a theme that links all the tracks. The idea was that the album was a live performance by Sgt. Pepper's Lonely Hearts Club Band, so should be played in one go, with the tracks in the order that they appeared. This idea was reinforced by features such as noises of an orchestra tuning up before the start of the first track and audience applause during the song.

2) The name of the album is the name of the fictional band that The Beatles used as their alter ego — pretending to be someone else gave them the chance to experiment with different styles of music.

3) The songs on the album use a wide variety of instruments — including a 40-piece orchestra who play a long, dissonant crescendo in the middle of 'A Day In The Life', a French horn quartet on the title track and classical Indian instruments on 'Within You Without You'.

In the '70s, **Songs** Became **Longer** and **Albums** Had **Themes**

- Queen's 'Bohemian Rhapsody' (released in 1975) lasts for a whopping 6 minutes. It doesn't have a chorus — it's made up of unrelated sections, including a slow ballad, a guitar solo, an operatic section and a heavy rock section. The song is through-composed (see p.56).
- 'Stairway to Heaven' (1971) by Led Zeppelin lasts for an even more whopping 8 minutes. It has different sections — the first is gentle, with a recorder and acoustic guitar accompaniment. The next section is a little faster, with electric guitars, and is followed by a long electric guitar solo. The final section is fast, hard rock (see page 113).
- Pink Floyd's 1973 album *The Dark Side of the Moon* is another example of a concept album.

Did some gardening yesterday — it was beetle-mania...

The Beatles broke up in 1970 and the members went their separate ways, continuing to record and perform their own projects. However, the music they created together has had a lasting impact on the world of pop.

Pop Music — 1990s-Today

*The next two pages are going to look at **pop music** from **1990 onwards** — both bands and solo artists.*

Girl Bands and Boy Bands Were Popular in the 1990s

1) As the name suggests, boy bands are groups with all male members and girl bands are all female. There are usually four or five members in the group, and they're generally quite young — i.e. in their late teens or early twenties. The bands tend to focus on singing (rather than playing instruments).

2) Although there have been boy and girl bands around for years (e.g. the Jackson 5 formed in the 1960s), they became really popular in the 1990s. British and Irish groups included Boyzone, Westlife, Take That, the Spice Girls and All Saints, while the USA had the Backstreet Boys, *NSYNC and Destiny's Child.

3) These bands particularly appealed to teenage girls, who fell in love with the boy bands, and wanted to be like the girl bands. The songs were written for this target audience — they ranged from ballads (songs that tell stories, often slow and emotional, where the voice is the main feature) to up-tempo dance numbers (which the bands would dance to themselves). Songs were often about love.

Britpop Came About in the Mid '90s

1) Britpop was a reaction to American grunge music (a fusion of punk rock and heavy metal — like the music of Nirvana), which was popular in the early '90s. Britpop was influenced by British bands from the '60s, '70s and '80s — such as The Beatles (see p.114), the Sex Pistols, and The Smiths. It had elements of glam rock, punk rock (see p.113) and indie rock.

2) Key Britpop bands include Pulp, Blur, Oasis and Suede — there was a rivalry between Blur and Oasis. Blur's album *Parklife* and *Definitely Maybe* by Oasis were important early Britpop albums.

3) Britpop music tended to be quite up-tempo and was played by a typical rock band (see p.112), with a focus on the guitar (rather than synthesized instruments). The lyrics were important — they were often quite witty and about everyday things, and the singers' British accents were noticeable.

4) Later bands described as post-Britpop include Coldplay, Radiohead and the Stereophonics.

A Solo Artist's Voice and Personality are Key Features

1) Solo artists have been popular throughout the '90s and '00s, but today's charts in particular are dominated by solo artists. Many solo artists have instantly recognisable vocal features.

- Michael Jackson was well known for his high (sometimes falsetto) singing voice. He also used 'vocal hiccups' (a short intake of breath) and vowel sounds (such as "ah" and "hee hee").
- Whitney Houston had an impressive vocal range and was capable of producing big sounds. She was famous for her use of melisma and riffing (see p.109).
- Adele's rich, soulful voice is capable of producing a range of timbres, from a gentle, raspy sound (like at the start of 'Turning Tables') to a big, powerful sound (like the chorus of 'Skyfall').
- Lana Del Rey has a sultry, dreamy voice. George Ezra, Amy Winehouse, Robbie Williams and Paloma Faith all have voices that are easy to recognise.

2) Image is important to all pop musicians, but solo artists really need their personalities to come across. Personality can help sell a song — charismatic solo artists can engage with an audience on a more personal level than a band. This can be particularly effective in live performances.

Adele's emotional live performance of 'Someone Like You' at the 2011 Brit Awards made both her and her music really popular. The song was about a break-up, and the personal experience evident in the song resonated with the audience. Her personality and emotions are clear in many of her songs (most of which she writes herself), which makes it easy for the audience to relate to her.

If only personality was enough to make up for my horrible singing...

More recent boy/girl bands include One Direction, The Wanted, Girls Aloud, The Saturdays and Little Mix.

Pop Music — 1990s-Today

There have been so many different pop artists from the 1990s onwards — this page covers a few examples.

The **Accompaniment** and **Structure** Varies

Pop artists use different <u>accompaniments</u> and <u>structures</u> depending on the <u>style</u> and <u>purpose</u> of the song.

1990s

- '<u>Black or White</u>' by <u>Michael Jackson</u> (released in 1991) has a <u>typical rock band</u> accompaniment (see p.112). The song has a number of different <u>sections</u>, including an <u>intro</u> featuring Jackson's distinctive <u>falsetto</u> '<u>ow</u>'s, <u>verses</u> that end with a <u>mini chorus</u> ('it don't matter if you're black or white'), a <u>half-chanted</u> section, a <u>rap</u> section and an <u>outro</u>, with <u>guitar interludes</u> in between.
- <u>Bryan Adams</u>' '<u>(Everything I Do) I Do It For You</u>' (also released in 1991) starts with a <u>simple piano accompaniment</u>, before the <u>rest</u> of the <u>rock band</u> comes in, building up the <u>texture</u>. This song also has a <u>guitar solo</u> in the middle.
- <u>Westlife's</u> 1999 hit '<u>Flying Without Wings</u>' is a typical <u>pop ballad</u>. It's fairly <u>slow</u>, and opens with a <u>solo voice</u> before a <u>gentle guitar</u> comes in. The accompaniment <u>builds up</u>, adding a <u>drum kit</u>, <u>strings</u>, <u>piano</u> and <u>backing vocals</u> as the song reaches its <u>emotional climax</u>.

2000s

- '<u>Can't Get You Out Of My Head</u>' by <u>Kylie Minogue</u> (released in 2001) has two memorable <u>hooks</u> — the repeated '<u>la la la</u>' and the first line of the <u>chorus</u> ('I just can't get you out of my head'). The song <u>doesn't</u> follow a standard structure — the <u>choruses</u> and sections with <u>long</u>, <u>held-on notes</u> are broken up by the '<u>la la la</u>' sections. The song uses <u>synthesized instruments</u> and has a <u>strong drumbeat</u>, which makes it ideal to <u>dance</u> to in a nightclub.
- <u>Britney Spears</u>' hit '<u>Toxic</u>' (2003) also uses <u>synthesized instruments</u>, <u>distorted guitars</u> and <u>wailing strings</u> to create a <u>futuristic</u> sound. It has a <u>strong</u>, <u>driving beat</u>.
- <u>Rihanna's</u> 2007 single '<u>Umbrella</u>' mixes pop with <u>hip-hop</u> and <u>R&B</u>. It starts with <u>rap</u> verse by <u>Jay-Z</u>, then follows a standard <u>verse-chorus</u> structure, with a <u>hook</u> (repeated 'ella's and 'eh's) after each <u>chorus</u>. The <u>accompaniment</u> is based around a hi-hat <u>drumbeat</u> and <u>synthesizers</u>.

2010s

- '<u>Someone Like You</u>' by <u>Adele</u> (released in 2011) has a <u>simple</u> accompaniment of a <u>piano</u> playing <u>broken chords</u> (see p.39). The song has a rough <u>verse-chorus</u> structure, but with some <u>variations</u> — the verses are <u>different lengths</u>, and one <u>repeated</u> verse has a <u>different melody</u>. There is a <u>bridge</u> with <u>backing vocals</u> sung by Adele herself (see below).
- For his 2014 single '<u>Sing</u>', <u>Ed Sheeran</u> accompanies himself on the <u>acoustic guitar</u>, but the song also has <u>electric guitars</u>, <u>percussion</u> and <u>backing vocals</u>. There are several <u>different sections</u> to the song — including <u>falsetto</u> sections, repeated '<u>oh</u>'s and a <u>half-sung</u>, <u>half-rap</u> verse.

Artists Use **Technology** to Create **Vocal Effects**

As well as synthesized instruments, many pop artists use different forms of <u>technology</u> and <u>vocal effects</u> to add <u>variety</u>. Here are a few examples:

- '<u>Can't Get You Out Of My Head</u>' was recorded using <u>MIDI technology</u> (see p.72).
- '<u>Someone Like You</u>' uses <u>overdubbing</u> in the <u>bridge</u> section. A <u>separate track</u> of Adele singing in <u>harmony</u> with the melody is recorded and then <u>mixed in</u>.
- '<u>Telephone</u>' by <u>Lady Gaga</u> (featuring <u>Beyoncé</u>) uses different vocal effects such as <u>delay</u>, <u>reverb</u> and <u>pitch bends</u>, as well as <u>samples</u> (see p.73) of a <u>telephone ringing</u> and a <u>telephone operator</u> speaking.

Pop music doesn't fit neatly into one box...

It's hard to make generalisations about pop music as it's so varied. You might be asked about the vocals, the accompaniment, technology or style — try and pick out the key features.

Musicals

Musical theatre is a lighter, more modern version of **opera**. *It's been* **developing** *since the 19th century. You need to know about* **Broadway musicals** *from the 1950s-1990s.*

Musicals Have **Songs**, **Dialogue** and **Dances**

1) Musicals came from <u>less serious</u> versions of <u>opera</u>, like <u>opéra comique</u> and <u>operetta</u> (see p.86). Towards the <u>end</u> of the <u>19th century</u>, <u>Gilbert and Sullivan</u> wrote lots of popular <u>comic operas</u>.

2) The type of musicals that are around <u>today</u> started in the <u>1920s</u>, and <u>developed</u> throughout the rest of the <u>20th</u> and into the <u>21st century</u>. They started out on <u>Broadway</u>, a famous theatre street in <u>New York</u>. Some started in <u>London's West End</u>.

3) Musicals use <u>singing</u>, <u>dancing</u> and <u>talking</u> to tell stories.

4) They usually have an <u>orchestra</u> to accompany the singers and play <u>incidental (background) music</u>.

5) Some musicals that started out on the <u>stage</u> have been made into really popular musical <u>films</u> — like *Grease*, *West Side Story* and *Sweeney Todd*. Sometimes, a film is <u>adapted</u> into a musical performed on <u>stage</u> — like *Spamalot* (based on Monty Python and the Holy Grail) and *Billy Elliot*.

6) Some musicals are based on <u>novels</u> — like *Les Misérables*, *Oliver!* and *Jekyll & Hyde*.

Musical Styles are Always **Changing**

Musicals are generally written in the style of the <u>popular music</u> that's around at the time — so musicals from <u>different times</u> sound very different. <u>Earlier</u> musicals were influenced by <u>jazz</u> and <u>swing music</u> (see p.131-132), while lots of musicals from the <u>1970s onwards</u> used <u>rock music</u> (see p.112-113). Have a listen to some of these musicals to hear the different styles they use:

1920s-1950s	**COLE PORTER**: *Paris, Anything Goes, Kiss Me, Kate, Silk Stockings*
1940s-1950s	**RODGERS & HAMMERSTEIN**: *Oklahoma!, South Pacific, The King and I, The Sound of Music*
1950s-2010s	**STEPHEN SONDHEIM**: *Follies, Sweeney Todd* and lyrics for *West Side Story*
1960s-1990s	**KANDER & EBB**: *Cabaret, Chicago, Kiss of the Spider Woman*
1970s-2010s	**ANDREW LLOYD WEBBER**: *Joseph and the Amazing Technicolour Dreamcoat, Jesus Christ Superstar, Evita, Cats, Phantom of the Opera, School of Rock*
1970s-2000s	**SCHÖNBERG & BOUBLIL**: *Les Misérables, Miss Saigon*

Some Musicals Contain **Pop Songs**

1) Songs from musicals sometimes hit the <u>charts</u>. In the UK, musicals by <u>Andrew Lloyd Webber</u> and <u>Tim Rice</u> have spawned a few chart hits, such as 'Don't Cry For Me Argentina' from *Evita*, 'Memory' from *Cats* and 'No Matter What' from *Whistle Down the Wind* (sung by Boyzone).

2) Sometimes chart hits find their way into musicals — *Mamma Mia!* was written around a collection of <u>ABBA</u> hits. The <u>plots</u> of these musicals often have <u>nothing</u> to do with the band, but use their songs to tell a <u>story</u>. Others <u>tell the story</u> of the <u>band</u> or <u>singer</u> (e.g. *Buddy — The Buddy Holly Story*).

Musicals Can Be About **Any Topic**

1) Some musicals deal with very <u>serious</u> subject matter — *Miss Saigon* is set during and after the <u>Vietnam War</u>, and *Cabaret* is set in <u>Nazi Germany</u>. These musicals are often <u>tragic</u> and <u>emotional</u>.

2) Other musicals are based on <u>Shakespeare's plays</u> — *West Side Story* is based on *Romeo and Juliet*, but set in <u>1950s New York</u>. The two <u>rival gangs</u> are the <u>Jets</u> (Americans) and the <u>Sharks</u> (Puerto Rican immigrants). The music has lots of <u>jazz elements</u>, a number of <u>dance scenes</u> and looked at <u>social problems</u> in America, which made it quite <u>different</u> to other musicals at the time.

3) Some musicals have quite <u>bizarre</u> plots, such as *Little Shop of Horrors* (which is about a <u>man-eating plant</u> — see p.119-120) and *Starlight Express* (which is about a <u>train set</u>, with the cast on <u>rollerskates</u>).

Musicals

Here's how to create that Broadway sound...

Most Musical Songs are **Easy on the Ear**

Musicals are meant to be <u>entertaining</u> and <u>easy to listen to</u>. This is how they do it...

1) The melodies are easy to <u>sing</u> — audiences tend to prefer songs they can sing along to.

2) The harmony is <u>diatonic</u> — it'll be in either a major or a minor key.

3) The song <u>structure</u> is often <u>simple</u>, with alternating verses and choruses
   and a middle eight (similar to the structure of a <u>pop song</u>).

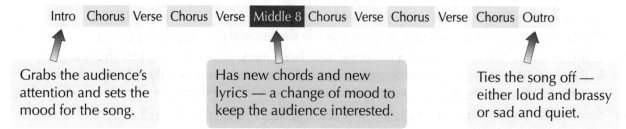

Intro — Grabs the audience's attention and sets the mood for the song.

Middle 8 — Has new chords and new lyrics — a change of mood to keep the audience interested.

Outro — Ties the song off — either loud and brassy or sad and quiet.

4) The chorus is often in <u>32-bar song</u> form. The 32 bars break down into 4 sections of
   8 bars each. Sections 1, 2 and 4 use the <u>main theme</u> (sometimes with slight variations).
   Section 3 has a <u>contrasting theme</u> (middle eight).

5) The chorus has a <u>hook</u> — a catchy bit of lyrics and melody that makes the song memorable,
   e.g. '<u>I like to be in America</u>' (*West Side Story*), '<u>It's the hard-knock life</u>' (*Annie*)
   or '<u>And all that jazz</u>' (*Chicago*). The hook is the bit that gets stuck in the audience's head
   (so they want to buy the soundtrack when they get home) and often becomes the title of the song.

There are **Four Basic Types** of Musical Song

When you hear a musical song you should be able to identify what <u>type</u> of song it is:

1) **SOLO CHARACTER SONG** — a character sings about how they're
   <u>feeling</u> — in <u>love</u>, full of <u>hate</u>, over the moon with <u>happiness</u>, etc.
   '<u>Maria</u>' from *West Side Story* and '<u>Maybe This Time</u>' from *Cabaret*
   are both solo character songs.

2) **DUET** — duets are basically the same as solo character songs, except
   there are <u>two people</u> singing so you get <u>two different reactions</u> to a
   situation. '<u>I Know Him So Well</u>' from *Chess* is a great example.

3) **ACTION SONG** — the words of the song tell you what's going on
   in the <u>plot</u> — they lead you into the next bit of the story.

4) **CHORUS NUMBER** — the whole <u>ensemble</u> get together and have
   a <u>big old sing-song</u>. Like at the end of *Grease* — 'We go together
   like ramma lamma lamma ka dinga da dinga dong...' and
   '<u>Food, Glorious Food</u>' at the beginning of *Oliver!*.

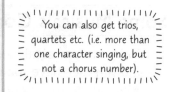

You can also get trios,
quartets etc. (i.e. more than
one character singing, but
not a chorus number).

All these styles of song developed from opera — solo songs are like <u>arias</u>, action songs are like <u>recitatives</u>.

The lyrics in a musical song tell part of the story. They're usually <u>written first</u>, so the composer has to fit
the music around them.

SUGGESTED LISTENING

It's showtime — let's see those jazz hands...

Listen to the quintet version of 'Tonight' from *West Side Story* — it features Tony, Maria, Anita
and the two rival gangs. At one point, all five different parts are sung at the same time.

Little Shop of Horrors

Your study pieces for this Area of Study are three songs from the 1982 musical 'Little Shop of Horrors'.

Little Shop of Horrors is a Rock 'n' Roll Musical

1) The plot centres around <u>Seymour Krelborn</u>, a flower shop employee who takes care of a <u>plant</u> that turns out to be from <u>outer space</u>. The plant, <u>Audrey II</u>, attracts <u>lots of customers</u> to the shop, but Seymour discovers that the only way of keeping Audrey II alive is by feeding it <u>human blood</u> (and later, <u>bodies</u>).

2) *Little Shop of Horrors* is based on a <u>horror-comedy</u> film from 1960. The music was <u>composed</u> by <u>Alan Menken</u>, with <u>lyrics</u> and <u>book</u> (the script) by <u>Howard Ashman</u>. The <u>musical</u> was also made into a film in 1986.

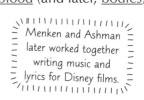
Menken and Ashman later worked together writing music and lyrics for Disney films.

3) As well as <u>rock 'n' roll</u>, the show features <u>other styles of music</u> that were popular in the <u>1960s</u>, including <u>doo-wop</u> and <u>Motown</u>.

4) The band is made up of standard <u>rock instruments</u> — <u>electric</u> and <u>bass guitars</u>, <u>keyboards</u> and <u>percussion</u>. The keyboards use different <u>synthesized</u> sounds, such as the <u>Hammond organ</u> and <u>cimbalom</u> (see p.155). Various <u>percussion instruments</u> are used as well as a standard <u>drum kit</u>, including <u>bongo drums</u> and <u>castanets</u>. Some of the <u>vocal parts</u> also use <u>scat</u> singing (see p.109). Later versions of the musical added <u>other instruments</u>, e.g. <u>clarinets</u>, <u>saxophones</u>, <u>flutes</u> and <u>trumpets</u>.

'Prologue/Little Shop of Horrors' is the Opening Song

1) The musical <u>opens</u> with long <u>drum rolls</u>. Then, chords are played on the <u>keyboards</u> — both <u>piano</u> and <u>organ</u> sounds are played together, creating a <u>homophonic</u> texture. A <u>deep</u>, <u>booming voice</u> is heard from <u>offstage</u>, speaking over the <u>chords</u> and giving an <u>ominous</u> feel.

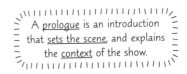
A <u>prologue</u> is an introduction that <u>sets the scene</u>, and explains the <u>context</u> of the show.

2) The <u>narrators</u> (Crystal, Chiffon and Ronette) enter, and sing together in the style of a <u>1960s girl group</u> (they are named after girl groups too). They act as a <u>Greek chorus</u> throughout the show, commenting on the <u>action</u>, providing <u>backing vocals</u> and sometimes <u>interacting</u> with the characters on stage.

3) After the <u>introduction</u>, the song has <u>two choruses</u> with a <u>contrasting</u> section in between, and an <u>outro</u>.

   - The <u>up-tempo</u> choruses are sung in <u>close harmony</u> (a style typical of <u>1960s girl groups</u>) by the three narrators. The <u>instrumentation</u> changes after the <u>introduction</u> — the <u>chorus</u> features standard <u>rock band</u> instruments. The <u>texture</u> is mainly <u>melody with accompaniment</u>.

   - The contrasting section has some <u>nonsense lyrics</u> and a <u>new chord pattern</u>. There is <u>call and response</u> between the <u>vocals</u> and the <u>guitars</u>, which leads into the <u>second chorus</u>.

   - The <u>accompaniment</u> gets more and more <u>dissonant</u>, with <u>sevenths</u> and <u>suspended chords</u> added for the second chorus and outro. The song ends with a <u>spooky-sounding</u> dissonant chord.

4) The phrase 'little shop of horrors' acts as a <u>title hook</u> — it has the <u>most memorable</u> melody in the song, as well as being the <u>name</u> of the musical.

5) The <u>introduction</u> of the song is in E♭ <u>major</u>. The opening chords have a <u>sense of foreboding</u> — they are played on an <u>organ</u> sound, which makes it sound a bit like a <u>funeral march</u>. This is <u>unusual</u> for a major key, which normally sounds <u>happy</u>. At the chorus, the key <u>abruptly changes</u> to <u>G major</u>.

6) The <u>chorus</u> mainly uses chords I, II, IV and V, with <u>added sevenths</u>. In the <u>contrasting section</u>, the chords move between <u>IV</u> and <u>I</u>, then chord <u>V</u> is used to lead back into the chorus.

7) There is a lot of <u>syncopation</u> in both the <u>melody</u> and the <u>accompaniment</u>. The emphasis is mainly on the <u>off-beat</u> — the <u>snare drum</u> often plays on beats <u>2</u> and <u>4</u> of the bar, which drives the music on. The chorus features <u>repeated quaver chords</u> — this pattern is used throughout the musical.

Pick out some typical rock 'n' roll features in these songs...

You only need to know about three songs in detail, but it's still a good idea to listen to the rest of the soundtrack to get a feel for the style of the musical, and to give these songs a bit more context.

Little Shop of Horrors

There are two more songs to learn about on this page, so you'd better keep reading...

'Mushnik & Son' is a Patter Song

> *Patter songs are very quick with fast rhythmic patterns. They're fun for the audience to listen to.*

1) 'Mushnik & Son' is a <u>duet</u> between <u>Seymour</u> and <u>Mr Mushnik</u>, the owner of the flower shop. The song is about Mushnik's attempt to <u>stop Seymour leaving</u> with Audrey II, taking the <u>fame</u> and <u>fortune</u> with him. He convinces Seymour to become his <u>adopted son</u> and run the shop together.

2) The tempo is <u>fast</u> with a <u>rapid rhythm</u>. It is mostly <u>syllabic</u> (see p.109) — each syllable is sung on one note, which makes the song feel even more <u>fast-paced</u>.

3) The style is influenced by <u>Jewish Klezmer</u> music — the keyboards uses a <u>cimbalom</u> sound, which is a typical Klezmer instrument. Mushnik is Jewish, and his lyrics contain some <u>Yiddish</u> words.

4) It has a <u>verse-chorus</u> structure and ends with a short <u>outro</u>. The choruses feel <u>slower</u> than the verses, with <u>fewer words</u> sung over <u>longer notes</u>. The <u>instrumentation</u> is different as well — the <u>chorus</u> features a <u>countermelody</u> on the <u>cimbalom</u>, and <u>castanets</u> are played in the <u>verses</u>.

5) A lot of the vocals are <u>half-spoken</u> and <u>half-sung</u>, which makes the song feel like a <u>conversation</u>. The two characters sing <u>back and forth</u> within the same line, as well as <u>finishing</u> each other's lines and singing in <u>unison</u>. By the end of the song, Seymour and Mushnik are singing in <u>harmony</u>.

6) The song is in <u>C minor</u> — the <u>minor key</u>, as well as the use of <u>diminished chords</u> and <u>dissonant notes</u>, reflects Mushnik's <u>fear</u> of losing the success that Audrey II has brought to the shop. The melody also uses a lot of <u>chromatic notes</u> and <u>scalic patterns</u>.

7) The <u>time signature</u> is $\frac{4}{4}$, with <u>syncopated rhythms</u> in the accompaniment that give it the feel of a <u>dance</u>.

'Feed Me (Git It)' Uses the 12-Bar Blues Pattern

1) In '<u>Feed Me (Git It)</u>', Audrey II tries to persuade Seymour to feed it <u>human flesh</u> and <u>blood</u>. The song is about Seymour's <u>moral dilemma</u> — Audrey II is offering him <u>fame</u> and <u>success</u>, but in exchange, he will have to <u>kill people</u> so the plant can <u>keep growing</u>. This song is the <u>first time</u> Audrey II talks.

2) There are sections of <u>dialogue</u>, mainly between <u>Seymour</u> and <u>Audrey II</u>. Seymour's coworker <u>Audrey</u> and her boyfriend <u>Orin</u> also have dialogue — Orin <u>mistreats</u> Audrey, so Seymour decides to <u>feed him</u> to Audrey II. The dialogue is sometimes <u>unaccompanied</u>, but at other points it is <u>spoken</u> over the <u>instrumental</u>. The song <u>alternates</u> between <u>spoken</u> and <u>sung sections</u>:

   - The <u>introduction</u> has a <u>different</u> style and feel to the rest of the song. It starts p with a gentle <u>piano</u> and <u>strings accompaniment</u> while Seymour <u>sings</u> about how lucky he is to have found Audrey II.

   - The <u>main section</u> uses the <u>blues scale</u>. It is in $\frac{4}{4}$, and is based around a <u>modified version</u> of the <u>12-bar blues</u> chord pattern (see p.130) — these are <u>common features</u> of <u>rock 'n' roll</u> music.

   - In the <u>bridge</u>, the <u>time signature</u> changes to a $\frac{12}{8}$ shuffle (see p.129). This section sounds similar to '<u>Da Doo</u>' (a song performed by Seymour <u>earlier</u> in the musical), but in a <u>minor key</u>.

   - When the <u>main section</u> returns, Seymour and Audrey II either sing <u>in harmony</u> or sing <u>alternate lines</u> to show that they've made the deal.

3) The <u>hook</u>, 'feed me', is an <u>ostinato</u> (see p.83) — the two notes repeat <u>throughout</u> the song. During the <u>dialogue</u>, the notes can be heard in the <u>accompaniment</u>, linking the <u>spoken sections</u> with the <u>choruses</u>. The ostinato emphasises the <u>tonic note</u> of the key — it is a <u>pedal note</u> (see p.39).

4) The <u>instrumentation</u> is <u>typical</u> of a rock band, featuring <u>electric guitars</u>, <u>bass guitars</u>, <u>keyboards</u> and <u>percussion</u>. <u>Drum</u> and <u>piano fills</u> and <u>guitar riffs</u> are used throughout the song. It has a <u>rock 'n' roll feel</u>, with <u>rhythms</u> that change to <u>match the lyrics</u>.

Learn this stuff or your exam will be scarier than Audrey II...

Watch out — there are loads of different versions of the soundtrack, and some of them have slightly different lyrics and instrumentation. Make sure it's the <u>1982 Off-Broadway</u> cast recording that you're listening to.

Film Music

SPOILER ALERT: the next three pages may contain spoilers. Consider yourself warned.
Composers who write **film music** have to write music to **fit** with the **action** already set by the **film makers**.

Look Out for **Leitmotifs** in Most Film Music

'Leitmotif' can also be spelt 'leitmotiv'.

1) A leitmotif is a tune that returns throughout the film (there's often more than one).

2) It represents a particular object, idea or character in the story, and often returns in the background or in an altered form.

3) Leitmotifs are used throughout the *Lord of the Rings* films — for example, the one that represents the group of characters who make up the Fellowship of the Ring is heroic, and appears less frequently after the Fellowship falls apart. The leitmotif for the Shire (the home of the hobbits) is a happy melody in a major key. It's light and playful, and reflects the comfort and safety of the Shire.

4) 'Hedwig's Theme' is the main leitmotif in the *Harry Potter* films — it's repeated in all the films and played by different instruments. It's associated with the world of magic and wizards.

5) Sometimes the leitmotifs give you a hint as to what will happen later in the film — if a character turns out to be a bad guy, their theme might have menacing chords being played in the background.

> In the final few bars of 'Anakin's Theme' from *Star Wars: Episode I — The Phantom Menace* (1999), you can hear echoes of 'Darth Vader's Theme' from *Episode V* (also by John Williams). This is a subtle hint that Anakin (who's good in this film) will become Darth Vader.

Composers Use Lots of **Repetition** in Film Music

1) Repeated sections of music can be used to link different parts of the film together — it can remind you of something that happened earlier in the film.

2) A leitmotif can be repeated throughout the film, but might be transformed to reflect what's going on. The instrumentation can be changed, or it can be repeated in a different key (e.g. it might come back in a minor key to show that things have started to go wrong). Sometimes just the rhythm of the leitmotif is played in the background — it might be so quiet it's hardly noticeable, but it all adds to the drama.

3) Often at the end of the film there's a triumphant modulation of the main theme (as long as the film has a happy ending). It ends in a happy, uplifting key with a drawn-out cadence (see p.42-43), to show that the story of the film has been resolved.

4) Of course, if the film doesn't have a happy ending (or if there's going to be a sequel), the theme may be left unresolved, giving the film a more open or darker ending.

5) Repetition can be used to create tension and suspense — a repeated sequence that's getting louder and louder can really have you on the edge of your seat.

Some Films Use **Pop Songs** to Get **Publicity**

1) Lots of films have pop songs as part of their soundtrack — they're usually released in the charts to generate publicity. They're often performed by famous pop stars — like Pharrell Williams' song 'Happy' for the film *Despicable Me 2* (2013).

2) Some films have pop songs over the opening or closing credits. These songs aren't always in the same style of music as the rest of the film, and often don't appear anywhere else in the film (e.g. Take That's 'Rule The World' is only heard over the closing credits of the 2007 film *Stardust*).

3) A song used as the title track might return in the background later. For example, the song 'My Heart Will Go On' by Celine Dion pops up many times in the film *Titanic* (1997).

A good excuse to watch some films...

Film music is written to create a certain atmosphere. Composers use it to set the scene, create a mood or describe a character. It should help the overall effect of the film and add to the drama of the story.

Film Music

*Film composers use music to **set the scene** — it helps you believe it's in a **different country** or **time**.*

Traditional Instruments Give You a Feel for Time and Place

1) Music can be used to create the mood of a different <u>time</u> or <u>place</u>.

2) <u>Westerns</u> are set in 19th century North America. They generally tell a simple story and they can often be very <u>dramatic</u> and <u>violent</u>.

3) Westerns use music <u>from the time</u> to <u>set the scene</u>. For example, <u>Ennio Morricone</u> composed some of the music for <u>Django Unchained</u> (2012). He used elements of <u>traditional music</u>, with <u>instruments</u> including the Spanish guitar, banjo, tin whistle, trumpet and percussion.

4) Films set in the <u>70s</u> or <u>80s</u> might use <u>pop songs</u> from the time to set the scene. People will <u>recognise</u> the songs and it'll <u>remind</u> them of that decade.

5) <u>Tim Rice</u> and <u>Elton John</u> composed the songs for Disney's <u>The Lion King</u> (1994). The songs have a lot of <u>African influences</u> (including <u>drumming</u>, <u>traditional instruments</u> and <u>isicathamiya singing</u> — see p.133), which helps the audience <u>imagine</u> the film's setting. <u>Hans Zimmer</u> composed the <u>orchestral</u> music for the film, and also used <u>traditional African music</u> and <u>singing</u>.

The Music in War Films Creates the Atmosphere

1) The music in war films needs to create an <u>atmosphere</u> for the <u>time</u> and <u>place</u> of the war, as well as showing the <u>action</u> and <u>emotion</u> of the plot. For example, the battle scenes of <u>Gladiator</u> (2000) are accompanied by <u>threatening music</u> (by <u>Hans Zimmer</u>), which creates tension.

2) <u>Sound effects</u> (like <u>explosions</u> and <u>gunfire</u>) can be incorporated into the music to suggest <u>war</u>.

3) <u>Saving Private Ryan</u> (1998) is set in the <u>Second World War</u>. The music (by <u>John Williams</u>) is only heard <u>between</u> the battle scenes (the battles have no musical accompaniment). However, the frequent use of the <u>snare drum</u> is a <u>constant reminder</u> of the fighting (it sounds like a <u>military march</u>). The music is generally quite <u>mournful</u> and <u>reflective</u>, focusing on the <u>cost</u> to life, rather than the <u>heroism</u> of war.

Unnatural Sounds Make Strange Places Seem Even Stranger

<u>Horror</u>, <u>science fiction</u> or <u>fantasy</u> films are often set in <u>strange places</u> or on other <u>planets</u>. Composers need to <u>transport</u> the audience to a <u>weird reality</u>, where nothing is quite what you'd expect.

1) <u>Unusual harmonies</u> and <u>time signatures</u> are used when things are a bit <u>weird</u> — they're not what you're expecting, so they sound odd.

2) <u>Synthesizers</u> and <u>samples</u> of bizarre <u>sounds</u> often have no relation to what's happening on-screen, but make the audience wonder what's going on and set their imagination racing.

3) <u>Instruments</u> or <u>voices</u> can be <u>distorted</u> using <u>computers</u>.

4) There's often no clear <u>structure</u> so it's hard to predict what's going to happen.

5) <u>Discords</u> and <u>diminished</u> chords make it difficult to listen to.

6) <u>Rapid scalic patterns</u> (going up and down scales) and <u>interrupted cadences</u> (see p.43) can make <u>pulse-raising</u> scenes feel more frantic.

7) In the famous <u>shower scene</u> in <u>Psycho</u> (1960), the <u>stabbing</u> of the <u>knife</u> is accompanied by (and emphasised by) the <u>violins</u> also <u>stabbing</u> out a <u>high-pitched tritone</u> (p.29). Each chord goes right through you, and makes what you're seeing on-screen feel much more <u>real</u>.

8) <u>James Horner's</u> music for <u>Avatar</u> (2009) combines <u>instruments</u>, <u>timbres</u> and <u>textures</u> from music from all over the world to create the <u>music</u> and <u>culture</u> of the <u>Na'vi people</u>.

Music revision can be used to put you in a mood...
There are loads of little tricks that film composers can use to help set the scene and create an atmosphere.

Film Music

*Sometimes, film music helps you **understand** what's happening. It can also help to **build tension**.*

The **Style** of Music **Changes** With the **Mood** of the Scene

1) The soundtrack for the film *Pirates of the Caribbean: The Curse of the Black Pearl* (2003) was written by Klaus Badelt.
2) There's a simple love theme to accompany the growing romance between Will and Elizabeth, using string and woodwind instruments playing quietly.
3) In the humorous scenes involving Captain Jack Sparrow, the music is playful to create a light-hearted mood and provides a contrast with the fight scenes.
4) During battle scenes, the mood is tense and dramatic — the music is played by low brass instruments.

Composers Can Keep You on the **Edge** of Your Seat

1) Ostinati keep the audience on edge. For example, in *The Thomas Crown Affair* (1999) an ostinato made up of clapping and a piano motif from Nina Simone's 'Sinnerman' is used to accompany a heist in an art museum.
2) In some sci-fi films there's background music with just drums and bass, generated on computers. It's played throughout the film to let the audience know that the danger is always there.
3) A good example of this is in *Tron: Legacy* (2010), which has music written by Daft Punk. They use computer-generated noises to mimic the sound of high-intensity computer games from the '80s, which helps create the virtual-reality setting.
4) Sustained notes create suspense (e.g. tremolo strings), and minor or dissonant chords make the audience feel uneasy. Suspensions that don't resolve (see p.41) are another good way of doing this.
5) Composers know how to build the tension and make you feel like something bad is going to happen:

> - Dynamics get louder.
> - Tempo gets faster — like the two-note motif in *Jaws* (1975), which speeds up (and gets louder) as the shark gets closer.
> - Pitch gets higher.
> - A tune played earlier in a scary bit sometimes comes back to remind you.
> - Sometimes they use silence before a loud bit just to make you jump.

Diegetic Music is Music the Characters Can **Hear**

1) In most films, the music is extra-diegetic — it's not actually part of the story. It's put 'over the top' of the action to increase the effect of the film. It's for the audience's benefit only.
2) Sometimes film-makers want to include music in the story for the characters (as well as the audience) to hear — this is diegetic music.

- In *The Hunger Games: Mockingjay — Part 1* (2014), Katniss sings a song for one of her companions. It is recorded and turned into a propaganda video by the rebels, and used as their battle song.
- In *Inception* (2010), the song 'Non, je ne regrette rien' by Édith Piaf is used diegetically as a plot device. The song helps wake a character up from a dream. Characters in a dream can hear a slowed-down version of the song, while in the real world it's heard at the original tempo. In fact, much of the soundtrack to the film is based on an extremely slowed-down version of the original.
- In *Baby Driver* (2017), Baby listens to music to counter the effects of tinnitus. Most of the music in the film is diegetic — the audience hears the song that Baby is listening to at that time. The soundtrack is also synchronised to the action seen on screen.

Game Music

From fairly basic origins, video game music has developed into a pretty important genre in its own right.

Early Video Game Music Was Very Simple

1) Due to limited technology, the music for early video games was very simple — it could only have a couple of different instruments or parts, so was often monophonic (or very basic polyphony).

2) The music wasn't usually played throughout the game — it would sometimes just be used as a theme tune at the start, or played in response to something happening in the game (e.g. completing a level).

> Space Invaders (created by Tomohiro Nishikado in 1978) was one of the first games to have music playing continuously throughout the game — it was based on a loop of four descending notes in the bass part, which changed speed to match the movements on screen.

3) Early video game music would often use synthesizers (see p.72), which could be integrated into the video game hardware to create and manipulate synthetic sounds (rather than recording real instruments).

4) MIDI (Musical Instrument Digital Interface) allowed composers to write for a range of instruments that played back consistently on different pieces of equipment (and different types of computer).

5) From the 1990s, video games were able to use higher quality music with more realistic instrumental timbres because of the technological advances in CD audio. Nowadays, soundtracks can be created very effectively using DAW (digital audio workstation) software like Logic Pro or Cubase.

Recent Game Music is More Like a Film Score

1) In modern video games, better technology has led to games with a more intricate plot or complicated mission for the player to complete. Better audio technology has enabled game music to become more like a film score. As well as synthesizers, it frequently uses orchestral and choral elements.

2) As there are often different locations within a game, composers will create music to go with each place or time — using similar methods to film composers (see p.121-122).

3) Games often use motifs (short melodic ideas), which can be developed to reflect the changing actions. Some ways of altering motifs include sequencing, playing inversions or retrograde versions (see p.83), augmentation and diminution (lengthening or shortening all note values or intervals — see p.18). These changes have different effects — e.g. diminution of the note values makes it sound more urgent.

4) Like films, there are different genres of game — e.g. sci-fi, fantasy, war or racing. The techniques that film composers use for these types of film can be used in game music too (see p.122).

5) Some well-known film composers have also written music for games — e.g. Harry Gregson-Williams (who composed some of the music for the *Metal Gear Solid*® series of games, the *Shrek* films and *The Martian*). As a result, some games have full soundtracks.

- In *Halo*®, the player takes on the role of the supersoldier Master Chief in a fight against an alien religious group called the Covenant. It is set on a range of planets in the 26th century.

- There have been a number of different composers for the games in the series, including Martin O'Donnell (the lead composer), Michael Salvatori, Stephen Rippy and Neil Davidge.

- The main theme opens with male voices singing (like monks chanting — this represents the Covenant), which sounds eerie and mysterious. A driving syncopated drum rhythm (playing an ostinato) builds up the intensity and creates a sense of excitement. Low strings enter playing the melody, which is based on the same rhythmic pattern over increasing intervals (the first time, it's a perfect octave, then a major ninth and so on) — it sounds a bit like a fanfare. Other string parts are introduced, creating a complex layering of orchestral parts and giving the music energy.

 I didn't know there was a video game version of Master Chef...
Next time you're playing a video game, pay attention to the music and see what effect it has. Careful not to get too distracted though — you don't want to fail your mission (or your exam).

Warm-up and Exam Questions

Before you get stuck into the exam-style questions, have a go at these warm-up questions first.

Warm-up Questions

1) What does a cappella mean?
2) Name one singer who sings falsetto.
3) When did rock 'n' roll become popular in the USA?
4) Describe four different sub-genres of rock music.
5) What is a concept album?
6) How can personality help a solo artist become popular?
7) Name two songs that were hits in the 2010s.
8) What is a musical?
9) Describe 32-bar song form.
10) Name the **four** main types of songs found in musicals.
11) What are the main instruments used in *Little Shop of Horrors*?
12) What is a prologue?
13) What style of music is 'Mushnik & Son' influenced by?
14) What musical pattern is the melody of 'Feed Me (Git It)' based on?
15) What is a leitmotif?
16) How is repetition used in film music?
17) Why are instruments from a particular time or place sometimes used in film music?
18) What is DAW software?

Exam Questions

To make sure you really know your stuff, here are a couple of exam questions.

These questions are about 'Prologue/Little Shop of Horrors' from the 1982 Off-Broadway cast recording of *Little Shop of Horrors*.

Unfortunately, we were unable to get permission to include this track on our playlist.

However, it's readily available to listen to online — you just need to listen from 0:50 to the end of the recording.

Play the excerpt **four** times. Leave a short pause between each playing.

a) What is the tonality of this excerpt?

....

[1 mark]

Exam Questions

b) Which word best describes the tempo of this excerpt?
Circle the correct answer.

rubato   **moderato**   **allegro**   **prestissimo**

[1 mark]

c) Which of the following words describes the vocals in this excerpt?
Circle the correct answer.

harmony   **unison**   **descant**   **falsetto**

[1 mark]

d) What is the texture of this excerpt?

....

[1 mark]

e) Identify three features of this excerpt that are typical of rock 'n' roll music.

....

....

....

....

....

[3 marks]

f) Identify one similarity and one difference between the first chorus and the final chorus.

....

....

....

....

[2 marks]

Exam Questions

Track 34 is an excerpt from 'She Has Funny Cars' by Jefferson Airplane.
Play the excerpt **four** times. Leave a short pause between each playing.

Track 34

a) What is the time signature of the excerpt?

....
[1 mark]

b) Suggest the decade in which this song was composed.

....
[1 mark]

c) Which two instruments play the riff in the introduction of the excerpt?

....
[2 marks]

d) Circle two words that describe the rhythm of the instruments
and vocals at the start of this excerpt.

  syncopation   **tango beat**   **swung rhythms**   **Bo Diddley beat**
[2 marks]

e) Describe how the vocals change throughout the excerpt.

....

....

....

....

....

....
[3 marks]

Revision Summary for Section Seven

That's the end of <u>Section Seven</u> — now, let's see which bits you can remember...
- Try these questions and <u>tick off each one</u> when you <u>get it right</u>.
- When you've done <u>all the questions</u> for a topic and are <u>completely happy</u> with it, tick off the topic.

Voices and Instruments in Pop (p.109-110) ☑

1) Describe four different ways backing vocals can be sung.
2) Describe: a) scat   b) riffing
3) Name two electronic effects that can be added to vocal parts.
4) Describe typical lead guitar, rhythm guitar and bass guitar parts in pop music.

Rock 'n' Roll, Rock and Pop Music (p.111-116) ☑

5) What were the two main influences on rock 'n' roll music?
6) Write down three things that rock 'n' roll songs were often about.
7) Name three early rock 'n' roll stars.
8) Describe punk rock.
9) Name two rock anthems.
10) What is arena rock?
11) What genre does the album *Sgt. Pepper's Lonely Hearts Club Band* by The Beatles belong to?
12) Name one boy band and one girl band.
13) Briefly describe Britpop.
14) Describe two different solo artists from the 1990s.
15) Describe one effect used on Lady Gaga's 'Telephone'.

Musicals (p.117-120) ☑

16) Give one example of a musical that was based on a book.
17) Name four different composers who wrote musicals.
18) In musical terms, what is a hook?
19) What does an action song in a musical do?
20) Name three musical styles used in *Little Shop of Horrors*.
21) Who wrote a) the music, and b) the lyrics, for *Little Shop of Horrors*?
22) Describe the singing style of the narrators in 'Prologue/Little Shop of Horrors'.
23) Which of the four types of musical songs is 'Mushnik & Son'?
24) How does the time signature change in 'Feed Me (Git It)'?

Film and Game Music (p.121-124) ☑

25) How did Tim Rice and Elton John create the African setting of *The Lion King*?
26) What type of films might use music with unusual harmonies or weird time signatures?
27) Describe how the music in *The Pirates of the Caribbean* films illustrates the different places and characters.
28) How are ostinati used in film music?
29) How do composers create suspense?
30) What is diegetic music?
31) Give three ways that motifs in game music can be altered.

The Blues

*You might not associate the blues with 'traditional music', but it took influences from traditional sources and reinterpreted them. It still has an **influence** on jazz, pop and rock 'n' roll music today.*

African Slaves in America Started Off the Blues

1) In the <u>1600s</u> and <u>1700s</u>, millions of Africans were captured and sold as <u>slaves</u>. Many were taken to work on plantations in <u>North America</u>.

2) To take their minds off their work, which was often brutally hard, they sang <u>work songs</u>, using their tools to give the music a <u>beat</u>. The lyrics were often about the <u>hardship</u> and <u>misery</u> of being a slave.

3) Over the years, <u>African musical styles</u>, such as <u>call and response</u> singing (p.55), blended with features of <u>European music</u>, especially <u>chords</u>. This combination was the beginning of the <u>blues</u>.

4) Even after slavery was finally <u>abolished</u> in the <u>1860s</u>, life remained hard for ex-slaves living in the <u>southern states</u>. The <u>lyrics</u> and <u>tone</u> of their songs carried on being <u>sad</u> and '<u>blue</u>'.

5) The traditional blues instruments are the <u>harmonica</u>, <u>guitar</u>, <u>banjo</u>, <u>violin</u>, <u>piano</u>, <u>double bass</u> and <u>voice</u>. They're all <u>acoustic</u> — electric instruments hadn't been invented when blues began.

6) In the <u>early twentieth century</u>, black Americans began to play the blues in bars <u>beyond</u> the southern states. By the <u>1920s</u>, blues was popular all over America with both white and black audiences.

7) In the <u>1940s</u> and <u>1950s</u> a style called <u>rhythm'n'blues</u> (R'n'B) was developed. It's a <u>speeded-up</u> version of blues played on <u>electric guitar</u> and <u>bass</u>.

Blues has its Own Scale

1) You get a blues scale by <u>flattening</u> the <u>3rd</u>, <u>5th</u> and <u>7th</u> of any major scale. The unflattened <u>5th</u> is played too.

2) The flattened notes are called <u>blue notes</u>. They're not always lowered by a <u>full semitone</u> — sometimes they're flattened by a <u>microtone</u> instead (see p.134).

3) Singers and players often <u>slide</u> up or down to blue notes — this is known as <u>pitch bend</u>. This feature comes from the '<u>bent</u>' notes used in African singing.

4) The <u>2nd</u> and <u>6th</u> notes are often left out.

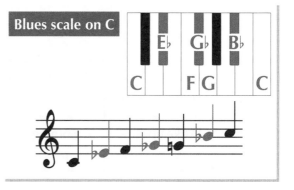

Blues Melodies have Swinging, Offbeat Rhythms

1) In normal '<u>straight</u>' rhythm the beats split up into <u>equal halves</u>.

I want chips and egg

I want <u>chips</u> and egg

2) In <u>swung</u> rhythm, the first bit of the beat is <u>longer</u>, as it <u>steals</u> time from the second bit to give the music a <u>swinging</u> feel. The rhythm shown on the left is a special type of swung rhythm called '<u>shuffle</u>'.

3) <u>Syncopation</u> creates an <u>offbeat sound</u> by avoiding the <u>strong beats</u> — it puts the <u>oomph</u> in <u>unexpected places</u>.

4) A <u>backbeat</u> is when beats <u>2</u> and <u>4</u> are emphasised.

Please don't make me beg

The blues have influenced almost all forms of popular music...

The blues doesn't have to be mournful, sad and depressing — it just sounds better that way...

The Blues

*There are lots of different types of blues, but the most popular song structure is the **12-bar blues**.*

Twelve-bar Blues has a **Repeated Twelve-Bar Structure**

12-bar blues uses a set <u>chord pattern</u> that is <u>12 bars long</u>. Singers like <u>Bessie Smith</u> and <u>Robert Johnson</u> made the 12-bar blues structure really popular in the 1920s. It's still one of the most popular styles today.

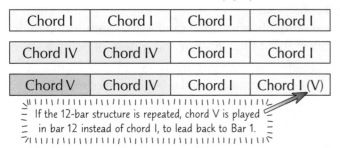

Chord I	Chord I	Chord I	Chord I
Chord IV	Chord IV	Chord I	Chord I
Chord V	Chord IV	Chord I	Chord I (V)

If the 12-bar structure is repeated, chord V is played in bar 12 instead of chord I, to lead back to Bar 1.

1) The only chords are <u>I</u>, <u>IV</u> and <u>V</u>.

2) The 12-bar pattern is <u>repeated</u> throughout the song.

3) You can make the chords even more <u>bluesy</u> by adding <u>minor 7ths</u> (see p.29).

12-bar blues has had a huge influence on other musical styles including <u>ragtime</u>, <u>jazz</u>, <u>rock and roll</u> and <u>R&B</u>. Loads of <u>pop songs</u> today still use the standard 12-bar structure.

Twelve Bars Break Nicely into **Three Lines of 4 Bars**

The <u>lyrics</u> of a 12-bar blues song usually stick to <u>three lines</u> for <u>each verse</u> of the song.

Lines 1 and 2 are usually the same. → *Woke up this morning feeling blue.*
→ *Woke up this morning feeling blue.*

Line 3 is different, but rhymes with lines 1 and 2. → *Feeling sad and lonesome without you.*

The words are usually pretty gloomy.

Each line of music lasts for 4 bars, but the words don't always fill up the whole line. The singer's part (the <u>call</u>) is followed by an instrument playing an answer (the <u>response</u>) in the gap before the next line.

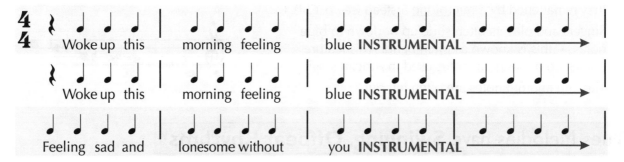

There are **Sixteen-Bar Patterns** too

1) Blues <u>doesn't have</u> to use a 12-bar pattern. <u>16-bar patterns</u>, based on the 12-bar structure, can be used.

2) There are a few <u>different versions</u> of the 16-bar pattern. Sometimes the <u>first line</u> of the 12-bar blues is <u>repeated</u> to make a 16-bar pattern. The rest of the pattern then follows the <u>12-bar</u> structure.

3) This variation is the same as the 12-bar pattern, except bars 9 and 10 are repeated <u>twice</u>. →

Chord I	Chord I	Chord I	Chord I
Chord IV	Chord IV	Chord I	Chord I
Chord V	Chord IV	Chord V	Chord IV
Chord V	Chord IV	Chord I	Chord I

'Hoochie Coochie Man', performed by Muddy Waters, uses the 16-bar blues.

4) 12-bar and 16-bar patterns can be used in the <u>same piece</u>, for example 16-bar <u>verses</u> with a 12-bar <u>chorus</u>. The 16-bar patterns are also <u>divided</u> into 4-bar lines, so it's easy to <u>switch</u> between the two.

Jazz

Jazz developed from a fusion of African and European influences.

Jazz has its Roots in African American Blues and Ragtime

1) Jazz is a type of music that developed in the USA in the early 20th century. It's a fusion of African and European influences that came from the music of the newly-freed slaves.

2) It started off as Dixieland jazz in New Orleans in the early 1900s. Dixieland jazz is a mix of brass band marches, ragtime (music with lots of syncopated melodies that was often played on the piano) and blues (see p.129-130). Dixieland jazz is polyphonic (different parts move at different times).

3) It was played in bars — one of the few places black musicians were allowed to perform because of segregation (black people weren't allowed to use the same places as white people).

4) In 1920, jazz moved to Chicago. This was the era of the Prohibition (from 1920-1933, alcohol was banned in the United States). Illegal bars (called speakeasies) often had jazz bands playing. Jazz started to get a bad reputation. Some people thought it was immoral.

5) The 1920s were known as 'the Jazz Age' or the 'Roaring Twenties'.

Jazz has Developed Over Time

1) Swing music is a type of jazz that can be danced to. It's played by a big band (see below).

2) It's usually quite fast, and rhythms are swung (see p.129). Most pieces are in $\frac{4}{4}$ time. It has regular phrases and an emphasis on the first and third beats of the bar to make it easier to dance to.

3) It was popular because it was played on the radio, which was more accessible and acceptable than going to illegal bars. The radio introduced swing to a wider audience.

4) In the 1940s, bebop (or just bop) developed from swing music. Bebop is fast with lots of improvisation. It has complex harmonies, exciting syncopated rhythms and irregular phrase lengths. Bebop is much less structured than swing.

5) Free jazz developed in the 1950s and 1960s as a reaction against the limits of swing and bebop.

6) It didn't follow the normal rules of tempo and rhythm — players within the same band would play at different speeds to each other. There wasn't a regular rhythm.

7) It involves lots of improvisation (see p.132). Soloists don't follow the chords or structure of the band.

> Jazz didn't stop developing in the 60s. There are even more experimental forms of jazz, such as avant-garde jazz, which pushes the boundaries of what's considered "normal".

Trumpets, Trombones and Clarinets are Used in Jazz

1) A typical jazz band has a trumpet, a trombone and a clarinet on the front row. Later, saxophones were included too. The front row instruments play improvised solos.

2) There's also a rhythm section with piano, drums, a double bass and sometimes a guitar.

3) Big bands are made up of saxophones, trumpets, trombones and a rhythm section. The saxophone section has alto, tenor and baritone saxophones and sometimes clarinets. Some big bands have a singer too.

4) A typical big band has 5 saxophones (2 altos, 2 tenors and a baritone), 4 trumpets, 4 trombones and a 4-piece rhythm section (piano, bass, guitar and drums).

Mmmmmm Jaaazz...

There's loads of different types of jazz out there — the best thing you can do to appreciate it is to listen to as much as you can get your hands on. You might discover that you're a massive jazz enthusiast...

Jazz

*Jazz has lots of features that mean you'll **recognise** it when you hear it — for example, it has a **swing** to it.*

Jazz is **Swung** and **Syncopated**

1) Early jazz music was based on a 12-bar blues structure (see p.130).
2) The rhythm section played the chords, and the front row instruments would improvise over them.
3) Jazz musicians use call and response and blue notes (see p.129) — key features of jazz and blues.
4) Syncopated and swung rhythms are common in jazz.

Jazz Often **Isn't Written Down**

1) Improvisation is where a performer makes up music on the spot. There are often improvised solo sections in jazz pieces. This means the same piece can be played in radically different ways — even if a piece is played twice by the same people, it won't sound the same.
2) The improvisations aren't totally random though — the soloist will know which chords to improvise over. This is often a 12-bar blues chord pattern (see p.130). Some improvisations use a mode (see page 27) instead of a chord pattern.
3) There are lots of different devices a soloist can use to make their solo interesting:

   - Triplets and dotted rhythms help the tune flow (see p.17).
   - Blue notes (see p.129) are often used in jazz improvisations.
   - Ornaments (like passing notes and appoggiaturas) make the tunes more lively (see p.41).
   - A range of dynamics and accents (see p.20) also bring variety to a solo.
   - Dissonant notes keep the solo interesting.
   - Some performers pinch bits of other tunes in their solos — it keeps the audience entertained when they spot them.

4) Jazz songs are a bit different — the singer has less chance to improvise, but they can use scat (a type of improvised singing with nonsense words and syllables).
5) In early jazz (and some today) the music wasn't written down.
6) The band follows the band leader, so they know when a new section's starting, or the piece is ending.
7) Jazz involves lots of interaction between the soloist and the band, such as call and response — the soloist plays a phrase (the call) and the band answers it (the response), or the other way around.

Jazz is Used in **Lots** of **Fusion Genres**

1) Jazz fusions take any element of jazz and add it to elements of other (often quite different) genres.
2) The elements of jazz that are often used in fusions are the instruments, free rhythms, chords and chord patterns, improvisation and call and response.

   - Salsa is a fusion of Cuban son music with big-band jazz. It uses son rhythms with jazz instruments such as the trumpet and trombone (see p.131).
   - Ska uses jazz instruments and elements such as a walking bass line with rhythms from Jamaican mento music and calypso from Trinidad and Tobago (see p.135).

Improvisation is important in jazz...

...and other genres as well. Make sure you learn the ways a soloist can make their solo exciting and that you can pick them out when you're listening. Oh, and learn everything else too...

African Music

*This page is about music in **sub-Saharan Africa**. It's different from North African music (see next page).*

Drums Play a Big Part

1) Drums are one of the <u>most widely-played instruments</u> in sub-Saharan Africa. They're used to play an <u>accompaniment</u> for <u>singing</u>, <u>dancing</u> and even <u>working</u>.

2) Drums can also be used to <u>call people together</u> for important <u>community events</u> like weddings and funerals — a bit like church bells in Europe. There are <u>different drumbeats</u> for different events.

3) Here are some of the main types of drum from West Africa:

- The <u>djembe</u> is played with the <u>hands</u>. It comes in different sizes. The <u>size</u> of the drum affects its <u>pitch</u> — <u>smaller</u> drums are <u>higher-pitched</u>.
- Dunduns are <u>cylindrical drums</u> played with <u>sticks</u>. They have a drum skin at each end. There are three types: the <u>kenkeni</u> (a high-pitched drum that keeps the beat), the <u>sangban</u> (a mid-pitched drum) and the <u>dundunba</u> (a large, low-pitched drum).

- The <u>donno</u> from Ghana is also known as the <u>talking</u> drum. It's played with a stick. The <u>strings</u> round the sides attach to the drumhead. The player can <u>squeeze</u> and <u>release</u> the strings as they play to change the <u>pitch</u> of the drum.

4) Most African music is passed on through <u>aural tradition</u> — it's not written down.

The Rhythms are Complex

1) The music is structured using <u>rhythmic cycles</u> of varying lengths, with <u>accents</u> on particular beats.

2) Rhythmic cycles with <u>accents</u> in <u>different places</u> are often played at the <u>same time</u> — this creates <u>polyrhythm</u> and <u>cross-rhythm</u> (see p.14), and adds <u>tension</u> to the music.

3) Notes that don't fall on a strong beat can be emphasised, giving a <u>syncopated</u> effect.

4) Although the music is based on repeated cycles, individual players introduce <u>small variations</u>. These gradually <u>develop</u> the basic patterns throughout the performance.

This means 'repeat the previous bar'.

A Cappella Singing is a Feature of Some African Music

1) <u>South African</u> all-male choirs (such as <u>Ladysmith Black Mambazo</u>) sing <u>a cappella</u>.

2) There are two main types of South African Zulu a cappella singing:

- <u>mbube</u> — <u>loud</u>, <u>powerful</u> singing, with <u>high-pitched</u> <u>lead vocals</u> over a <u>four-part harmony bass line</u>.
- <u>isicathamiya</u> — <u>softer</u> and <u>gentler</u> singing, with <u>four-part harmonies</u> singing <u>call and response</u>.

Ladysmith Black Mambazo feature in the Paul Simon study pieces (p.139-140).

3) <u>Techniques</u> such as <u>glissandos</u> (slides in pitch, also called <u>portamento</u>), whistles and yodels are used.

African Music

Let's have a look at some more sub-Saharan instruments, before getting onto North African music.

The **Thumb Piano**, **Balafon** and **Kora** are Popular

These are some of the most popular instruments in sub-Saharan Africa.

A balafon is a wooden xylophone. The lumpy things hanging under the keys are dried gourds. They create a warm, mellow sound.

The kora is made and played by the Mandingo people. It's got 21 strings and you play it by plucking — a bit like a harp.

The mbira or thumb piano is really popular — partly because it's pocket-sized. It makes a liquid, twangy sound.

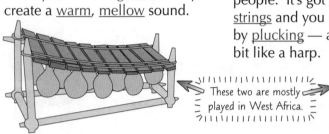

These two are mostly played in West Africa.

The thumb piano is played all over sub-Saharan Africa.

1) In West Africa, the balafon, kora and ngoni (a lute with 4-7 strings) are played by griots.

2) The griots have been around for centuries. They use music to tell stories about the history of the village and region they live in, including recording births, deaths and marriages.

3) They go through years of training to memorise the stories and master their instruments.

4) Senegalese griots play a type of drum called a sabar (a bit like a djembe) at weddings and naming ceremonies. Different rhythms have different meanings in sabar music.

North African Music is **Influenced** by **Arabic** Music

1) North African music is different to music from sub-Saharan Africa.

2) It's strongly influenced by Arabic and Andalusian music. Muslim Arabs came to North Africa from the Middle East and Al-Andalus (Spain and Portugal's name when they were part of the Islamic empire).

3) Arabic and Arab-influenced music is characterised by an emphasis on rhythm and melody, rather than harmony as in Western music. Musicians often improvise over a drone — a continuous bass note.

4) Microtones are also an important feature — they're any size of interval smaller than a semitone.

5) Andalusian classical music has a precise structure — it is performed in nubas (sets of different pieces), which each have a certain mode.

6) Each nuba is performed in five 'movements', called mizan, which each have a different time signature.

A Libyan nuba mode. The flat sign with a line through it means the note is a quartertone flat — it's a microtone.

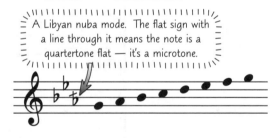

7) Improvisation is key in North African music — musicians use the modes as a basis for improvising.

Some North African instruments

The ney is a flute made from a type of cane. It has a breathy sound.

The oud is similar to a lute. It tends to have 5 or 6 pairs of strings, with each pair tuned to the same pitch. It has a rich, resonant sound.

The rabab is a bowed string instrument with a small body and long neck. It tends to only have 1-3 strings, so it has been partially replaced by the violin, which has a greater range.

REVISION TIP

It's worth listening to what these instruments sound like...

Have a listen to some African music and try to see if you can pick out the instruments described above. Make sure you learn to recognise features such as call and response.

Caribbean Music

Caribbean music has indigenous, Latin American, African and European influences.
Different styles have developed on different islands, based on what the mix of influences has been.

Caribbean Music is Rich in Variation

1) Caribbean music's <u>diversity</u> is due to its <u>history</u>. People inhabited the islands for centuries before they were colonised by <u>Spain</u>, <u>France</u>, <u>Britain</u> and the <u>Netherlands</u>. The European nations brought millions of <u>Africans</u> to the Caribbean as slaves. Each of these people had <u>different influences</u> on the <u>music</u>.

2) <u>Steel pans</u> are well-known Caribbean instruments. They were originally made from large oil drums, and produce a <u>bright</u>, <u>ringing</u> sound. They're played using <u>sticks</u> with rubber heads.

3) Modern pans are often made from sheet metal. They come in <u>various sizes</u> and are named in line with their <u>range</u>, e.g. a <u>bass</u> pan plays the <u>lowest</u> notes. <u>Oval-shaped dents</u> in the pans give different notes.

4) The instruments reflect the <u>diversity</u> of the music.

Caribbean instruments <u>Percussion</u> (especially <u>drums</u>) is important in Caribbean music due to the <u>African</u> influence.	The <u>guiro</u> makes a scrapy noise. 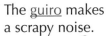	<u>Maracas</u> come from the Caribbean. 	Types of <u>guitar</u> introduced by the Spanish are common. The <u>tres</u> has 3 sets of 2 or 3 strings, while the <u>cuatro</u> can have 4 or 5 pairs of strings.

 <u>Bongos</u> are paired drums played with the hands. <u>Congas</u> and <u>timbales</u> are also paired drums.

 <u>Claves</u> (wooden sticks) are often used to beat out a rhythm to <u>set the tempo</u> (see p.136 and p.141).

Calypso comes from Trinidad

1) <u>Calypso</u> music has its origins with <u>African slaves</u> who were brought to Trinidad. They used music to <u>communicate</u> with each other. The <u>lyrics</u> had a big role in <u>traditional</u> calypso songs — the songs had <u>funny</u> or <u>mocking lyrics</u> that the plantation owners couldn't understand. They told <u>stories</u> about important topics such as <u>social issues</u> or <u>relationships</u>, and were often <u>improvised</u>.

2) Over the centuries, the island came under the rule of <u>Spain</u>, <u>France</u> and <u>Britain</u>. Calypso music was <u>influenced</u> by the cultures of those countries, in addition to its <u>African roots</u>.

3) The <u>French</u> introduced <u>carnival</u> — it's still held <u>each year</u>, just before the start of <u>Lent</u> (the period before Easter). <u>Calypso</u> plays a big part, and <u>steel pan bands</u> and <u>singers</u> compete for <u>prizes</u>.

4) Calypso bands use a <u>wide range</u> of instruments, mixing the percussion mentioned above with instruments such as guitars, brass and woodwind instruments. <u>Steel pans</u> are important in calypso.

- Calypso music is usually in $\frac{2}{2}$ or $\frac{4}{4}$ time.
- The rhythms are <u>syncopated</u> (see p.129), and mostly follow a <u>3-3-2 pattern</u>. Each bar has <u>three beats</u>, but the final beat is <u>shorter</u> than the others.
- The songs can have a <u>verse-chorus</u> or <u>strophic</u> structure.
- The texture can be <u>melody with accompaniment</u>, or <u>polyphonic</u> with melodies and countermelodies (see p.47).

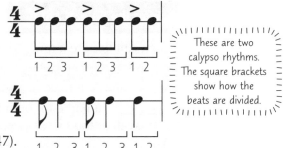

These are two calypso rhythms. The square brackets show how the beats are divided.

Cooking with steel pans is not recommended...

Have a listen to some calypso — listening to it will help you remember what the key features of it are.
Try picking out the rhythms and the 3-3-2 pattern, as well as the distinctive sound of the steel pans.

Caribbean Music

You may not be familiar with the styles of music on this page, but they influenced some genres that you've probably heard of — reggae and salsa, among others.

Mento is a Type of Jamaican Folk Music

1) Mento is similar to calypso, and was very popular in Jamaica in the first half of the 20th century.
2) It draws on musical traditions brought by West African slaves, as well as European influences.
3) It usually features acoustic instruments, including:

   - acoustic guitar
   - banjo — a plucked string instrument with a long neck and small body
   - drums
   - a rhumba box — a type of large mbira (see p.134) that can be sat on while it's being played

4) The lyrics were often lighthearted and witty, dealing with everyday life as well as political issues.
5) It's in strophic form — all the verses have the same melody (but different lyrics). See p.56 for more.

Son is Music from Cuba

Son is a type of dance music from Cuba. These are its key features:

1) A basic repeated rhythm pattern called a clave (pronounced *clah-vey*) is played on claves (*clayves*).
2) Other rhythmic patterns are played on instruments such as the maracas and bongos. These parts are often syncopated and form complicated cross-rhythms and polyrhythms against the clave part.
3) The melody is played by brass instruments, such as trumpets.
4) Call and response between the lead singer (called the sonero) and the chorus (the choro).
5) The lyrics in son music often talk about love, or comment on life in Cuba.

Salsa (see p.141) is a mix of son and big-band jazz (see p.131).

Merengue and Zouk are also Types of Dance Music

Merengue is from the Dominican Republic (there's a similar form called méringue from Haiti). It has African and Spanish influences. Caribbean instruments such as the cuatro and tambora (a double-headed drum) and 'Western' ones such as the accordion and saxophone are used to play it. It has a fast $\frac{2}{4}$ or $\frac{4}{4}$ beat, and uses catchy melodies with a simple harmony. It's sung in Spanish.

Zouk comes from the French Antilles

1) The French Antilles are a group of eastern Caribbean islands that were colonised by France.
2) Zouk is a mix of African styles, Caribbean music such as cadence (Haitian pop) and calypso, and American funk (a mix of soul, jazz and R'n'B).
3) It uses gwo ka — a name for both drums from Guadeloupe and the rhythms played on them — as well as the use of synthesizers and backing singers. It tends to have a fast beat.
4) Its modern sound has helped it become popular worldwide, especially in France.

Don't mix up clave and clave...

Phew, there were a lot of different styles on that page. Make sure you're clear on which one is which, and what the key features of each one are. You'll need to know about some of them for the fusions pages.

Fusions

Fusions are a combination of two or more styles of music.
The musical styles on this page fuse Western music with genres of music from Africa.

Styles Can Be **Combined** to Create **Fusions**

1) <u>Fusion</u> is when two or more <u>styles</u> of music are <u>merged</u> to create a new style.

2) It can happen <u>gradually</u> and <u>naturally</u> over time as two cultures become <u>mingled</u>, or it can be done <u>deliberately</u> when musicians <u>experiment</u> with different styles.

3) There are <u>different ways</u> of combining styles — e.g. you can mix the <u>rhythms</u> of one with the <u>melodies</u> of another, or use the <u>instruments</u> of one culture to play the <u>melodies</u> of another.

4) Some fusion styles have since been fused <u>again</u> to create even more new types of music.

Mbalax comes from **Senegal** and **the Gambia**

1) Mbalax is a form of <u>dance</u> music from <u>Senegal</u> and <u>the Gambia</u>.

2) It developed from a fusion of the drumming tradition of <u>sabar</u>, played by Senegalese <u>griots</u> (see p.134), <u>Western</u> popular music and <u>Afro-Caribbean</u> influences. Mbalax is also the name for the <u>rhythms</u> used in sabar music.

3) It's characterised by the <u>complex rhythms</u> and the <u>percussion</u> instruments used in sabar music.

4) 'Western' instruments such as <u>electric guitars</u> are used, as well as <u>synthesizers</u>.

5) The lyrics are usually in <u>Wolof</u> (spoken by the Wolof people of Senegal), <u>French</u> or <u>English</u>.

6) <u>Youssou N'Dour</u> made the genre famous with his 1994 duet with Neneh Cherry, '7 Seconds'. He also plays <u>percussion</u> on some of the Paul Simon study pieces — see p.140.

Raï is **Pop Music** from **Algeria**

1) Some Algerian musicians wanted to create something <u>different</u> to North African classical music (p.134) — <u>raï</u> was the result. It developed over time from the <u>early 20th century</u>, but became more <u>popular</u> in the <u>1980s</u>. Eventually, it got fused with <u>pop</u>, <u>rock</u> and <u>jazz</u> to create a form of popular <u>dance</u> music.

2) <u>Trumpets</u>, <u>saxophones</u> and <u>accordions</u> are used alongside <u>North African</u> instruments (see p.134).

3) Some Western instruments used in raï are <u>fixed-pitch</u>, so they can't produce the <u>microtones</u> common in North African music. This makes the <u>tonality</u> a bit different to the classical music raï comes from.

4) <u>Rock instruments</u> such as <u>electric guitars</u> and <u>drum kit</u> are used as well. <u>Synthesizers</u>, <u>drum machines</u> and techniques such as <u>reverb</u> (an echo effect) are used in raï to create a <u>modern</u> sound.

5) Raï lyrics often discuss <u>everyday life</u> and <u>political issues</u>.

6) Raï is popular in <u>France</u>, which is home to many people with a North African background.

Fusions can be Quite **Specific**

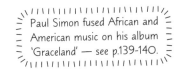
Paul Simon fused African and American music on his album 'Graceland' — see p.139-140.

Fusions can be the work of just one <u>band</u>, or a single <u>track</u> or <u>album</u>.

Afro Celt Sound System

1) The band <u>Afro Celt Sound System</u> play a fusion of <u>sub-Saharan African</u> and <u>Celtic</u> music.

2) They use traditional <u>Irish</u> and <u>African musical styles</u> (e.g. an <u>Irish air</u> with an <u>African drumbeat</u>).

3) They play a mixture of <u>Irish</u> and <u>African instruments</u> (e.g. a <u>bodhrán</u> and a <u>djembe</u>).

4) The music's based on <u>pentatonic scales</u> (a Celtic influence) and complex African rhythms.

5) An <u>electronic dance beat</u> ties the music together.

Fusions

Ska and reggae are two types of fusion that combine Caribbean and American musical styles.

Ska is a Fusion of R'n'B and Mento

Ska is a type of <u>dance</u> music that combines <u>rhythm 'n' blues</u> (R'n'B — see p.129) from the United States with rhythms from <u>mento</u> and <u>calypso</u>. It emerged in the 1950s. Here are some of its <u>key features</u>:

1) It uses <u>jazz instruments</u> such as trumpets and saxophones with electric guitars, percussion and piano or keyboard — this lineup is influenced by R'n'B.

2) There's a <u>walking bass line</u> — usually in <u>crotchets</u>, a walking bass line is improvised by the bassist around the <u>notes of the chords</u> being played. It's common in jazz and the blues.

3) It's usually in $\frac{4}{4}$ time with <u>offbeat</u> rhythms, an influence of <u>mento</u>. There's often a drumbeat on the 2nd and 4th beats, and the rhythm guitar plays offbeat 'skank' rhythms (see below).

4) Ska hits include purely <u>instrumental</u> music as well as <u>songs</u> with lyrics.

Reggae Came After Ska

<u>Rocksteady</u> is like a much <u>slower version</u> of <u>ska</u>. Reggae developed from this by mixing rocksteady with <u>new effects</u> and a <u>slightly faster</u> beat, driven by the <u>bass guitar</u>. Reggae tracks tend to have singers.

1) Electric and bass guitars, drum kit and keyboard or an electric organ are usually used. The bass guitar plays <u>riffs</u> — repeated patterns only a few bars long.

2) The lyrics are often <u>political</u>. The songs are usually in verse and chorus form.

3) <u>Simple</u> chord sequences are used. Reggae's played in $\frac{4}{4}$ time:

'Skank' rhythm, played by the rhythm guitar.

The rhythm guitar plays an offbeat pattern. It has a 'choppy' sound created by the guitarist strumming upwards rather than down — known as 'upstroke'.

'Bubble' rhythm, played by the keyboard.

The keyboard plays repeated offbeat chords, alternating between left and right hands. The rhythm above is often used.

- Reggae uses a fair amount of music <u>technology</u> and <u>effects</u>.
- The bass guitar sound is adjusted so that higher frequencies are <u>less prominent</u> and lower frequencies are <u>emphasised</u>, giving it a characteristic <u>heavy</u> sound.
- Remixing techniques are often used, particularly <u>delay</u>. A delay is a bit like an <u>echo</u> — it's a short recording of a bit of music which is then repeated over the top of the piece.
- Reggae musicians began to release versions of their tracks with added effects, in which they used '<u>toasting</u>' — speaking over the top of the music. <u>Hip-hop</u> and <u>rap</u> followed on from this.

4) <u>Bob Marley</u> is one of the most famous <u>reggae</u> artists — his compilation album '<u>Legend</u>', released in 1984, is a great example of <u>reggae music</u>:

- The band started as a <u>ska</u> group, <u>The Wailers</u> — some of the songs on the album, such as '<u>Get Up Stand Up</u>', are ska tracks that were originally sung by The Wailers.
- It also includes the famous <u>reggae</u> hits 'Three Little Birds', 'No Woman No Cry' and 'Jammin'' — try to pick out some <u>key features</u> mentioned on this page in these songs.

5) <u>Reggaeton</u> is an urban style of music similar to hip-hop or rap. It's dance music, popular in <u>clubs</u>. It's a blend of <u>reggae</u> and <u>dub</u> (a DJ rapping over bass guitar and drums) with American <u>R'n'B</u>, <u>rap</u> and <u>hip-hop</u>, as well as <u>Latin American influences</u>.

I hope you're not fused out after all that...

With fusions, it's important you know which genres of music were combined to make them and what the main features of these genres are. Then you can spot which bits have been used to make the fusion...

Paul Simon — Graceland

Paul Simon is an American singer and songwriter. His album 'Graceland' fuses American and African musical styles. Three songs from 'Graceland' are study pieces, so make sure you read this stuff carefully...

Graceland is Paul Simon's **Most Successful** Studio Album

1) Paul Simon's album 'Graceland' was released in 1986 — it has sold about 16 million copies. Simon is also known as half of the folk-rock duo Simon & Garfunkel.

2) The songs are a fusion of pop, rock and folk music with a cappella singing. The album combines the sounds of American popular music with African music styles like mbaqanga (a type of South African jive music that originated in the 1960s), mbube and isicathamiya (see p.133). There's a strong focus on percussion, a key feature of African music.

3) Simon worked with many South African musicians on the album, including the all-male a cappella group Ladysmith Black Mambazo, guitarist Ray Phiri and bassist Bakithi Kumalo.

4) The initial recordings took place in Johannesburg, South Africa. When it was released, the album was criticised for breaking the cultural boycott imposed against South Africa due to its apartheid policy.

- Apartheid was a political and social system in South Africa which strictly enforced racial discrimination against non-white people. It lasted from 1948 to the early 1990s.
- By the late 1980s, many countries (including the USA) had imposed economic sanctions on the country. Artists were asked not to perform or present their work in South Africa.

5) Simon claimed he wanted to support the South African musicians, and they have songwriting credits on some tracks on the album. This helped their careers, which had been limited under apartheid — Ladysmith Black Mambazo had more international success following the album's release.

'Graceland' **Combines** Elements of **Country** and **African** Music

1) The song 'Graceland' is about a road trip Paul Simon took from Louisiana to Graceland, the home of Elvis Presley in Memphis, Tennessee. The lyrics tell a story, which is common in country music, and reference locations in the south of America such as the Mississippi Delta.

2) The rhythms used in the song are typical of American country music. Other features of country music include the slapback echo, the almost-spoken lyrics and the irregular rhythms of the vocal part.

3) It has a typical verse-chorus structure, with a long instrumental introduction. The melody varies between verses — unusually, it also varies between the choruses.

Simon was influenced by music from Sun Records, a rock 'n' roll and country record label.

4) The song mainly uses major chords I, IV and V, and the minor chord VI. Minor chords are used a lot in country music but are rare in African music.

5) The track 'Graceland' features a range of instruments:

- Nigerian musician Demola Adepoju played pedal steel guitar, a common instrument in country music. Adepoju had introduced the pedal steel guitar into west African music in the late 1970s.
- Bakithi Kumalo played the fretless bass — you can hear a slide played on it in the intro.
- The bass and electric guitar riffs, a key part of the chorus, are typical of American music. Sometimes, the guitars play broken chords and at other times, the chords are strummed.

6) In the first chorus, the bass plays a similar pattern to the vocal melody, which is a feature of mbaqanga. Later in the track, there is call and response between the electric and bass guitars and the lead vocals — the guitars finish the vocal line. Call and response is common in African music.

7) The texture is mainly melody with accompaniment. It has a clear $\frac{4}{4}$ metre, emphasised by the kick drum and shaker. The instrumental parts are syncopated, with triplets played by the electric guitar in the chorus.

Try to pick out some of the individual instrumental parts...

The title track of the album came from a single lyric Simon had in his head — just the word 'Graceland'. At first, he didn't see a link between the lyric and the music he'd created for the album, so he dismissed it.

Paul Simon — Graceland

'Diamonds on the Soles of Her Shoes' Features **A Cappella** Singing

1) The song is about a romance between a <u>rich girl</u> and a <u>poor boy</u>.

2) The song has a <u>long introduction</u> (about one minute) that has a <u>different style</u> to the rest of the track.

- It features <u>a cappella singing</u> in <u>Zulu</u> by <u>Ladysmith Black Mambazo</u>, who are known for singing in <u>mbube</u> and <u>isicathamiya</u> styles. The group of voices singing <u>homophonically</u> creates a <u>dense texture</u>. <u>Joseph Shabalala</u>, the founder of Ladysmith Black Mambazo, <u>wrote</u> the song with Paul Simon.
- Simon's vocals enter <u>later</u> in the intro — at first, he sings over the a cappella part, but then begins to interact with Ladysmith Black Mambazo in a <u>call and response</u> style.
- The introduction is in <u>E major</u>, but the key changes to <u>F major</u> for the rest of the song.

3) The main part of the song has a <u>verse-chorus</u> structure. There are also several <u>instrumental sections</u> which feature instruments such as <u>trumpets</u> and <u>saxophones</u>, the <u>electric guitar</u> and the <u>fretless bass</u>.

4) The verse, chorus and instrumental sections are played <u>twice</u> before the song moves to the <u>outro</u> — the same two-bar pattern is <u>repeated</u> multiple times to the end of the track as it gradually <u>fades out</u>.

5) The main melody uses elements of the <u>pentatonic scale</u>. The vocal line <u>improvises</u> around the main idea, and the phrasing is often <u>irregular</u>. The bass guitar part includes <u>improvised fills</u>, and <u>interacts with</u> and <u>imitates</u> the vocal line, which is typical of <u>mbaqanga</u>.

6) The <u>electric guitar riff</u> is repeated throughout the song. Senegalese singer-percussionist <u>Youssou N'Dour</u> contributed <u>percussion</u> on the track, providing <u>shaker</u> and <u>drum layers</u>. The rest of the band includes <u>guitar</u>, <u>bass</u>, <u>drums</u>, <u>alto</u> and <u>tenor saxophones</u> and <u>trumpet</u>, alongside Simon's <u>lead vocals</u>.

7) The music is in $\frac{4}{4}$, heard clearly when the instruments start, and has a <u>steady tempo</u>. Both the lead and the a cappella vocals are <u>syncopated</u>, and a snare drum is used to create an <u>off-beat click</u>.

'You Can Call Me Al' Has Lots of **Recording Effects**

1) The song tells a story of a man having a <u>mid-life crisis</u>. Throughout the track, the meaning shifts — by the end, the <u>lyrics</u> refer to Simon's <u>own experience</u> of travelling to South Africa.

2) The song has a <u>verse-chorus</u> structure, with the well-known <u>synthesiser</u>, <u>trumpet</u> and <u>trombone hook</u> as an <u>introduction</u>. It also includes <u>bass</u> and <u>electric guitars</u>, a <u>drum kit</u> and <u>percussion</u>. There are two <u>instrumental solos</u> — one for the <u>penny whistle</u> (common in African music) and one for the <u>bass guitar</u>.

3) Towards the end of the track, there are lots of <u>drum fills</u> and <u>improvisations</u> on the bass guitar, along with African-influenced <u>vocal hums and slides</u> and <u>repetitions</u> of the main trumpet riff as the track fades out.

4) The vocal melody has a flexible, sometimes <u>improvised</u>, rhythm with lots of <u>syncopation</u>. The lyrics are <u>almost spoken</u> in the verses — the biggest leap in pitch is a <u>perfect fifth</u> in the second chorus.

5) Ladysmith Black Mambazo also provide backing vocals. The <u>harmony</u> in the verses is based around the <u>major chords</u> I and V, as well as occasionally chord II.

6) The texture is mainly <u>melody with accompaniment</u>. The chorus has a more interesting texture than the verses, as the synths, trumpets and trombones play the hook as a <u>countermelody</u> against the lead vocal.

7) Lots of <u>effects</u> were used when the song was <u>recorded</u> and <u>mixed</u>:

- The <u>penny whistle</u> solo uses <u>delay</u> to make the instrument sound <u>fuller</u> than it would live.
- The first half of the bass solo was played, then <u>copied</u> and <u>reversed</u> to make the solo longer.
- In many places, Paul Simon <u>overdubbed</u> the backing vocals himself.
- Two different <u>tape delays</u> were used to <u>thicken</u> the lead vocal — this was used to make sure Simon's vocals could be <u>heard clearly</u> over the rest of the music.

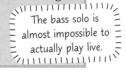
The bass solo is almost impossible to actually play live.

You could call him Paul, but it's just not as catchy...

Make sure you can pick out specific examples of both the American and African influences in these three tracks — for example, think about the instruments used or the styles of singing.

Salsa

Salsa is a popular form of dance music, particularly in Latin America and the Caribbean.

Salsa Grew Out of Son and Big-Band Jazz

1) Latin American musicians living in New York combined <u>Cuban son</u>
   (see p.136) with <u>big-band jazz</u> to create <u>salsa</u> in the 1960s and 1970s.

2) Taking the basic structure of son, <u>salsa bands</u> added the harsher,
   brass-based arrangements of <u>big band jazz</u>. The <u>trombone</u> was a big focus.

3) Salsa also took inspiration from <u>Puerto Rican</u>, <u>Brazilian</u> and <u>African</u> music.
   It soon became popular throughout <u>Latin America</u> and <u>beyond</u>.

Clave is the Rhythm of Salsa

1) The <u>clave</u> is the <u>basic rhythm</u> of a piece of salsa music. The most common rhythm is the <u>son</u> clave.

2) The son clave rhythm has a group of <u>three</u> notes and a group of <u>two</u>.

It goes like this...   ...or like this...

3) A salsa piece doesn't have to use the same clave <u>throughout</u>.
   It might switch to a <u>different clave</u> half-way through.

4) All the other parts are <u>built around</u> the clave — the clave is the <u>foundation</u> of the piece.

5) The '<u>Bo Diddley beat</u>' originates from the <u>son clave</u> rhythm.
   It is used a lot in <u>rock</u> and <u>pop</u> music.

The Structure of Salsa is Flexible

There are <u>three main chunks</u> in a salsa tune. The three different chunks
can appear in <u>any order</u>, and they can all be used <u>more than once</u>.

1) In the <u>verse</u>, you hear the <u>main tune</u>, usually sung by the <u>sonero</u> or played by an instrumentalist.

2) The <u>montuno</u> is a kind of <u>chorus</u> where the sonero or lead instrumentalist <u>improvises</u>
   and the choro or other instrumentalists <u>answer</u>.

3) There is a <u>break</u> between choruses, called the <u>mambo</u>, with new musical material —
   e.g. different chords or a different tune. It's often played by the <u>horn section</u>.

4) There's usually an <u>introduction</u> and <u>ending</u>.

5) There could also be a '<u>break</u>' — a bit where the main tune <u>stops</u> and just the rhythm section plays.

Here's a fairly <u>typical</u> salsa structure:

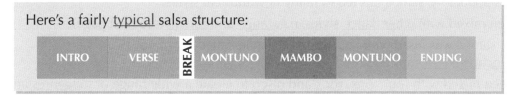

If only all genres were named after food...

...'salsa' means 'sauce' in Spanish. I guess you can just think of it as a mix of different foods, to remind you
it's a fusion. Make sure you're clear on the clave rhythms and the structure — they're pretty important.

Samba

Samba is one of the most popular forms of dance music in South America, and around the world.

Samba Comes from **Brazil**

1) Samba is a Brazilian street carnival dance. Some of the famous Brazilian carnivals, such as the Rio Carnival, have made samba popular all over the world.

2) It's usually in either $\frac{2}{4}$ or $\frac{4}{4}$. It sounds cheery and is played at a fast tempo in a major key.

3) Samba instruments include a big variety of percussion, Portuguese guitar (a bright-sounding guitar with 12 strings), keyboards, whistles and, in larger street bands, saxophones and trumpets.

4) Samba is played by huge bands at carnivals, and by smaller bands for dancing samba-salão in ballrooms, or to accompany samba-canção (samba songs).

The **Samba Beat** Sounds like **Footsteps**

1) The main samba beat is played by a pair of loud, resonant bass drums called surdo drums.

2) The basic surdo rhythm sounds like steady marching footsteps. The surdo players alternately hit the drum with a stick then damp it with the hand. This muting and unmuting gives the effect of offbeat springy notes in between the main beats.

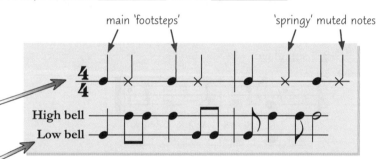

3) Over the basic surdo beat you hear many other complex syncopated, ostinato rhythms, such as this agogo bells rhythm:

4) Other common percussion instruments include: shakers (known as ganzás, caxixis, or shekeres), scrapers (the reco-reco) and tambourines (pandeiros).

The **Whistle Player** is **In Charge** of a Samba Band

1) Large samba bands are controlled by a leader playing a two-toned samba whistle and a drum.

2) The whistle sets the tempo and signals call and response sections. In the call and response bits, the leader plays a rhythm (usually on a drum called a repinique) and is answered by the rest of the band.

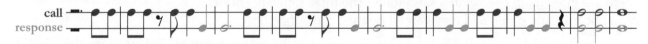

3) The call and response sections contrast with the sections where everyone plays repeated rhythms.

4) Sometimes the whole band stops and then starts again. This is called a break.

5) Samba melodies are usually very catchy and repetitive. They also build up — parts get added on top.

Samba has been **Fused** to Make **New Styles**

1) Because of its popularity, samba has led to many new musical styles.

2) Samba is often mixed with other dance styles, e.g. tango and rumba (see next page).

3) In the 1950s, samba was fused with jazz to make a style called bossa nova, which has syncopated rhythms and usually features a guitar and vocals.

4) It has also been mixed with soul, funk, rock and disco to create a wide range of subgenres and fusions.

Put 2nd December in your diaries — it's Brazil's National Samba Day...

Just like any type of music, the typical rhythms of samba can be changed or added to, so that it doesn't become too boring and repetitive. The rhythms on this page are common, but there are loads of others.

Contemporary Latin American Music

Lots of Latin American music is intended to be danced to, much the same as salsa and samba...

The **Cuban Habanera** Influenced Many Types of Dance Music

1) The <u>habanera</u> is a <u>Cuban dance</u> from the <u>19th century</u>. It has Spanish and African influences, as well as origins in a <u>European country dance</u> called the <u>contradanza</u>, brought via <u>Haiti</u>.

2) The habanera is usually in $\frac{2}{4}$ and has a distinctive <u>dotted rhythm</u>: It's quite <u>slow</u> and <u>deliberate</u>.

3) Lots of other styles of <u>Latin American dance music</u> have <u>developed</u> from the habanera, including:

- <u>Danzón</u> — a type of dance for <u>pairs</u>, with <u>set steps</u>. The music was traditionally played by an <u>orquesta tipica</u> — a band made up of <u>wind</u> and <u>brass instruments</u>, with a few <u>string instruments</u> as well. The danzón is usually <u>slow</u> and <u>elegant</u>.
- <u>Cha-cha-cha</u> — a dance style that evolved from danzón in the 1950s. It's a <u>mid-tempo</u> dance (so is slightly faster than the danzón or habanera), in $\frac{4}{4}$ with the 'cha-cha-cha' on beats <u>3 and 4</u>.
- <u>Tango</u> — see below.

4) The <u>Cuban rumba</u> is an <u>Afro-Cuban dance</u>, accompanied by <u>percussion</u> (including <u>maracas</u>) and <u>voices</u>. There are a few different <u>types</u> of rumba, each with <u>different rhythms</u>.

Tango is **Dance Music** from **Argentina**

1) Tango has a mix of African, Latin American and European influences, including <u>Italian</u> melodies, <u>Cuban habanera</u> rhythms (see above), <u>milonga</u> (syncopated music from <u>Argentina</u> and <u>Uruguay</u>) and <u>candombe</u> (<u>Uruguayan</u> music with African rhythms).

2) Tango instruments include <u>flute</u>, <u>violin</u> and <u>guitar</u>, accompanied by <u>bandoneons</u> (a type of accordion made in Germany) and a rhythm section of <u>piano</u>, <u>double bass</u> and <u>percussion</u>.

3) Tangos have <u>2</u> or <u>4</u> beats in the bar. These are some of the <u>basic rhythms</u>:

4) The main melody often uses a <u>slow rhythmic pace</u> with <u>triplets</u> and <u>syncopation</u> (see p.129). <u>Staccato</u> notes (see p.19) give the music <u>precision</u>.

5) Tango has <u>simple harmonies</u>, often in a <u>minor key</u>, based on the <u>tonic</u> and <u>dominant</u> chords (for example, A minor and E major). Prominent and repeating <u>dotted rhythms</u> in the bass often move between the <u>tonic</u> and the <u>dominant</u> notes, as shown below:

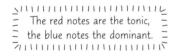
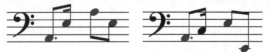

The red notes are the tonic, the blue notes the dominant.

This is an habanera rhythm used in early tango music.

Santana Blends **Latin American** and **Rock** Music

1) Carlos Santana was born in <u>Mexico</u>, but he moved to the <u>United States</u>. This <u>influenced</u> his music, which is a <u>fusion</u> of Latin American styles with North American genres such as blues and rock music. He is known for <u>virtuosic guitar playing</u>, and formed the band <u>Santana</u> in 1966.

2) The band includes <u>rock</u> instruments alongside <u>trumpets</u> and <u>trombones</u> — a nod to its <u>Latin</u> influences. They also use Latin <u>percussion</u> instruments and <u>Spanish lyrics</u> in some of their songs. Their music is <u>varied</u>, with <u>jazz</u>, <u>hip-hop</u>, <u>rock</u> and even <u>Classical</u> influences.

3) Santana often use music from <u>other genres</u> and give it a <u>Latin twist</u> — 'Migra' is a cover of a song by <u>rock/raï</u> musician (see p.137) <u>Rachid Taha</u> but with different lyrics, and 'Jingo' is a <u>cover</u> of a song by <u>Nigerian</u> percussionist <u>Babatunde Olatunji</u>.

Celtic Music

Every country has its own type of folk music, which uses local languages, dialects and instruments.

Folk Music was Played by **Ordinary People**

1) Folk music's still around nowadays but it used to be <u>much more popular</u>. In olden times, before radios and record players, the <u>only</u> music ordinary people had was music they played themselves.

2) The tunes tend to be quite <u>simple</u> and work with just a <u>few</u> instruments or voices. This made them <u>easier</u> for people in the <u>pub</u>, <u>field</u> or <u>factory</u> to learn and play.

3) Folk music was hardly ever <u>written down</u>. It survived through the <u>aural tradition</u> — people <u>heard</u> a song or tune they liked and <u>memorised</u> it.

4) Folk music changes over time as people add <u>new ideas</u>. Sometimes they're being deliberately <u>creative</u>, sometimes they <u>can't remember</u> exactly what they've heard and make up a new bit.

5) The <u>instruments</u> used to play along with folk songs and dances tend to be <u>small</u> and <u>easy to carry</u>. The most popular ones are the <u>pipe and tabor</u> (a three-holed recorder and a drum, played together for a one-man band effect), the <u>fiddle</u>, the <u>hurdy-gurdy</u>, the <u>bagpipes</u>, the <u>accordion</u> and the <u>concertina</u>.

6) The main types of folk music are <u>work songs</u> (sung by <u>labourers</u> to help them to work as a <u>team</u> and take their <u>minds</u> off their work), <u>ballads</u> (they tell <u>stories</u> of <u>love</u>, <u>real-life events</u> or <u>legends</u>) and <u>dance</u> music (see next page).

Folk Tunes are Fairly **Simple**

1) A lot of folk melodies are based on <u>pentatonic scales</u> (see p.27). They've only got five notes, which makes writing tunes with them a lot easier.

2) A <u>major pentatonic</u> scale uses notes <u>1</u>, <u>2</u>, <u>3</u>, <u>5</u> and <u>6</u> of an ordinary <u>major scale</u>.

3) A <u>minor pentatonic</u> scale uses notes <u>1</u>, <u>3</u>, <u>4</u>, <u>5</u> and <u>7</u> of a <u>natural minor scale</u>.

4) There are <u>no semitone intervals</u> in pentatonic scales. It makes it much easier to add a <u>harmony</u> because the notes don't clash. It also makes them <u>easy to sing</u>.

> The <u>structure</u> in folk tunes tends to be pretty simple too. <u>Songs</u> are often <u>strophic</u> — the tune stays the same for each verse. Strophic songs can either be a number of <u>musically identical</u> verses (with different words), or can have a <u>chorus</u> that's just a <u>slight variation</u> on the verse (so the structure is A A' A A' A...). Phrases have even numbers of bars — usually <u>four</u>. Often each phrase begins with an <u>anacrusis</u> (upbeat).

Lots of **Celtic Folk Music** Comes From **Scotland** and **Ireland**

1) Lots of places in <u>Western Europe</u> have traditional Celtic folk music — like <u>Wales</u>, <u>Cornwall</u> and <u>Brittany</u> in France.

2) Celtic folk music also includes <u>traditional Scottish</u> and <u>Irish</u> music.

3) The songs are often sung in <u>Gaelic</u> — Celtic languages spoken in Scotland and Ireland. The two most common forms are <u>Scots Gaelic</u> and <u>Irish Gaelic</u>.

4) Traditional Celtic instruments include <u>fiddles</u> (violins), <u>bagpipes</u>, <u>tin whistles</u> and <u>accordions</u>. An Irish framed drum called the <u>bodhrán</u> is also used.

5) <u>English</u> folk is a bit separate from <u>Celtic</u> folk. English folk uses instruments such as the <u>recorder</u> and <u>Northumbrian pipes</u> (a kind of <u>bagpipe</u>) as well as many of those mentioned above.

Folk songs were often just passed from person to person...

Folk music is often about simplicity — pentatonic scales, simple structure and instrumentation. This made it easier to pass on. The use of pentatonic scales gives folk music a pretty distinctive sound.

Contemporary British Folk

This page focuses on folk music that's been mixed with different kinds of popular music to create various fusions. However, there's still a lot of 'traditional' folk around today as well.

Some **Folk** Music is Influenced by **Popular** Music...

1) <u>Modern</u> Irish dance music combines <u>folk rhythms</u> with <u>contemporary beats</u>. It uses both <u>live instruments</u> and <u>MIDI sequencers</u>.

2) A good example of this is the music from <u>Riverdance</u>. It's a sell-out show featuring <u>Irish dancers</u>, a <u>choir</u> and a band using <u>folk instruments</u> alongside others such as the <u>drum kit</u>. It uses techniques such as <u>reverb</u> to enhance the music.

3) Some bands turn folk music into a more <u>modern</u> style by adding a <u>bass line</u> and <u>drum kit</u>.

- The Scottish band <u>Capercaillie</u> combine folk music and instruments with <u>funk</u> bass lines, <u>synthesizers</u> and electric and bass guitars to create a <u>fusion</u>. Capercaillie's album *Beautiful Wasteland* is a good example of Celtic folk rock music.
- Another Scottish band, <u>Runrig</u>, is well-known for its mix of <u>Gaelic folk</u> with <u>rock</u> music. They also use folk instruments with electric and bass guitars and drum kit to create a <u>rock</u> sound. Their lyrics are sung in <u>English</u> and <u>Scots Gaelic</u>. Their rock cover of the song 'Loch Lomond' is very popular.

...and Some **Popular** Music is Influenced by **Folk** Music

1) Irish pop artists like <u>The Corrs</u>, <u>Westlife</u> and <u>Van Morrison</u> sometimes use <u>elements</u> of Irish music.

2) For example, The Corrs use <u>traditional Irish instruments</u> in some of their songs, but their use of <u>music technology</u>, particularly synthesizers, and <u>pop instruments</u> (such as electric guitar) gives their songs a mostly pop music sound.

3) Westlife used the <u>Irish</u> tune '<u>The Londonderry Air</u>' (also used in the song <u>Danny Boy</u>) in their hit single '<u>You Raise Me Up</u>'.

4) Some of <u>Van Morrison's</u> albums were influenced by Irish music — particularly *Astral Weeks* (his second album) and *Irish Heartbeat*, a collaboration with the traditional Irish group <u>The Chieftains</u>.

English Folk is **Less Well-Known**

1) English folk has often had a <u>lower profile</u> than Scottish or Irish folk. However, there are a few examples of it around in <u>mainstream music</u>. This form of modern folk is often known as '<u>nu-folk</u>'.

2) <u>Mumford & Sons'</u> first two albums are known for their folk-influenced sound, created by their use of instruments such as the <u>banjo</u> and <u>double bass</u>. Their lyrics sometimes reference rural topics such as the <u>harvest</u> and <u>owning land</u>. Many of their songs are <u>ballads</u>, a song format often used in folk.

3) They used to play as the backing band to <u>Laura Marling</u>, a folk-influenced singer. Her music, along with that of the band <u>Noah and the Whale</u>, represented a '<u>folk revival</u>' in British music. They brought folk music to a new <u>generation</u> of listeners.

The group <u>The Imagined Village</u> aims to revive interest in English folk. They bring together a diverse group of musicians, such as <u>Afro Celt Sound System</u> band members (see p.137) and a <u>sitar</u> player. The group takes old folk songs and makes them <u>current</u> — for example, they turned a song about the <u>Napoleonic wars</u> into one about the war in <u>Afghanistan</u>.

Folk fusions usually use folk instruments and melodies...

Have a listen to a traditional recording of 'Loch Lomond' and Runrig's version so you can hear how they've fused the folk melody with rock. It's well worth listening to the other bands too.

Warm-up and Exam Questions

Phew, what a long section. Now it's time to see how much you've remembered. Have a go at the warm-up questions to get yourself in the swing of things, and then try the exam questions...

Warm-up Questions

1) Who first created blues music?

2) What is syncopation?

3) Write out the chord pattern used for 12-bar blues.

4) Name four instruments commonly played by jazz musicians.

5) What is scat?

6) What is a kora?

7) What is a microtone?

8) Which two time signatures are usually used in calypso?

9) Where does mento come from?

10) What is a fusion?

11) What styles of music does ska come from?

12) What technique does the rhythm guitar use in reggae?

13) What is the song 'Graceland' about?

14) What is the texture of the introduction to 'Diamonds on the Soles of Her Shoes'?

15) Where does samba come from?

16) What kind of scale is often used in folk music?

17) What is a bodhrán?

Exam Questions

Have a go at these exam-style questions.

These questions are about 'You Can Call Me Al' from the album *Graceland* by Paul Simon.

Unfortunately, we were unable to get permission to include this track on our playlist.

However, it's readily available to listen to online —
you just need to listen to the first 1 minute of the recording.

Play the excerpt **four** times. Leave a short pause between each playing.

a) Which word best describes the texture at the start of the excerpt?

   Circle your answer.

   Polyphonic   **Monophonic**   **Homophonic**   **Heterophonic**

   [1 mark]

Exam Questions

b) Describe the rhythm of the instrumental parts at the start of the excerpt.

....

....

[1 mark]

c) What is the time signature of this track?

....

[1 mark]

d) The drums start in bar 3. On which beat of the bar does the snare drum play?

....

[1 mark]

e) Which of the following technology effects is used on the lead vocals in the chorus?
Circle your answer.

   Overdubbing   **Flanger**   **Chorus**   **Distortion**

[1 mark]

f) Describe how the texture changes as the music moves into the chorus.

....

....

....

....

[3 marks]

Exam Questions

Track 35 is an excerpt from 'She Bangs' by Ricky Martin.

Play the excerpt **four** times. Leave a short pause between each playing.

Track 35

a)   What is the tonality of this excerpt?

....

[1 mark]

b)   List the order in which the following instruments are first heard
     in this excerpt by writing the numbers 1-4 in the boxes below.

Percussion ☐   Lead vocals ☐

Spanish guitar ☐   Trumpets ☐

[2 marks]

c)   'She Bangs' is a Latin dance track. Identify one feature of this excerpt that is
     typical of Latin music, and one feature that is typical of dance music.

....

....

[2 marks]

d)   Decide whether each of the statements below is true or false. Write T or F in the boxes.

The trumpets play a mainly syncopated rhythm. ☐

The lead vocal part is disjunct. ☐

The lead vocals and piano play in a call and response style. ☐

There is a drum roll before the trumpets enter. ☐

[4 marks]

e)   Describe how the dynamics change in this excerpt.

....

....

[2 marks]

Revision Summary for Section Eight

That's the end of Section Eight — put your knowledge to the test by giving these questions a go.
- Try these questions and tick off each one when you get it right.
- When you've done all the questions for a topic and are completely happy with it, tick off the topic.

The Blues and Jazz (p.129-132) ☐

1) What are blues lyrics like? ☐
2) What is the blues scale? ☐
3) Explain the difference between straight and swung rhythms. ☐
4) Why is it easy to switch between the twelve-bar and sixteen-bar blues patterns? ☐
5) Name two different types of jazz. ☐
6) List five devices that could be used in improvisation. ☐
7) What is call and response? ☐

African and Caribbean Music (p.133-136) ☐

8) Name three types of African drum. ☐
9) Describe mbube and isicathamiya singing. ☐
10) Name two features of North African music. ☐
11) Name two types of Caribbean percussion instrument. ☐
12) Write down one calypso rhythm. ☐
13) Give the two definitions of the word 'clave' in Cuban son. ☐
14) What is: i) a sonero?   ii) a choro? ☐
15) Which genres does zouk come from? ☐

Fusions (p.137-140) ☐

16) Name two features of mbalax. ☐
17) How is a modern sound created in raï music? Give two details. ☐
18) How is the heavy bass guitar sound created in reggae? ☐
19) Which musical styles are fused in the album 'Graceland'? ☐
20) Name three instruments used in 'Diamonds on the Soles of Her Shoes'. ☐
21) Explain how the bass guitar solo in 'You Can Call Me Al' was recorded. ☐

Salsa, Samba and Contemporary Latin American Music (p.141-143) ☐

22) What is a mambo? ☐
23) What are the typical time signatures of samba? ☐
24) What is the role of the whistle player in a samba band? ☐
25) What two styles make up bossa nova? ☐
26) Describe the origins of the habanera. ☐
27) Give two features of the harmony in tango. ☐

Celtic Music and Contemporary British Folk (p.144-145) ☐

28) Which notes of a natural minor scale does a minor pentatonic scale use? ☐
29) What is strophic form? ☐
30) List three bands that play folk fusions. ☐

Orchestral Music of Aaron Copland

Aaron Copland was a twentieth-century American composer.

Copland Wrote Several **Well-Known Pieces**

1) <u>Aaron Copland</u> was an <u>American</u> composer who lived from <u>1900-1990</u>. He studied composition in <u>France</u> for a few years, before <u>returning</u> to America to work as a <u>composer</u>, <u>conductor</u> and <u>lecturer</u>.

2) Although he used <u>different styles</u> in his compositions during his lifetime, such as <u>jazz</u> and <u>serialism</u> (see p.151), he's most well-known for his <u>American-influenced</u> music.

3) He wrote for different <u>ensembles</u> and <u>purposes</u>, including <u>symphonies</u>, <u>ballet</u> music and <u>film scores</u>. His most <u>famous</u> pieces include his <u>third symphony</u>, the ballets *Billy the Kid*, *Appalachian Spring* and *Rodeo*, several film scores (including *Of Mice and Men)* and '<u>Fanfare for the Common Man</u>'.

> '<u>Fanfare for the Common Man</u>' is often used for <u>ceremonial occasions</u> in America, such as at the celebrations for the inaugurations of the presidents <u>Bill Clinton</u> and <u>Barack Obama</u> and the opening of the museum commemorating the <u>9/11 attacks</u>. It's written for a <u>brass</u> and <u>percussion</u> ensemble.

Copland Created Music that Sounded **American**

Copland wanted to create music that had an <u>American sound</u>. It had a <u>more traditional</u> feel than the music of some other <u>20th century</u> composers, such as <u>Stravinsky</u> or <u>Schoenberg</u>.

1) Copland's music is <u>tonal</u> — it's in a <u>major</u> or <u>minor</u> key. Other music at the time was more <u>atonal</u>.

2) He makes use of <u>simple</u> melodic and rhythmic material, such as American <u>folk tunes</u>.

3) His pieces often celebrate American <u>history</u> and <u>culture</u>. For example, '<u>Lincoln Portrait</u>' is about the American president <u>Abraham Lincoln</u>, and includes quotes from his <u>speeches</u> alongside the music.

4) Some of his music captures the spirit of the <u>Wild West</u> and America's <u>landscapes</u>. For example, *Appalachian Spring* portrays life in the Appalachian Mountains.

- Copland's <u>ballet</u> *Appalachian Spring* was first performed in <u>1944</u>. It's set on the <u>wedding day</u> of a young couple on a <u>Pennsylvania farm</u>.

  Both Appalachian Spring and Rodeo (see below) have been turned into orchestral versions (without dancers).

- It's written for a <u>small orchestra</u> (only <u>13</u> instruments), as that's all there was room for in the orchestra pit of the ballet's original venue.

- The ballet has a <u>gentle opening</u>, representing <u>dawn</u>. Copland later uses a <u>Shaker hymn</u> called '<u>Simple Gifts</u>' as the <u>theme</u> for a set of <u>variations</u> (see p.82).

Rodeo is a **Ballet** About **Life on a Ranch**

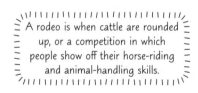

A rodeo is when cattle are rounded up, or a competition in which people show off their horse-riding and animal-handling skills.

1) *Rodeo* is another <u>ballet</u> by Copland, first performed in <u>1942</u>. It's set in the <u>Wild West</u> (as was Copland's earlier ballet, *Billy the Kid*), on a <u>ranch</u> — a farm where <u>cattle</u> are raised.

2) The ballet is in <u>five</u> sections: '<u>Buckaroo Holiday</u>', '<u>Ranch House Party</u>', '<u>Corral Nocturne</u>', '<u>Saturday Night Waltz</u>' and '<u>Hoe-Down</u>'. You can see the <u>influence</u> of the <u>cowboy theme</u> in the names. 'Buckaroo' is another word for <u>cowboy</u>, while a 'corral' is a <u>pen</u> for cattle or horses.

3) Copland used a <u>large</u> orchestra, with lots of <u>brass</u>, <u>woodwind</u> and <u>percussion</u> ('<u>Hoe-Down</u>' uses <u>timpani</u>, <u>xylophone</u>, <u>snare drum</u>, <u>woodblock</u>, <u>bass drum</u> and <u>cymbals</u>). However, he uses <u>fewer</u> instruments in the slower movements, such as '<u>Corral Nocturne</u>' and '<u>Saturday Night Waltz</u>'.

4) He often uses <u>American folk tunes</u> in *Rodeo* — for example, the main theme of '<u>Saturday Night Waltz</u>' is based on the American folk song '<u>I Ride an Old Paint</u>' (a paint is a type of <u>horse</u>).

A ranch house party sounds like a wild night in...

The first few bars of 'Saturday Night Waltz' sound like an orchestra <u>tuning</u> up. The <u>string section</u> play <u>two</u> or <u>three</u> open strings at once (<u>double-</u> or <u>triple-stopping</u>), as they often do when tuning.

Serialism

*Serialism is a twentieth century method of composition — one of the main composers who developed and used this system was **Arnold Schoenberg** (1874-1951). He invented the **12-tone system** in the 1920s.*

The **12-Tone System** Arranges Notes in a **Certain Order**

1) To use the 12-tone system, start by arranging the 12 chromatic notes of an octave into a set order (any order you like), written out horizontally — this is called a tone row.

The initial arrangement is called the prime order:

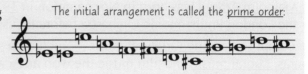

2) Now rearrange the prime order. There are a few different ways of doing this — the first is to play the notes in reverse order (or retrograde).

3) Take the prime order again and turn the intervals between the notes upside down — this is known as an inversion.
E.g. if the prime order goes up a semitone, in the inversion you go down a semitone.

4) For the last type of arrangement, take your inversion and play the notes in reverse order to give a retrograde inversion.

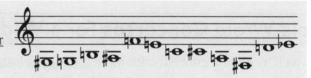

5) These four different tone rows can be transposed — each one can start on any of the 12 different notes. This gives you 48 different tone rows to use in your composition (see below).

6) As it uses all the notes of a chromatic scale, this music is not written in any key — it's atonal.

Use the **Tone Rows** as the **Building Blocks** of the Piece

1) Pick any tone row — the notes can be played in the bass line or melody and in any octave.

2) Once a row has been started, you have to use all the notes in it (i.e. you can't just use half a row). However, rows can be passed between parts and can overlap.

3) Notes can be combined to make motifs — memorable bits of melody that reappear through the piece.

4) Groups of notes can be piled up to make chords. Notes that were next to each other in the original rows would be played all at once by different instruments. This is called verticalisation — notes that were written out horizontally in the rows are written out vertically in the score.

5) The prime order could be designed to create decent-sounding chords with triads, or to create cluster chords with notes really close together.

6) Serialist music is quite complicated to write, so most pieces are only for small groups of instruments.

'Moses und Aron' by Schoenberg and Alban Berg's Violin Concerto are good examples of serialist pieces.

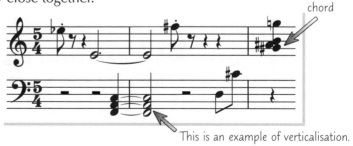

cluster chord

This is an example of verticalisation.

Not to be confused with cerealism — eating your breakfast in order...

Although this page is all about ordering the notes, serialism can order other elements too — such as metres, dynamics or rhythms. Total serialism, which came a bit later, is when every aspect of a piece is ordered.

British Music — Arnold and Britten

*There have been lots of **British classical composers** from 1910 to today — but the ones you need to know about for this AoS are **Malcolm Arnold**, **Benjamin Britten**, **Peter Maxwell Davies** and **John Tavener**.*

Malcolm Arnold was a Trumpet Player and Composer

1) Sir Malcolm Arnold was born in Northampton in 1921. He played principal trumpet for the London Philharmonic Orchestra before focusing on composition. He died in 2006.

2) He composed a wide variety of music — including symphonies, ballets, overtures, concertos, operas, choral music and film music (he won an Academy Award for the 1957 film *The Bridge on the River Kwai*). He also wrote music specifically for wind bands and brass bands.

3) Arnold lived in Cornwall for a number of years, which inspired some of his compositions — such as *Four Cornish Dances* (he also wrote suites of English, Irish, Welsh and Scottish dances). He composed 'The Padstow Lifeboat' (a brass band march) to celebrate the launch of a new lifeboat.

4) The *Tam O'Shanter Overture* is based on a poem by Robert Burns (it's a piece of programme music — see p.99). It has Scottish elements — for example, the clarinets imitate bagpipes. The drunken Tam is represented by a trombone and bassoons, giving the overture a light-hearted, comedic feel.

5) Arnold's music was quite conservative compared to other composers of the time — he was influenced by late Romantic/early 20th century composers such as Berlioz, Sibelius, Mahler and Bartók (see p.158), rather than atonal and experimental styles. His love of jazz also influenced his work.

Arnold Wrote Concertos For a Wide Range of Instruments

1) As well as writing concertos for more traditional instruments (such as cello, piano, flute and horn), some of Arnold's concertos were written for instruments not usually featured in concertos — including guitar, recorder (recorder concertos were more common in the Baroque era) and harmonica.

2) Many of his concertos were written for specific performers — for example, the Harmonica Concerto was written for Larry Adler, and Clarinet Concerto No.2 was commissioned by Benny Goodman:

> Clarinet Concerto No.2 has both typical and non-typical features of a concerto. It has the traditional three-movement, fast-slow-fast structure (the movements are marked Allegro vivace, Lento and Allegro non troppo). However, the concerto is unusual in that it has many jazz influences (see p.131-132), as Goodman was a jazz musician. Arnold uses dissonance frequently, and the third movement is a ragtime piece (it's called the Pre-Goodman Rag). The cadenza is marked with the instruction 'as jazzy and way out as you please'.

Benjamin Britten Wrote Both Vocal and Orchestral Music

1) Benjamin Britten was born in Lowestoft, Suffolk in 1913. He started composing at a young age, and continued until his death in 1976.

There's more on Britten on the next page.

2) Britten wrote a lot of orchestral music — including the *Simple Symphony* (its movements have the light-hearted titles 'Boisterous Bourrée', 'Playful Pizzicato', 'Sentimental Saraband' and 'Frolicsome Finale'). *The Young Person's Guide to the Orchestra* is variations and a fugue (see p.82) on a theme by Purcell, and is often used to teach children about the instruments of the orchestra.

3) He is also well known for his vocal music — he wrote a number of operas and song cycles (see p.102). The sizes of the operas vary — some are written for large companies, while others are written for chamber ensembles. Perhaps his most famous choral work is the *War Requiem* (see next page).

I'm going to call my composition 'Morbid Minuet'...

Have a listen to *The Tam O'Shanter Overture* — the poem that it's based on tells the story of Tam, who's making his way home from the pub when he comes across the devil and some dancing witches. When the witches notice him, they chase him until he escapes on his horse, Meg.

British Music — Britten and Maxwell Davies

You're part-way through the section on music from Britain — and coincidentally, part-way through the section on music by Britten as well. It's time to have a look at a couple of his pieces in a bit more detail.

Peter Grimes is an Opera by Britten

1) *Peter Grimes* was first performed in 1945. Britten composed the music, and Montagu Slater wrote the libretto (based on a poem written by George Crabbe in 1810). It tells the story of the title character, a fisherman who is shunned by the people of his town after the suspicious deaths of his two apprentices.

2) Britten later arranged the music used in between the acts into a suite called *Four Sea Interludes*: 'Dawn', 'Sunday Morning', 'Moonlight' and 'Storm'. All four interludes are very descriptive (for example, Britten uses horns playing in thirds to imitate church bells in 'Sunday Morning', and frantic low brass and strings to represent the fury of the storm in the fourth movement). All four movements have a sense of doom to reflect the overall mood of the opera.

War Requiem Was First Performed in 1962

1) A requiem is a mass for the dead (see p.103). Britten wrote his *War Requiem* for the opening of the new Coventry Cathedral (the old one was destroyed by a bomb in World War II).

2) He used Latin words from the Requiem Mass alongside war poems by Wilfred Owen (who was writing about World War I). Owen's poems, such as 'Anthem for Doomed Youth' and 'Futility', highlight the hopelessness of war.

3) Britten varies the instrumentation throughout — a soprano soloist is accompanied by a chorus and full orchestra, while a boys' choir is accompanied by an organ. A tenor and a baritone soloist (who sing the war poems) are accompanied by a chamber orchestra. These three groups are combined in the final section for maximum impact.

Peter Maxwell Davies Was Influenced by Different Genres

1) Sir Peter Maxwell Davies was born in Salford in 1934. He was knighted in 1987 and was made Master of the Queen's Music in 2004. He continued composing until his death in 2016.

2) Throughout his career, he explored many different styles of music — including medieval and Renaissance techniques (especially the use of plainsong, a monophonic chant) and serialism (he used sequences of both pitch and note length — see p.151). He was also influenced by expressionism:

> Expressionism is an early twentieth century artistic movement that followed Romanticism. Artists believed their works should express their inner feelings. To do this, they moved away from conventional forms which they felt were too restrictive. Expressionist music (such as some of Schoenberg's compositions) is characterised by intense emotions, angular, spiky melodies, dissonance and atonality.

3) He composed a large number of orchestral pieces, including ten symphonies and a number of concertos and string quartets.

There's more on Maxwell Davies on the next page.

4) He also wrote a variety of vocal works, such as the chamber opera *The Lighthouse* and the musical drama *Eight Songs for a Mad King*. This is a piece about the madness of King George III — it's written for a baritone and a chamber orchestra of six musicians (who are on stage with the singer and form part of the action).

I prefer the lesser-known 'Six Songs for a Mad GCSE Student'...

A lot of these pieces are 'programme music' — they 'tell a story'. Have a listen to some of the pieces, such as *Four Sea Interludes*, and see if you can pick out how the composer has portrayed the story using music.

British Music — Maxwell Davies and Tavener

You're nearly done with British composers — just a bit more on Peter Maxwell Davies, then a bit on John Tavener as well (not to be confused with the Renaissance composer John Taverner).

Peter Maxwell Davies Was **Inspired** by the **Orkney Islands**

1) Maxwell Davies moved to the <u>Orkney Islands</u> (off the north-eastern tip of <u>Scotland</u>) in the early 1970s. Many of his compositions from the 1970s onwards have <u>Scottish influences</u> (for example, the orchestral piece *An Orkney Wedding, with Sunrise* has a <u>bagpipe solo</u>).

2) He often had strong <u>political opinions</u> — which led him to write *Farewell to Stromness*:

> - *Farewell to Stromness* is from a larger work called *The Yellow Cake Revue*, which Maxwell Davies composed in 1980 to <u>protest</u> against a potential <u>uranium mine</u> on Orkney.
> - *The Yellow Cake Revue* is a collection of pieces for <u>piano</u> and <u>voice</u> — *Farewell to Stromness* is a <u>solo piano interlude</u>.
> - The piece is <u>slow</u> and <u>gentle</u>, with lilting <u>Scottish rhythms</u> that sound a bit like a <u>Scotch snap</u> (see p.17), though they're written differently.
> - It starts with a steady <u>ostinato bass line</u> (see p.83) made up of crotchets — this is thought to represent people having to <u>leave their homes</u> after the mine opened.

'Yellowcake' is the powder taken from uranium ore.

John Tavener Wrote a Lot of **Religious** and **Vocal Music**

1) <u>Sir John Tavener</u> was born in London in <u>1944</u> and <u>died</u> in <u>2013</u>.

2) He came from a religious family, and much of his music has <u>religious influences</u>. In 1977, he converted to the <u>Russian Orthodox</u> church, which inspired some of his later music.

3) Whilst at school, Tavener sang in <u>choirs</u> — much of his work is <u>vocal music</u>. He achieved early success with *The Whale* — a <u>cantata</u> that tells the story of <u>Jonah and the whale</u>. A cantata is similar to an <u>oratorio</u>, with <u>arias</u> and <u>recitatives</u> (see p.86) but uses words from <u>books</u> or <u>poems</u>.

4) His *Song for Athene*, a piece for <u>SATB choir</u>, was performed at the <u>funeral</u> of <u>Princess Diana</u> in 1997.

5) Some of his choral works are settings of <u>poems</u> by <u>William Blake</u> — including *The Lamb* (see below).

6) He wrote some <u>instrumental</u> music too — such as *The Protecting Veil*, a piece for <u>cello</u> and <u>strings</u>.

The Lamb is Often Sung at **Christmas**

The Lamb is a <u>four-part choral piece</u>, based on the <u>poem</u> of the same name from <u>William Blake's</u> *Songs of Innocence* (a collection of poems). It was written for Tavener's <u>three-year-old nephew</u>.

> - The <u>score</u> for *The Lamb* is <u>unusual</u>, as it has <u>no time signature</u> and <u>no bar lines</u> (bars are indicated by <u>dotted lines</u>, like in <u>traditional plainsong</u> (see p.85).
> - The piece is <u>slow</u> and <u>gentle</u> — the <u>melody</u> is quite <u>simple</u>, and made up of just a few notes.
> - It's written for an <u>SATB choir</u> singing <u>a cappella</u>, which adds to the <u>gentle</u>, <u>simple</u> feel. It is <u>quiet</u> throughout (the dynamics range from ***pp*** to ***mp***).
> - Tavener creates <u>contrast</u> by varying the <u>texture</u> of the voices — at the beginning, the voices are in <u>unison</u>, then the second part enters in <u>contrary motion</u> (where one part goes <u>up</u> as the other goes <u>down</u>). Finally, all four parts sing in <u>parallel harmony</u> (see p.45).
> - In the section in contrary motion, the second part is singing an <u>inversion</u> of the first part (see p.83). This creates <u>dissonance</u>.

Say Farewell to the British composers...

There's a lot of detail about different pieces on the British music pages. Write down the names of the pieces, then shut the book and note down as much info about them as you can...

Zoltán Kodály — Háry János

Zoltán Kodály (pronounced 'cod-eye') was a Hungarian composer. He lived from 1882 to 1967. Two movements from his Háry János suite are the study pieces for this Area of Study.

Kodály Collected Folk Tunes

Kodály was interested in music education — he created a method for learning music.

1) Like many early 20th century composers, Kodály, along with Bartók (another Hungarian composer — see p.158), continued the Romantic trend of expressing his national identity by using folk music in his work.

2) Kodály encouraged Bartók's interest in the genre, and together they collected lots of Eastern European folk tunes. They contributed to ethnomusicology — the study of music from different cultures.

3) Kodály's well-known works include *Concerto for Orchestra*, *Psalmus Hungaricus* (a work for tenor solo, choir and orchestra), the *Háry János Suite* and his *Symphony in C*.

Kodály Mixed Hungarian Folk With Western Classical Music

1) Elements of Hungarian folk music can be seen in much of Kodály's work.

> Hungarian folk melodies are often based on pentatonic scales (see p.27). The texture tends to be melody with accompaniment. The music often contains contrasting slow and fast sections. Dotted rhythms are a distinctive feature.

2) Kodály also took inspiration from Debussy's impressionist music.

> Like impressionist art, impressionist music creates an overall impression or mood, rather than focusing on details. Impressionist composers created different timbres or 'colours' by experimenting with new playing techniques and using contrasting combinations of instruments. They moved away from large-scale pieces (such as symphonies) towards smaller works. The tonality tended to be ambiguous, with dissonant harmonies and unusual extended chords.

> Kodály was more influenced by the impressionist use of different timbres than the harmony — his music was often tonal (though he did experiment with other types of harmony as well).

Háry János was Originally a Comic Opera

1) Kodály's opera Háry János was first performed in 1926. Háry, the main character, is a likeable rascal who tells tall tales of his life. Kodály used the opera to showcase Hungarian folk music.

2) Later, Kodály took some of the material from his opera to create an orchestral suite (see p.91), which was first performed in 1927. The suite has become more well-known than the original opera — two of the movements of the suite are your study pieces. The six movements of the orchestral suite are:

- Prelude; The Fairy Tale Begins
- Viennese Musical Clock
- Song
- The Battle and Defeat of Napoleon
- Intermezzo
- Entrance of the Emperor and His Court

'The Battle and Defeat of Napoleon' and 'Intermezzo' are the study pieces.

3) The first movement of the suite opens with a dramatic crescendo to a chord — a musical representation of a sneeze. In Hungary, a sneeze traditionally indicates that what follows is true, but here the composer is using it ironically as Háry's stories are wildly exaggerated (but he manages to convince his listeners).

4) The suite is written for a large orchestra: 3 flutes (who also play piccolos), 2 oboes, 2 clarinets, a saxophone, 2 bassoons, 4 French horns, 3 trumpets, 3 cornets, 3 trombones and a tuba. There's also a full string section, a piano and a large range of percussion instruments, including timpani, a celesta (which sounds a bit like a glockenspiel), tubular bells and a cimbalom. The cimbalom is a Hungarian instrument that's played by hitting its horizontal strings with sticks.

5) The use of contrasting percussion in the suite creates lots of 'colour' in the piece — an impressionist feature.

HABRDA/Shutterstock.com

Zoltán Kodály — Háry János

'The Battle and Defeat of Napoleon' is the fourth movement of the suite. If you've chosen the study pieces from this Area of Study, make sure you read the next two pages carefully.

This Movement Mainly Uses **Brass, Percussion** and the **Saxophone**

1) 'The Battle and Defeat of Napoleon' tells the story of a <u>battle</u> between the <u>Emperor of Austria</u> and <u>Napoleon</u>, and how Háry <u>defeats</u> Napoleon, who creeps off the battlefield.

2) The <u>instrumentation</u> of this movement does <u>not</u> included the <u>full orchestra</u>. There is an emphasis on <u>brass</u>, <u>percussion</u> and <u>saxophone</u>, and there are <u>none</u> of the lower woodwind instruments, French horns, strings or keyboards.

3) There's a lot of <u>dynamic contrast</u> in this movement, with sections varying from ***ppp*** to ***fff***, and long <u>crescendos</u> and <u>diminuendos</u> to add drama.

'The Battle and Defeat of Napoleon' uses Different **March Styles**

This movement is in <u>three sections</u>, and each section is a different type of <u>march</u>.

Section A: The arrival of the French (bars 1-70)

1) The movement starts with a <u>military march</u>. It's in $\frac{2}{4}$ and is marked *alla marcia* (in a march style), with a tempo of ♩ = 108.

2) The movement starts with four bars of <u>percussion</u> (<u>bass drum</u> and <u>cymbals</u>), followed by the <u>trombones</u> playing the <u>main theme</u> of the first section from bar 5 in <u>unison</u>. The <u>trumpets</u> then enter, playing the theme in <u>octaves</u> with the trombones — so the <u>texture</u> for this opening section is <u>monophonic</u>. The <u>staccato quavers</u> give the theme a <u>military</u> feel.

3) In bar 22, the <u>piccolos</u> and <u>saxophone</u> enter. The piccolos play <u>tremolos</u> and the trombones play <u>glissandos</u>, and the trumpets and trombones play <u>tritones</u>, which makes it sound as if the orchestra is <u>shrieking</u>. This also introduces notes which are <u>not</u> in the key signature of the movement (<u>C major</u>).

4) The 'shriek' leads into <u>descending chromatic scales</u> and a quiet pleading sound played by the <u>saxophone</u> (alternating between notes a <u>semitone apart</u>), before the music comes to a <u>pause</u> in bar 30. A ***ff*** <u>brass fanfare</u> leads into the rest of Section A, where the theme is <u>repeated</u> at a <u>higher pitch</u> (one trumpet plays the theme an <u>octave higher</u>, and is then joined by the piccolos and saxophone). The trombones and another trumpet provide <u>quaver accompaniments</u>, and the third trumpet plays <u>semiquavers</u> on the <u>off-beat</u>. This creates a <u>thicker texture</u>, which, along with the <u>crescendo</u>, represents the <u>approaching army</u>.

Section B: The entry of Napoleon (bars 71-100)

1) Section B is a <u>processional march</u>. It's in $\frac{4}{4}$ and is slightly <u>slower</u> (*poco meno mosso*). It uses the same <u>melodic pattern</u> as the <u>French national anthem</u> (with a <u>different rhythm</u>) to show <u>Napoleon</u> is arriving.

2) Again, it starts with <u>percussion</u> leading into <u>trombone glissandos</u> before they play the main melody of this section at a <u>low pitch</u>. The trumpets play <u>triplets</u> in a <u>fanfare style</u> as the <u>tonality</u> becomes more <u>ambiguous</u> between <u>C major</u> and <u>C minor</u>. From bar 90, the music modulates to <u>B major</u>.

3) As this section develops, the <u>quavers</u> in the trombone melody against the <u>triplets</u> in the trumpets create <u>polyrhythms</u> (see p.14) and a thicker <u>polyphonic texture</u>. The polyrhythms, along with an <u>increase in tempo</u>, give it a <u>frantic</u> feel.

Section C: Funeral March in which Napoleon leaves (bars 101-114)

1) The movement finishes with a <u>funeral march</u>. It's marked ♩ = 54 (exactly <u>half the tempo</u> of section A), so is much <u>slower</u> than the other sections and has a <u>thinner texture</u>.

2) The <u>saxophone</u> is the main instrument here with its <u>gentle, pleading timbre</u>. The low brass instruments only move between the notes B♭ and F, again making the tonality <u>ambiguous</u>.

Zoltán Kodály — Háry János

'Intermezzo' is the fifth movement of the suite. In the original opera, it was an instrumental interlude.

'Intermezzo' is in Ternary Form

'Intermezzo' has a fairly straightforward <u>ABA structure</u> — it's in <u>ternary form</u> (see p.81).

<u>Section A</u> (bars 1-40) is in <u>two halves</u>:

1) The first half starts with a <u>lively 8-bar melody</u>, which is <u>repeated</u> in bars 9-16. The violins, violas and cellos play the melody in <u>octaves</u>, and although the melody is <u>doubled</u> by the clarinets (with the flutes and oboes joining for the second 4-bar phrase, which is an <u>octave higher</u>), the strings dominate this section.

2) A notable feature of the melody is the <u>dotted rhythm</u>, which also includes <u>Scotch snaps</u> (see p.17) — instead of the long note being followed by the shorter one, the short note is followed by the longer one. This is common in <u>folk music</u>.

3) In this part of the movement, the <u>cimbalom</u> has a <u>fast</u>, <u>virtuosic countermelody</u> which is more elaborate than the main melody, creating a <u>polyphonic texture</u>.

1) The second half of Section A (bars 17-40) consists of a repeated <u>12-bar melody</u>. This melody starts with a <u>slow</u> bar (marked *pesante*, which means 'heavily') before returning to the previous tempo.

2) The instrumentation <u>differs</u> each time this melody is played — the first 12 bars have the melody in the <u>first violins</u>, lightly doubled by <u>some</u> of the woodwind. In contrast, bars 29-40 have a <u>larger</u>, <u>fuller orchestration</u>, with the melody played by the <u>first and second violins</u> and <u>all</u> the woodwind (except the bassoons). The <u>trumpets</u> are heard for the first time here as well. Apart from the odd bar of semiquavers, the cimbalom has a largely <u>accompanying</u> role here.

3) The <u>Scotch snap</u> is again noticeable, but Kodály uses <u>quavers</u> and <u>triplets</u> as well as <u>dotted rhythms</u> in this section. He also uses a number of <u>ornaments</u>, such as <u>acciaccaturas</u> (e.g. bar 24) and <u>turns</u> (e.g. bar 26) — see p.84.

<u>Section B</u> (bars 41-72) <u>contrasts</u> with Section A:

1) Section B has a <u>slower tempo</u>, <u>quieter dynamic</u>, <u>thinner texture</u> and more <u>song-like melody</u> than Section A.

2) This melody is first heard on a <u>solo French horn</u> with a <u>light string accompaniment</u>. A <u>second</u> French horn joins in after four bars, playing in <u>harmony</u>. Later, the <u>clarinets</u>, <u>bassoons</u>, <u>violas</u>, <u>cellos</u> and finally the <u>flutes</u> all play the melody. The orchestration <u>increases</u> through this section, creating a <u>fuller texture</u>, before dying away to leave a <u>solo clarinet</u>, and then a few bars later, a <u>solo flute</u>.

3) <u>Triplets</u> and <u>acciaccaturas</u> are heard frequently in Section B.

From the end of bar 72, Section A <u>returns</u>. The movement <u>finishes</u> with three ***ff*** <u>chords</u>.

This Movement has lots of Hungarian Folk Influences

1) The <u>rich</u> string sound, <u>variations</u> in <u>tempo</u> and <u>syncopation</u> are all <u>typical</u> of Hungarian folk music — as is the <u>cimbalom</u>. The <u>triplets</u>, <u>dotted rhythms</u> and <u>ornaments</u> also help create a Hungarian sound.

2) The <u>tonality</u> of this movement is more straightforward than in the fourth movement. Section A is mainly in <u>D minor</u> in the first half and <u>F major</u> (the <u>relative major key</u>) in the second half, returning to <u>D minor</u> before the end. Section B is mainly in <u>D major</u> (the <u>tonic major</u>). However, in some places, the music is more <u>modal</u> (e.g. the harmony of bar 17, which looks like F major but with a B♮ — a <u>Lydian</u> mode).

3) The <u>dynamics</u> are <u>varied</u> and <u>dramatic</u>, with <u>long crescendos</u> and <u>sudden changes</u>.

Liar, liar, cimbalom on fire...

Listen to these movements plenty of times so you're really familiar with them. Make sure you can pick out the key features mentioned on these pages, especially the Hungarian influences.

Orchestral Music of Bartók

*Béla Bartók is another **Hungarian** composer — he lived from **1881-1945**.
Like Kodály, he was interested in folk music, but he also tried out **new ideas**.*

Bartók's Music Was **More Experimental** Than **Kodály's**

1) In the twentieth century, some composers moved away from traditional forms of harmony and structure.

   - Composers in the late Romantic period often used so many chromatic notes that the music began to lose the character of the main key. A lot of early twentieth century music was atonal (p.26).
   - Classical forms (see p.91-93) relied on fixed keys to create contrast between different sections. Now fixed keys were gone, traditional structures were used less frequently.

2) Bartók experimented with these ideas. He often didn't use key signatures — he used accidentals (see p.11) instead. Sometimes he made up his own key signatures, e.g. one with a C♯ but no F♯.

3) Some of his pieces frequently change time signature, and use unusual time signatures such as $\frac{4+2+3}{8}$.

4) Like other modern composers, he experimented with using instruments in new ways. A type of pizzicato, where the string is lifted vertically and released to give a snapping sound, is named after him. You can hear it in the third movement of his *Divertimento for Strings*.

5) Bartók shared Kodály's interest in Eastern European folk music, but he also took inspiration from further afield — his *String Quartet No. 2* was influenced by folk music from North Africa.

Bartók's **Concerto for Orchestra** Mixes **Old** and **New**

The 1943 work **Concerto for Orchestra** was one of the last pieces Bartók wrote. Each section of the orchestra is given a chance to shine — hence the name. It has many of the features described above.

- Although *Concerto for Orchestra* has a non-standard five-movement structure, the first and last movements make use of sonata form (see p.92), used in classical concertos.
- It has simple, folk-like melodies. An oboe tune in the fourth movement is based on just 4 notes.
- The time signature often changes — the start of the fourth movement switches between $\frac{2}{4}$ and $\frac{5}{8}$.
- The tonality is ambiguous — there's no key signature in the first movement. There's lots of dissonance — near the start, the cellos and double basses play a C♯ against a C♮ in the violas.
- The timpani have a chromatic line, requiring them to retune quickly to be able to play the notes.

Some of Bartók's music was more influenced by folk music than by 20th century classical music. His **Romanian Folk Dances for Orchestra** are a good example of this.

- Each movement is based on a Romanian folk tune. The melodies are clear, with a simple accompaniment and harmony. The music is much more tonal than *Concerto for Orchestra*.
- In the second movement, the tempo changes frequently — a feature of Hungarian folk music.

Bartók's **Divertimento** for string orchestra has elements of Baroque, Classical and folk music.

- It features five soloists along with a string orchestra — like a Baroque concerto grosso (see p.81).
- It uses Classical structures — sonata form in the first movement and rondo form in the third.
- Despite this, it has a modern feel. The first movement features loud, dissonant chords, and frequently switches between $\frac{6}{8}$ and $\frac{9}{8}$. The syncopated rhythms are a folk influence.
- The second movement is sombre. The timbre is varied using mutes and harmonics (see p.64).
- In the third movement, the solo first violin plays a folk-influenced cadenza (see p.57).

Bartók — a mad scientist of the music world...

Don't think you can just make up key signatures in your compositions — the examiners won't approve...

Minimalism

Minimalist music is music that changes a small subtle bit at a time. It's all about slow, gradual changes.

Minimalism Builds Music out of Repeated Patterns

1) Minimalism is a Western art music style that developed during the 1960s and 1970s.

2) It was a reaction against twentieth century styles such as expressionism (see p.153) and serialism (see p.151) which were atonal, dissonant and complex. Minimalism was a return to more basic concepts — minimalist composers constructed their music from simple note or rhythm patterns, known as cells.

3) The cells are continuously repeated, with occasional slight changes. They're layered on top of each other, so although the individual cells tend to be short and simple, the music can sound complicated.

4) There's often no clear melody. Harmony is created by layering patterns on top of each other. It develops gradually — there are no sudden changes.

5) In contrast to the atonality of serialism, minimalism is usually diatonic. Broken chords are often used to form cells. Common chords (chords shared between multiple keys) are also used.

6) Rhythm is important — some minimalist pieces are purely rhythmic, e.g. *Clapping Music* (see p.162).

Minimalism Uses Musical Ideas from All Over the World

Minimalist composers often borrowed ideas from other countries and cultures.

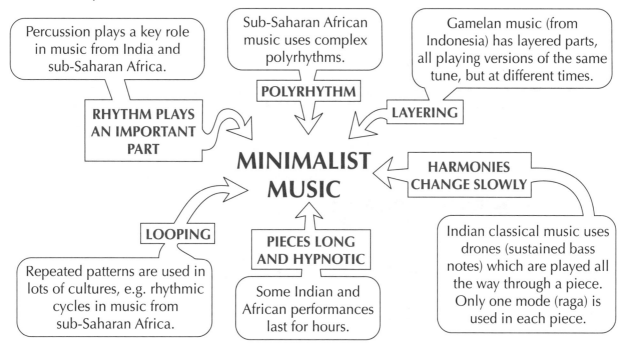

Percussion plays a key role in music from India and sub-Saharan Africa.

Sub-Saharan African music uses complex polyrhythms.

Gamelan music (from Indonesia) has layered parts, all playing versions of the same tune, but at different times.

POLYRHYTHM

LAYERING

RHYTHM PLAYS AN IMPORTANT PART

MINIMALIST MUSIC

HARMONIES CHANGE SLOWLY

LOOPING

PIECES LONG AND HYPNOTIC

Repeated patterns are used in lots of cultures, e.g. rhythmic cycles in music from sub-Saharan Africa.

Some Indian and African performances last for hours.

Indian classical music uses drones (sustained bass notes) which are played all the way through a piece. Only one mode (raga) is used in each piece.

Minimalism is Often Used in Film Music

1) The short cells of music used in minimalism can work well as leitmotifs in films (see p.121).

2) Minimalism works well as a way of gradually developing a film's atmosphere over time.

3) Film music often involves repetition (a feature of minimalism) — a gradual crescendo through a repeated bit of music is a great way of increasing tension.

4) Even film music that doesn't 'sound minimalist' can have minimalist elements. For example, the 'Chariots of Fire' theme features a constant pulse throughout to represent the characters running.

- Michael Nyman and Philip Glass are minimalist composers who have written lots of film scores.
- Philip Glass composed for the film *The Hours*. The film is set in three different time periods, but Glass's music gives it a sense of whole using repetition and layering.

Minimalism

Minimalist composers use different techniques to bring about gradual changes in their music.

The **Cells** Change **Gradually**

There are different ways of changing the cell patterns, as well as the way they fit together. These changes can happen every time the patterns are repeated, or after the same pattern has been repeated a few times.

Gradually adding or taking away notes

The pattern is changed by adding a single note — this is called additive melody. Another similar idea is to replace one note with a rest, or one rest with a note.

Gradually changing the notes of the pattern

This technique's called metamorphosis — another word for 'changing'. Small changes to one note, or one bit of the rhythm, are made to the pattern.

The changes often go full circle — the pattern ends up the same or nearly the same as it was at the start.

Adding or removing notes or rests

Two or more performers start with the same pattern. A note or rest is added or taken away from one of the parts. They move gradually out of sync and then gradually back in. This is known as phase shifting.

Layering patterns of different lengths together

Cells of different lengths, e.g. a 4-beat cell and a 5-beat cell, are played at the same time. This has a similar effect to phase-shifting — the patterns move apart then come back together.

Music Technology Plays a **Big Part** in **Minimalism**

1) Minimalist composers often use music technology to create continuously repeating cells called loops.

2) Composers used to create loops by recording music (or other sounds) onto tape, carefully cutting the bit of tape that contained the music they needed, and sticking the ends together to create a physical loop that could be played continuously. Modern sequencers (p.72) make this process much easier.

3) The different loops are recorded, one on top of another, using multi-track recording (see p.72). This helps create the layered sound of minimalism.

4) The layers can be edited to achieve different effects. For example, two identical loops can be played at the same time but at two slightly different speeds — this effect is another form of phase-shifting.

5) Live performances of minimalist music are often accompanied by recorded backing tracks (p.162).

Riley, Reich and Adams

Terry Riley, Steve Reich and John Adams have all used minimalism in their work.

Riley's In C was One of the First Minimalist Pieces

1) Terry Riley was born in 1935 in the USA — he is one of the founders of minimalism.
2) His influences include jazz (p.131-132) and Indian classical music
   — he studied in India with the singer Pran Nath.
3) Riley's work *In C* is one of the best-known early minimalist pieces. His other famous works include
   A Rainbow in Curved Air, *Uncle Jard* and *Salome Dances for Peace* (a set of five string quartets).

Riley's Compositions Are Quite Varied

- *In C* can be played by any combination of instruments and/or voices.
- It's made up of 53 cells. The cells are numbered and should be played in order, but each performer can choose how many times they repeat each cell. Some cells are only one quaver in length, but others are much longer. The layering of the cells creates polyrhythm (see p.14).
- Constant C quavers keep the piece together and give it a strong, driving rhythm.
- To finish, all the performers repeat the 53rd pattern together, then each stops when they're ready.

- *A Rainbow in Curved Air* is different from *In C*. Terry Riley performed it by recording each track and then layering them over each other. It has three movements.
- The piece is based on repeated cells of music, but also has more 'traditional' melodic lines.
- It uses a variety of instruments to explore different timbres and textures — it features an electric organ, electric harpsichord, a tambourine and a doumbek (a goblet-shaped drum).

- *Uncle Jard* shows the influences of jazz, blues and Indian classical music on Riley's work.
- In the first movement, influences from Indian music are seen in the modal tonality, singing style and drones (played by saxophones). A harpsichord imitates a sitar (an Indian string instrument).
- In the second movement, syncopated and swung rhythms played on the saxophone and piano create a jazz feel. Riley sings blues-style lyrics over the top (see p.130).
- *Salome Dances for Peace* has these influences, as well as elements of Western classical music.
- It's more melodic than Riley's early music, but still has minimalist features. It has repeated cells of music which are layered over each other, e.g. in the *Ceremonial Night Race* section.

Reich was Influenced by Riley

1) Steve Reich is an American composer who was born in 1936.
2) He did a degree in Philosophy, then studied composition with the experimental composer Luciano Berio. He tried writing serial music (see p.151), but preferred composing tonal pieces.
3) Reich began writing minimalist music, and was influenced by Terry Riley's compositions.
4) His works are also influenced by jazz, music from sub-Saharan Africa (especially drumming — see p.133), Balinese gamelan (tuned percussion music from Indonesia) and Middle Eastern singing.
5) Some of his best-known works are *Clapping Music*, *Electric Counterpoint* and *Different Trains*.

You could try composing a minimalist piece...

...and impress the examiners with something different. However, though minimalist music is repetitive, it's not easy to write — all the cells have to work together and the piece needs shape.

Riley, Reich and Adams

Let's have a look at some of Reich's music in a bit more detail.

Reich Wrote a Piece Based Only on Rhythm

1) Reich's *Clapping Music* is written for two performers who clap throughout the piece.
   - It's made up of one rhythm. The first player claps this rhythm throughout the piece. The second player claps the same rhythm, but after twelve repetitions they shift so they're one quaver behind.
   - This happens every twelve repetitions until the players end up in sync again. This is a good example of phase-shifting.

2) *Electric Counterpoint* is for a solo guitarist accompanied by a 14-piece guitar ensemble.
   - It has three movements. For live performances, the solo guitarist often plays along with a recording of the ensemble parts made before the performance.
   - The movements don't have titles — they're just marked ♩ = 192, ♩ = 96 and ♩ = 192. People tend to call them 'Fast', 'Slow' and 'Fast'. The middle movement's half the speed of the others, so there's a constant pulse. There should be no breaks between the movements.
   - It's made up of short cells that are repeated lots of times.
   - Because the guitars all have a similar sound, the timbre (see p.74) doesn't really change. This means the parts all blend together.

Different Trains is one of Reich's best-known works. It was written as a reaction to the Holocaust. It uses samples of people talking about train journeys, then imitates their voices with instruments.

John Adams Uses Minimalist Elements

1) John Adams was also born in the USA, in 1947. He is a composer and conductor.
2) Adams' work is influenced by minimalism, but elements of pop and jazz are also incorporated into his compositions. Some of his pieces are more recognisably minimalist than others.
3) His orchestral works include *Harmonielehre*, *Shaker Loops* and *Short Ride in a Fast Machine*.
4) Adams has also written a number of operas. Some of these deal with political issues — *Nixon in China* is about the US President Richard Nixon's visit to China in 1972 and *Doctor Atomic* is about the construction of the first atomic bomb.

Adams Uses Music to Paint a Picture

- *Shaker Loops* was originally written as a string quartet called *Wavemaker*. It features lots of tremolo, which represents ripples on water.
- Adams rewrote it and changed it into a string septet (though it can also be played by a string orchestra). The shaking action used to create tremolo inspired the name *Shaker Loops*.
- It features lots of repetition of short cells of music, and it's tonal.
- It becomes rhythmically complex as different instruments enter, adding more layers.

- *Short Ride in a Fast Machine* was inspired by a ride Adams had in a sports car.
- The woodblock plays crotchets throughout almost the whole piece — a constant pulse is often a feature of minimalist pieces. The rest of the orchestra is forced to keep up, creating a sense of the tension involved in travelling at high speed. When the pulse stops, the orchestra feels freer.
- The brass play a key role, with some fanfare-like sections. The strings are also important, and combine with a variety of percussion and woodwind to create a number of different timbres. The orchestra is large — it features thirteen different types of percussion.
- Although it has repeated cells, the piece changes quite rapidly. It lasts less than five minutes.

Warm-up and Exam Questions

Well, that was a whistle-stop tour through twentieth century styles of music. Try these warm-up questions to get yourself in the zone, and then have a go at the exam-style questions.

Warm-up Questions

1) Where is the ballet *Rodeo* set?

2) What is a tone row?

3) Name two musical genres which influence Malcolm Arnold's music.

4) For which occasion was Britten's *War Requiem* written?

5) Describe two features of expressionism.

6) Name a piece by John Tavener.

7) Describe three features of Hungarian folk music.

8) Name the three different types of march used in 'Battle and Defeat of Napoleon'.

9) What is the structure of 'Intermezzo'?

10) Give two ways in which Bartók was experimental in his composing.

11) In minimalist music, what are cells?

12) Give two ways in which cells can be varied to create gradual change in a minimalist piece.

13) Name two pieces by Terry Riley.

14) Which composition by Steve Reich is based only on rhythm?

15) Which technique creates the 'shaking' in *Shaker Loops*?

Exam Questions

Have a go at these exam-style questions.

Track 36 is an excerpt from 'Intermezzo' by Zoltán Kodály.

Play the excerpt **four** times. Leave a short pause between each playing.

Track 36

a) i) What is the traditional Hungarian instrument heard in this excerpt?

....

[1 mark]

ii) Describe its part in this excerpt.

....

....

....

[2 marks]

Exam Questions

b) What rhythmic feature is heard in this excerpt? Circle the correct answer.

hemiola   **cross-rhythms**   **Scotch snap**   **phase shifting**

[1 mark]

c) Identify two similarities and two differences between the first and second parts of this extract.

....

....

....

....

....

....

[4 marks]

d) What does the following symbol tell the performer to do?   ⌒

....

[1 mark]

e) Name **two** different types of ornament heard in the second half of the excerpt.

....

....

[2 marks]

Exam Questions

Track 37 is an excerpt from 'Hoe-Down' by Aaron Copland.

Play the excerpt **four** times. Leave a short pause between each playing.

Track 37

a) What are the violins playing in the first section of the excerpt?
Circle the correct answer.

the melody   offbeat chords   constant quavers   downbeat crotchets

[1 mark]

b) Name **two** percussion instruments that play in the excerpt.

....

....
[2 marks]

c) Explain how contrast between the first and second sections of the excerpt is achieved.
You might want to mention the following musical features:
* Instrumentation
* Rhythm
* Texture

....

....

....

....

....

....

....

....
[4 marks]

d) What is the tonality of the second section?

....
[1 mark]

Revision Summary for Section Nine

That wraps up <u>Section Nine</u> — time to put yourself to the test and find out <u>how much you really know</u>.
- Try these questions and <u>tick off each one</u> when you <u>get it right</u>.
- When you've done <u>all the questions</u> for a topic and are <u>completely happy</u> with it, tick off the topic.

Aaron Copland and Serialism (p.150-151) ☑

1) Name two ballets by Aaron Copland.
2) Give two ways in which Aaron Copland created an American feel in his music.
3) Give two ways in which a tone row can be rearranged.
4) Describe the tonality of serialist music.
5) What is verticalisation?

British Music — Arnold, Britten, Maxwell Davies and Tavener (p.152-154) ☑

6) Name one feature of Malcom Arnold's Clarinet Concerto No. 2 that is typical of a concerto.
7) Name the opera by Benjamin Britten that is about a fisherman.
8) The lyrics for Britten's *War Requiem* come from two sources. What are they?
9) Give three details about the instrumentation in *War Requiem*.
10) Why did Peter Maxwell Davies write *The Yellowcake Revue*?
11) In *The Yellowcake Revue*, what does the bass line represent?
12) What is a cantata?
13) How does John Tavener create contrast in *The Lamb*?

Kodály and Bartók (p.155-158) ☑

14) What is ethnomusicology?
15) Give three features of impressionist music.
16) What does the crescendo at the start of Zoltán Kodály's *Háry János Suite* represent?
17) Name two percussion instruments used in the *Háry János Suite*.
18) What are the two main families of instruments used in 'Battle and Defeat of Napoleon'?
19) Describe the texture at the start of 'Battle and Defeat of Napoleon'.
20) Describe the structure of 'Intermezzo'.
21) Give three features of 'Intermezzo' that are typical of Hungarian folk music.
22) Describe the unusual type of pizzicato used in Béla Bartók's *Divertimento for Strings*.
23) Describe the tonality in Bartók's *Concerto for Orchestra*.
24) In what way is Bartók's *Divertimento for Strings* similar to a concerto grosso?

Minimalism, Riley, Reich and Adams (p.159-162) ☑

25) What tonality do minimalist pieces tend to have?
26) i)   Where does gamelan music come from?
     ii) Which feature of gamelan is used in minimalist music?
27) How many cells is Terry Riley's *In C* made up of?
28) Describe two elements of Indian classical music used in the first movement of Riley's *Uncle Jard*.
29) Name two musical genres which influenced Steve Reich's music.
30) For which instrument is Reich's *Electric Counterpoint* written?
31) Name an opera written by John Adams.
32) How is the idea of travelling at high speed created in Adams' *Short Ride in a Fast Machine*?

General Certificate of Secondary Education

GCSE Music

CGP Practice Exam Paper
GCSE Music

Listening
and Contextual
Understanding Exam

Centre name				
Centre number				
Candidate number				

Time allowed: 1 hour 30 minutes

Surname	
Other names	
Candidate signature	

Instructions
- Write in black ink or ballpoint pen.
- Answer the questions in the spaces provided.
- Answer **all 8** questions in Section A.
- In Section B, answer **Question 9** and **one** of Questions 10-12.
- Give all the information you are asked for, and write neatly.
- Do all rough work in this book. Cross through any work you do not want marked.

Information
- The marks are shown by each question.
- The maximum mark for this paper is 96.
- There are 68 marks available in Section A and 28 marks available in Section B.
- For each question in Section A, you will need to play one or more tracks from the online audio. You will be told how many times to play each track.
- You do **not** need to listen to any tracks for Section B.
- Read through the question before you play the track(s).
- Leave a gap between each playing to give yourself time to write.

Instructions for playing the audio tracks:
- The tracks can be accessed via the Online Edition of this book.
- There are 8 questions in Section A, covered by tracks 38-50.

Question No.	1	2	3	4	5	6	7	8
Track No.	38, 39	40	41, 42	43, 44	45, 46	47, 48	49	50

- Leave 3 minutes at the start to read through the exam.
- Play one track at a time, stopping after each track.
- Each question will tell you how many times the track should be repeated.
- Allow a short pause between each playing for writing time.
  After the final playing of each track, allow some time for writing.

Section A: Listening

60 minutes
68 marks
Answer **all** the questions in Section A

1   Area of Study 1: Western classical tradition 1650-1910   7 marks
For this question, there are two excerpts, track 38 and track 39.
Play each track **three** times.

(Track 38)

1.1   What type of vocal ensemble is performing this piece? Circle the correct answer.

Male voice choir   SATB choir   Octet   SSA choir

[1 mark]

1.2   This piece was composed for the coronation of a king.
Identify **two** features of the excerpt that make it suitable for this occasion.

....

....

....
[2 marks]

1.3   What is the cadence heard at the end of this excerpt?

....
[1 mark]

(Track 39)

1.4 Name one of the instruments playing the melody at the start of the excerpt.

....

[1 mark]

1.5 This movement is in $\frac{2}{4}$. Suggest a suitable tempo for this excerpt.

....

[1 mark]

1.6 Which of the words below best describes the texture created by the first
and second violins towards the end of the excerpt? Circle the correct answer.

       unison   antiphony   counterpoint   monophony

[1 mark]

Turn over ▶

2   Area of Study 2: Popular music   8 marks
Play the track **four** times.

(**Track 40**)

2.1   In the introduction of the song, what technique does the vocalist use on the word 'in'?
Circle the correct answer.

       scat   falsetto   riffing   belting

[1 mark]

2.2   i) What is the tonality of this excerpt?

....

[1 mark]

ii) The piano part alternates between two chords.
On the first two beats of each bar, chord I is played.
What chord is played on the third and fourth beats of each bar?

....

[1 mark]

2.3   The bars in the table below are numbered from where the piano quavers start.

The time signature of the excerpt is $\frac{12}{8}$.

Read each statement below and put letters in the appropriate box to show
where each feature is heard.

- Write the letter A in the bar in which backing vocals are first heard.
- Write the letter B in the bar in which percussion is first heard.
- Write the letter C in the bar in which the bass drum is first heard.
- Write the letter D in the bar in which the bass drum plays 6 quavers
  in the second half of the bar.

1	2	3	4	5	6	7	8

[4 marks]

2.4   The solo artist also provides some of the backing vocals herself.
Which recording technique is used to achieve this? Circle the correct answer.

      sampling   overdubbing   phase shifting   reverb

[1 mark]

3   Area of Study 3: Traditional music   10 marks
For this question, there are two excerpts, track 41 and track 42.
Play track 41 **four** times and track 42 **three** times.

(Track 41)

3.1   Name the family of instruments used at the start of the excerpt.

....
[1 mark]

3.2   Tick the rhythm played by the first drum you hear at the start of the excerpt.

[1 mark]

3.3   Which phrase below correctly describes the device used in the vocal section?
Circle the correct answer.

       a cappella   singing in unison   polyphony   vibrato
[1 mark]

3.4   Name the region of the world this music comes from.

....
[1 mark]

3.5   Some of the percussion rhythms don't fit perfectly into the $\frac{4}{4}$ bars.
What is the technical term for such a combination of rhythms?

....
[1 mark]

Turn over ▶

Track 42

3.6 What type of bass line is used in this excerpt?

....

[1 mark]

3.7 i) To which genre of music does this excerpt belong?

....

[1 mark]

ii) Identify **three** features of the excerpt that are typical of this genre.

....

....

....

[3 marks]

4   Area of Study 4: Western classical tradition since 1910   9 marks
For this question, there are two excerpts, track 43 and track 44.
Play each track **four** times.

(Track 43)

4.1   Suggest a suitable tempo for this excerpt.

....

[1 mark]

4.2   Suggest a suitable composer for this piece.

....

[1 mark]

4.3   In the first seven bars, on which beat of the bar can pizzicato be heard?

....

[1 mark]

4.4   What family of instruments is playing in this excerpt?

....

[1 mark]

(Track 44)

4.5   Circle the word that best describes the harmony provided by the horns.

          dissonance   unison   consonance   suspension

[1 mark]

4.6   About halfway through the excerpt, the violins and woodwind play
a descending scale. What type of scale is it?

....

[1 mark]

Turn over ▶

4.7 After this scale, the mood of the excerpt changes.
Describe **three** ways in which this change of mood is achieved.

....

....

....

....

[3 marks]

5   Area of Study 1: Western classical tradition 1650-1910   10 marks
For this question, there are two excerpts, track 45 and track 46.
Play track 45 **three** times and track 46 **four** times.

(Track 45)

5.1   This excerpt is from a concerto. What is the name of the part
of the concerto heard in the first section of the excerpt?

....
[1 mark]

5.2   i) To which period of Western classical music history does this piece belong?

....
[1 mark]

ii) Give **one** reason for your answer to part i).

....

....
[1 mark]

(Track 46)

5.3   Fill in the missing notes in bars 2-3 on the score below,
using the rhythm given above the stave.

[6 marks]

5.4   Describe the tonality of this excerpt.

....

....
[1 mark]

Turn over ▶

6   Area of Study 2: Popular music   9 marks

For this question, there are two excerpts, track 47 and track 48.
Play each track **four** times.

(Track 47)

6.1   i) This excerpt comes from a Romantic symphony which is used in a film.
           What genre of film do you think this excerpt was used for? Circle the correct answer.

           horror   romance   comedy   action

                                                                                        [1 mark]

       ii) Describe **two** features of the excerpt that make it suitable for this genre.

           ....

           ....

           ....
                                                                                        [2 marks]

6.2   Describe the texture of this excerpt.

       ....
                                                                                        [1 mark]

6.3   In the film, this excerpt is actually played on synthesized instruments.
       Suggest **one** reason why this might have been done.

       ....

       ....
                                                                                        [1 mark]

(Track 48)

6.4 This excerpt comes from a different movement of the same symphony.
It has been used in an historical film.

    i) What is the time signature of this excerpt?

    ....

    [1 mark]

    ii) Suggest a type of dance this music would be suitable for.

    ....

    [1 mark]

6.5 Describe the tempo in this excerpt.

....

....

....

[2 marks]

178

7   Area of Study 3: Traditional music   7 marks
      Play the track **four** times.

(Track 49)

7.1 From which region of the world does this style of music originate?
      Circle the correct answer.

         Latin America   Africa   Middle East   Caribbean

[1 mark]

7.2 Which of these rhythms shows the main beat or pulse in the first half of this excerpt?
      Tick the box next to the correct answer.

[1 mark]

7.3 About halfway through the excerpt, the music changes.
      Describe the rhythmic differences between the two sections.

....

....

....

....

[3 marks]

7.4 The title of this piece is 'Carnivale'. Identify two features of this excerpt
      that make it suitable for a carnival.

....

....

....

[2 marks]

8 Area of Study 4: Western classical tradition since 1910   8 marks
Play the track **four** times.

(**Track 50**)

8.1 Suggest a suitable dynamic marking for this excerpt.

....
[1 mark]

8.2 Describe the rhythm at the beginning of the excerpt.

....
[1 mark]

8.3 i) To which genre of 20th century classical music does this piece belong?

....
[1 mark]

ii) Describe the features of this excerpt that are typical of this genre.

....

....

....

....

....

....

....

....

....
[5 marks]

Section B: Contextual Understanding

30 minutes
28 marks
Answer **Question 9**

9   Area of Study 1: Western classical tradition 1650-1910
This question is about the third movement of Mozart's Clarinet Concerto.

9.1   Name the instrument that Mozart originally began writing this concerto for,
and briefly describe how it differs from a clarinet.

....

....

[2 marks]

9.2   Describe **two** features of the accompaniment that are typical of a Classical concerto.

....

....

....

[2 marks]

9.3   Describe the structure of the third movement of this concerto.

....

....

[2 marks]

9.4   Explain how Mozart creates similarities and contrasts
between the different sections of this movement.

....

....

....

....

....

....

....

....

....

....

....

....

....

....

[8 marks]

Answer **one** of Questions 10-12

10   Area of Study 2: Popular music

10.1 Identify **two** 1960s musical influences used in the musical *Little Shop of Horrors*.

....

....

....

[2 marks]

10.2 Identify **two** musical techniques that are used to give 'Mushnik and Son'
        the feel of a conversation.

....

....

....

[2 marks]

10.3 The song 'Feed Me (Git It)' features repetitions of the words 'feed me'.
        Describe **two** of the musical techniques used with these words.

....

....

....

[2 marks]

10.4 Explain how 'Prologue/Little Shops of Horrors' uses musical elements
        to establish the genre and set the scene for the rest of the musical.

....

....

....

....

....

....

....

....

....

....

....

....

....

....

[8 marks]

11 Area of Study 3: Traditional music

11.1 Identify **two** electronic effects that were used on 'You Can Call Me Al'.

....

....

[2 marks]

11.2 Identify **two** elements of American country music that feature in 'Graceland'.

....

....

[2 marks]

11.3 Describe **two** differences between the introduction of 'Diamonds on the Soles of Her Shoes' and the rest of the song.

....

....

....

[2 marks]

11.4 Explain how 'Diamonds on the Soles of Her Shoes' fuses elements of American and African music.

....

....

....

....

....

....

....

....

....

....

....

....

....

....

[8 marks]

12   Area of Study 4: Western classical tradition since 1910

12.1   Describe **two** features of 'Intermezzo' that are typical of Hungarian folk music.

....

....

[2 marks]

12.2   Identify **one** feature of 'The Battle and Defeat of Napoleon' which
        suggests it was written by a 20th century composer.

....

....

[1 mark]

12.3   Describe the differences in instrumentation between 'The Battle and Defeat of Napoleon'
        and 'Intermezzo'.

....

....

....

....

[3 marks]

12.4   Explain how Kodály creates contrasts between the different sections in
        'The Battle and Defeat of Napoleon'.
        You may wish to refer to tempo, tonality, texture and any other musical features.

....

....

....

....

....

....

....

....

....

....

....

....

....

....

[8 marks]

END OF TEST

Answers

Section Two — Reading and Writing Music

Page 15 (Warm-up Questions)

1)

2) A sharp sign raises the pitch of the note (and other notes of the same pitch later in the bar) by one semitone.
A flat sign lowers the pitch of the note (and other notes of the same pitch later in the bar) by one semitone.
A natural sign cancels out a flat or sharp sign in the key signature or earlier on in the bar.

3)

4) Three beats

5) In simple time, the main beats are divided into 2, 4, 8, etc. but in compound time the beats are divided into 3, 6, 9, etc.

6) Regular, irregular and free

Page 15 (Exam Question)

Track 1

a)

(1 mark for each correct note or correct interval between two adjacent notes, up to 8 marks)

b) *(1 mark)*

c) *(1 mark)*

d)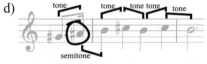

(up to 3 marks, one for each different feature identified)

Page 21 (Warm-up Questions)

1) (semibreve)

2)

3) Dotted crotchet, one and a half beats
Quaver, half a beat
Dotted minim, three beats

4) A tie joins two or more notes of the same pitch together.
A slur joins two or more notes of different pitch together.

5) Presto, allegro, moderato, andante, largo

Pages 21-22 (Exam Question)

Track 2

a) dotted notes *(1 mark)*

b) allegro *(1 mark)*

c) forte *(1 mark)*

d) energico *(1 mark)*

Section Three — Keys, Scales and Chords

Page 31 (Practice Questions)

Track 10 a) natural minor   b) melodic minor
c) whole tone   d) major

Track 11 Pentatonic (major isn't wrong, but pentatonic is more accurate)

Track 12 a) unison   b) perfect 5th   c) major 3rd
d) minor 3rd   e) major 7th   f) perfect 4th
g) minor 6th   h) augmented 4th/diminished 5th

Track 13 a) minor 2nd   b) major 3rd   c) perfect 4th
d) octave   e) major 6th   f) perfect 5th
g) minor 7th   h) major 2nd

Page 32 (Warm-up Questions)

1) Eight

2) They tell you what sharps or flats to play.

3) They are relative scales – they have the same notes/same key signature.

4) Natural, harmonic and melodic

5) Major pentatonic

6) It includes every white and black note on a keyboard.

7) A harmonic interval.

8) Diminished 7th

Pages 32-33 (Exam Question)

Track 14

a) i)   Four *(1 mark)*
ii)   Perfect fourth *(1 mark)*
iii) Minor third/augmented second *(1 mark)*

b) C♯ minor *(1 mark)*

c) Tenuto — played full length or longer *(1 mark)*

Page 40 (Practice Questions)

Track 17 a) major   b) minor   c) major
           d) augmented e) minor   f) diminished
           g) diminished h) minor

Track 18 a) root   b) 2nd   c) root
           d) 2nd   e) 1st   f) 2nd
           g) root   h) root

Pages 49-50 (Practice Questions)

Track 21 a) perfect   b) plagal   c) interrupted
           d) imperfect e) interrupted f) perfect
           g) imperfect h) perfect

Track 22 a)

           b) first inversion
           c) plagal

Track 23 a)

           b) homophonic
           c) perfect
           d) A

Track 24 a)

           b) F sharp
           c) interrupted

Track 25 a)

           b) (see above)
           c) Relative minor

Track 26 a)

           b) E flat major
           c) G minor
           d) pivot chord
           e) V, III

Page 51 (Warm-up Questions)

1) e.g. piano, guitar

2) I, IV and V or tonic, subdominant, dominant

3) First inversion

4) Block chords, rhythmic chords, broken / arpeggiated chords

5) Diatonic

6) Any three of the following: auxiliary notes, passing notes, appoggiaturas, suspensions, trills or other sensible answer.

7) In the middle of a piece, or at the end of any phrase except the last phrase.

8) Contrapuntal

Pages 51-52 (Exam Question)

Track 27

    a) Piano *(1 mark)*

    b) Alberti bass / broken chords / arpeggios *(1 mark)*

    c) Imperfect *(1 mark)*

    d) G major *(1 mark)*

    e) Accidental *(1 mark)*

    f) Staccato *(1 mark)*

    g) Melody with accompaniment *(1 mark)*

Section Four — Structure and Form

Page 59 (Warm-up Questions)

1) *Conjunct* — melodies move mainly by step. Notes are a major 2nd (a tone) or a semitone apart.

   Disjunct — melodies have a lot of jumps. Notes are more than a major 2nd apart.

   Triadic — melodies made up of the three notes in a triad.

   Scalic — melody moves up and down the notes of a scale.

2) A form where each verse has different music.

3) A repeated bass part, usually four or eight bars long that is played by the left hand on the piano or harpsichord, or by cello and double bass in an orchestra.

Pages 59-60 (Exam Questions)

Track 28

    a) i) D major *(1 mark)*

       ii) Perfect fifth *(1 mark)*

    b) Call and response/question and answer *(1 mark)*

    c) Any three of:

      - Starts off with longer notes (minims and crotchets), then changes to semiquavers.
      - Violin plays chords (double/triple stopping) in the first few bars, then single notes for the semiquavers.
      - Staccato in first few bars, then legato/slurred later on in excerpt.
      - Big intervals between the notes at first (disjunct), then smaller intervals in semiquaver section (conjunct).
      - Short rising and falling semiquaver runs at the end with staccato crotchets.
      (1 mark for each, up to a maximum of 3 marks)

Track 29

a) Baroque period *(1 mark)*

b) Oboe, bassoon, violin, viola, harpsichord.
   (1 mark for each instrument, up to 2 marks)

c) i)

   (1 mark for each correct note or correct interval between two adjacent notes, up to 7 marks)

   ii) Conjunct *(1 mark)*

d) Basso continuo *(1 mark)*

e) Bassoon / Harpsichord *(1 mark)*

Section Five — Instruments

Page 76 (Warm-up Questions)

1) E.g. slide — trombone
   Single reed — clarinet or saxophone
   Double reed — oboe or bassoon
   Pizzicato — violin, viola, cello, double bass
   Wooden bars — xylophone

2) *Tremolo* — trembling sound on string instrument (fast, short, light strokes with the bow). Guitars can also produce this type of sound.
   Con sordino — 'with mute', mute placed on the bridge of string instruments to make them sound further away. Brass instruments can also be muted.
   Tenor — higher male voice.
   Falsetto — someone with a lower voice singing much higher than their normal range.

3) Acoustic guitar — e.g. played by strumming or plucking six or twelve strings.
   Electric guitar — e.g. needs an amplifier and loudspeaker to be heard.
   Bass guitar — e.g. has only four strings, is pitched lower than electric and acoustic guitar, needs amplification.

4) Baroque

5) A military band is a marching wind band, with woodwind, brass and percussion. A brass band has brass and percussion. A jazz band can include woodwind, brass, percussion and any other instruments too, and sounds quite different.

6) Piano trio — piano, violin, cello.
   Clarinet quintet — clarinet, first violin, second violin, viola, cello.

7) MIDI — musical instrument digital interface
   Sampler — record, process and play back samples of music
   Remix — mixing together samples of pop or dance music to a fast drumbeat, often speeded up
   Sequencer — computer program that records and replays many tracks of music together

Pages 76-78 (Exam Question)

Tracks 30 and 31

a) Flute *(1 mark)*

b) Piano *(1 mark)*

c) Shape B *(1 mark)*

d) The left hand of the piano has chords, the right hand melody imitates the flute part. One follows the other around. / The melodies interweave in a two-part texture at a similar pitch. / The parts are contrapuntal.
   (1 mark for each sensible comment up to a maximum of 2 marks)

e) Flute, clarinet *(1 mark for each)*

f) Strings *(1 mark)*

g) Chromatic *(1 mark)*

h) Shape C *(1 mark)*

i) Crescendo *(1 mark)*

Section Six
— Western Classical Tradition 1650-1910

Page 104 (Warm-up Questions)

1) There were sudden changes in dynamics (no crescendos or diminuendos).

2) a) A small group of solo instruments.
   b) A larger group of accompanying instruments (often a string orchestra).

3) A set of variations played over a repeated bass part (basso ostinato).

4) A note that clashes with a chord, but which is followed by a note belonging to the chord (usually a tone or semitone away from the first note).

5) Treble, countertenor (or alto), tenor, bass

6) A solo vocal piece, backed by an orchestra — it's used to show the thoughts and emotions of the main characters.

7) Handel

8) E.g. clarinet

9) Three movements — first movement in sonata form (quick), second movement in ternary or variation form (slow), third movement in rondo, variation or sonata form (quick).

10) A basset horn can play notes four semitones lower than a standard clarinet.

11) It is in rondo form, with a main theme and three episodes. Two of the episodes are based on the same material.

12) E.g. Haydn, Beethoven.

13) Approximately 1820-1910

14) In an undertone.

15) A song for one singer and a piano.

16) E.g. *Introit, Dies Irae, Pie Jesu*

Pages 104-107 (Exam Questions)

Track 32

a) Any one of: horn, flute, bassoon *(1 mark)*

b) Trill, acciaccatura *(1 mark)*

c) Any four of:
Similarities:
- The metre doesn't change between the sections.
- The tonality is the same (major) / the key signature is the same (A major) in both sections.
Differences:
- The first episode is more chromatic than the main theme.
- The texture is thinner in the first episode.
- The accompaniment in the first episode is based more around the strings and uses fewer woodwind instruments than the main theme.
- The dynamics in the first episode are quieter.
- The clarinet plays at a lower pitch in the first episode.
(1 mark for each, up to a maximum of 4 marks. If only similarities or only differences have been discussed, award no more than 3 marks.)

d) Sequence *(1 mark)*

e) Any two of:
- The type of instruments/size of the orchestra are typical of the Classical period.
- The main focus in the orchestra is on the strings.
- The harmony is mainly diatonic.
- The texture is melody with accompaniment.
- The use of the clarinet, which was a new instrument in the period.
- The different sections indicate that it is in rondo form, which was common for the final movement of a concerto in the Classical period.
(1 mark for each, up to a maximum of 2 marks)

f) Any two of:
- The melody moves chromatically.
- The pitch is lower than elsewhere in the excerpt.
- The melody falls in pitch/uses a descending sequence.
- The notes are slurred.
- It has a crotchet-quaver rhythm, rather than semiquavers.
- It forms the response part of a call and response.
- It is played softly/quietly/piano.
(1 mark for each, up to a maximum of 2 marks)

Track 33

a) i) Requiem *(1 mark)*

ii) Day of wrath *(1 mark)*

b) The excerpt opens with homophonic chords. — T
The bass drum plays on the off-beats. — T
The choir sing in unison. — F
The strings play ascending runs between the choral sections. — F
(1 mark for each, up to a maximum of 4 marks)

c) Any three of:
- When the orchestra is playing alone, the music is mainly homophonic (playing in chords).
- The sections with choir and orchestra are more polyphonic (the choir are singing overlapping parts, while the brass play fanfare-like melodies underneath).
- The texture is rich and thick throughout.
(1 mark for each, up to a maximum of 3 marks)

d) Quick/lively and agitated *(1 mark)*

e) i) Romantic period *(1 mark)*

ii) Any four of:
Instrumentation:
- The music uses a full choir, with a lot of singers — this has a dramatic impact, which was typical of Romantic music.
- The choir is accompanied by a large orchestra, with prominent brass and percussion playing accented notes. This is typical of Romantic music — the development of new instruments meant that composers could write for large orchestras, and composers used these to add drama.
Dynamics:
- Dynamics are generally loud throughout, with crescendos to increase impact — the use of very loud dynamics (even up to *ffff*) to add drama was common in Romantic music.
Harmony:
- This piece involves lots of dissonance/clashing chords and complex harmonies. This was typical of Romantic music — complex harmonies allowed composers to show emotions like pain (which is appropriate for a piece entitled Day of Wrath).
Pitch:
- There is a range of pitch — the female voices in the choir sing in a very high range, while the male voices, brass and lower strings are much lower. Romantic composers used a large range of pitch to add drama and emotion to their works. In the instrumental parts, this was often made possible by developments in instruments.
Tempo:
- The music is quick — it feels frantic and desperate, which adds drama.
Mood:
- This piece is very dramatic and emotional and has a big impact — this is a key feature of Romantic music.
(Award 1 mark for a correct feature that is typical of Romantic music, and award a further mark for a suitable explanation of the use of that feature, up to a maximum of 8 marks.)

Section Seven — Popular Music

Page 125 (Warm-up Questions)

1) Singing without accompaniment
   (i.e. no instrumental backing).

2) E.g. Michael Jackson

3) 1950s

4) An album with a theme linking all the tracks.

5) E.g. hard rock — loud and aggressive,
   dominated by distorted electric guitar.
   Glam rock — theatrical and glitzy, with costumes and
   make up. It has a rock 'n' roll feel with catchy hooks.
   Heavy metal — harder and more distorted than
   hard rock, with longer guitar solos.
   Progressive rock — experimental and
   complicated, albums often had a theme.

6) E.g. it helps them engage with their fans.

7) E.g. 'Someone Like You' by Adele
   'Sing' by Ed Sheeran

8) A lighter, more modern version of opera.

9) 4 sections of 8 bars. Sections 1, 2 and 4 use the
   main theme, section 3 has a contrasting theme.

10) Solo character song, duet, action song,
    chorus number

11) Rock band instruments e.g. electric and bass guitars,
    keyboards and percussion.

12) An introduction section that sets the scene
    and gives the audience context.

13) Jewish Klezmer music

14) 12-bar blues

15) A phrase of music that represents a character,
    place or emotion.

16) E.g. to link parts of the film together.

17) To create the mood of a specific time or place.

18) Digital audio workstation software,
    such as Logic Pro or Cubase.

Pages 125-127 (Exam Questions)

a) Major *(1 mark)*

b) Allegro *(1 mark)*

c) Harmony *(1 mark)*

d) Melody with accompaniment *(1 mark)*

e) Any four of:
   - The 4/4 time signature
   - Use of typical rock 'n' roll instruments e.g. electric
   and bass guitars, keyboards and percussion
   - Repetitive/catchy melody
   - Catchy hook
   - Up-tempo
   (1 mark for each, up to a maximum of 3 marks)

f) Any two of:
   Similarities:
   - Same rhythm in the accompaniment/quavers played
   on the piano.
   - The harmony in the vocals is the same.
   Differences:
   - The 'no's in the final chorus are repeated/extended.
   - There are seventh chords/dissonance in the
   accompaniment in the final chorus.
   - The lyrics are slightly different.
   (1 mark for a similarity and 1 mark for a difference)

Track 34

a) 4/4 *(1 mark)*

b) 1960s (allow 1970s) *(1 mark)*

c) Electric guitar *(1 mark)* and bass guitar *(1 mark)*

d) Syncopation *(1 mark)* and Bo Diddley beat *(1 mark)*

e) Any three of:
   - At the start, the vocals sing the same rhythm
   as the instruments/there is homophonic texture.
   - At the start, only the male vocalist is singing.
   - The male vocalist then sings in harmony with dubbed
   vocals/another male voice.
   - Female vocals enter in the third line of the verse,
   singing in harmony.
   - In the chorus, the male and female vocals sing
   separate overlapping melodies/the female vocals sing a
   countermelody/they sing polyphonically.
   - The male and female vocals sing in harmony
   at the end of the excerpt.
   (1 mark for each, up to a maximum of 3 marks)

Section Eight — Traditional Music

Page 146 (Warm-up Questions)

1) African slaves in America.

2) Syncopation is when the accent is shifted from a strong
   beat onto a normally weaker beat.

3) I I I I IV IV I I V IV I I (V)

4) E.g. trumpets, trombones, saxophones, piano.

5) Improvised singing with nonsense words and syllables.

6) A West African instrument with 21 strings.

7) Any interval smaller than a semitone.

8) 2/4 or 4/4

9) Jamaica

10) When two or more styles of music are combined to
    create a new style.

11) R'n'B, mento, calypso

12) Upstroke

13) A road trip Paul Simon took from Louisiana
    to Graceland in Memphis, Tennessee.

14) Homophonic

15) Brazil

16) Pentatonic

17) An Irish framed drum.

Pages 146-148 (Exam Questions)

a) Homophonic *(1 mark)*

b) The rhythm is syncopated. *(1 mark)*

c) 4/4 *(1 mark)*

d) 4th beat *(1 mark)*

e) Overdubbing *(1 mark)*

f) Any three of:
   - There are more layers in the chorus.
   - The texture in the chorus is richer/thicker than in the verse.
   - The riff, played by the trumpets and synthesizers, returns, providing a countermelody in the chorus.
   - Overdubbed backing vocals are added behind the lead vocals, making the texture thicker.
   (1 mark for each, up to a maximum of 3 marks)

Track 35

a) Minor *(1 mark)*

b) Percussion   2   Lead vocals   4

   Spanish guitar   1   Trumpets   3

(2 marks for all four correct, otherwise 1 mark for at least two correct)

c) Latin music:
   Any one of:
   - Traditional Latin instruments e.g. Spanish guitar
   - Latin rhythms / syncopation
   Dance music:
   Any one of:
   - A fast tempo
   - Disco beat
   (1 mark for a feature from Latin music and 1 mark for a feature from dance music)

d) The trumpets play a mainly syncopated rhythm. — T
   The lead vocal part is disjunct. — F
   The lead vocals and piano play in a call and response style. — F
   There is a drum roll before the trumpets enter. — T
   (1 mark for each, up to a maximum of 4 marks)

e) Any two of:
   - The guitar and percussion are quiet at the start.
   - There is a crescendo just before the trumpets enter.
   - It gets louder when the trumpets enter.
   - The instruments get quieter as the lead vocals start.
   (1 mark for each, up to a maximum of 2 marks)

Section Nine — Western Classical Tradition since 1910

Page 163 (Warm-up Questions)

1) In the Wild West/on a ranch

2) The twelve chromatic notes in an octave arranged in any order.

3) Any two of:
   - jazz
   - classical music from the late Romantic period
   - early twentieth century classical music
   - British folk music

4) The opening of the new cathedral in Coventry.

5) Any two of:
   - intense emotions
   - angular/spiky melodies
   - dissonance
   - atonality
   - unconventional forms

6) Any piece by Tavener, e.g.:
   - Jonah and the Whale
   - Song for Athene
   - The Lamb
   - The Protecting Veil

7) Any three of:
   - pentatonic scales
   - slow and fast sections
   - dotted rhythms
   - melody with accompaniment
   - instruments such as the cimbalom
   - syncopation
   - rich string sound
   - triplets
   - ornaments

8) Military march, processional march and funeral march

9) ABA structure / ternary form

10) Any two of:
    - no clear key signature
    - unusual time signatures
    - new instrumental techniques

11) Short, repeated note or rhythm patterns

12) Any two of:
    - additive melody
    - metamorphosis
    - phase shifting
    - layering

13) Any two pieces by Riley, e.g.:
    - In C
    - Uncle Jard
    - A Rainbow in Curved Air
    - Salome Dances for Peace

14) Clapping Music

15) Tremolo

<u>Pages 163-165 (Exam Questions)</u>

Track 36

   a) i) Cimbalom *(1 mark)*

      ii) Any two of:
- virtuosic
- countermelody
- semiquavers
- separate to rest of orchestra
- mostly conjunct
(1 mark for each, up to a maximum of 2 marks)

   b) Scotch snap *(1 mark)*

   c) Similarities:
     Any two of:
- largely the same instrumentation
- dotted rhythms/Scotch snaps in both
- string dominated melody
- crescendos in both parts
- both use repeated melodies
- tempo is largely similar in both
     Differences:
     Any two of:
- cimbalom stands out in first half but not in second
- quavers/triplets in second half, mainly dotted rhythms in first half
- first half minor, second half mainly major
(1 mark for each similarity, up to a maximum of 2 marks. 1 mark for each difference, up to a maximum of 2 marks.)

   d) Pause/hold the note (or rest) on *(1 mark)*

   e) Any two of:
- Turn
- Acciaccatura
- Trill
(1 mark for each, up to a maximum of 2 marks)

Track 37

   a) Offbeat chords *(1 mark)*

   b) Any two of:
- cymbal
- xylophone
- woodblock
- piano
(1 mark for each, up to a maximum of 2 marks)

   c) Any of:
     Instrumentation:
- In the first section, only the strings, piano and woodblock play.
- In the second section, the whole orchestra plays.
     Rhythm:
- In the first section, strong offbeat chords are played.
- Despite the offbeat chords in the first section, the rhythm is clear/the section is quite rhythmic.
- In the second section, there is a strong downbeat.
- The second section also features some syncopation in the accompaniment.
- The second section melody has triplet flourishes.

Texture:
- The first section is an accompaniment section without a clear melody.
- The second section sounds almost monophonic at the beginning, with nearly all of the orchestra playing the tune and only a few instruments accompanying.
- Throughout the second section, multiple instruments play the melody.
- The second section becomes more homophonic after the start.
Tempo:
- The tempo in the first section is slower than in the second.
Dynamics:
- The first section is quite quiet (*mp*/*mf*).
- Most of the second section is louder (*f*).
Articulation:
- The first section is mostly staccato.
- The second section is less staccato/more legato.
(Award 1 mark for a correct statement about one section of the excerpt, and award a further mark for a correct comparison with the other section of the excerpt, up to a maximum of 4 marks.)

   d) Major *(1 mark)*

Page 167-187 — Practice Exam

Pages 168-179 — Section A

1 *Track 38*

1.1 SATB choir *(1 mark)*

1.2 Any two of:
- It's in a major key so it sounds happy.
- The trumpet fanfare sounds celebratory.
- The fast tempo (allegro) makes it sound joyful and upbeat.
- The word 'rejoice' is repeated.
- The timpani make the piece sound grand.
(1 mark for each, up to a maximum of 2 marks)

1.3 Perfect *(1 mark)*

Track 39

1.4 Violin or flute *(1 mark for one correct instrument)*

1.5 Andante (allow adagio, moderato) *(1 mark)*

1.6 Antiphony *(1 mark)*

2 *Track 40*

2.1 Riffing *(1 mark)*

2.2 i) Minor *(1 mark)*

ii) V7 (allow V) *(1 mark)*

2.3
1	2	3	4	5	6	7	8
		A, B		C			D

(1 mark for each letter in the correct box)

2.4 Overdubbing *(1 mark)*

3 *Track 41*

3.1 Percussion *(1 mark)*

3.2

(1 mark)

3.3 Singing in unison *(1 mark)*

3.4 (Sub-Saharan) Africa *(1 mark)*

3.5 Cross-rhythm *(1 mark)*

Track 42

3.6 Walking bass *(1 mark)*

3.7 i) Blues *(1 mark)*

ii) Any three of:
- blue notes/blues scale
- swung rhythms
- syncopated rhythms
- sad/mournful lyrics (e.g. dead, evil spirits, devil)
- walking bass
- the lyrics are 3 lines long with the first line repeated
- piano finishes off vocal line
(1 mark for each, up to a maximum of 3 marks)

4 *Track 43*

4.1 Moderato (allow andante/quite slow/ adagio/larghetto) *(1 mark)*

4.2 Bartók (allow Kodály) *(1 mark)*

4.3 The first beat *(1 mark)*

4.4 Strings *(1 mark)*

Track 44

4.5 Dissonance *(1 mark)*

4.6 Chromatic *(1 mark)*

4.7 Any three of:
- The dynamics are quieter.
- The music is more tonal/less atonal/less dissonant.
- The strings play a legato melody (they played staccato before).
- The string melody is more conjunct.
- The strings play longer notes.
- The woodwind add light-hearted/bird-like flourishes above the melody.
- The horns are no longer playing.
(1 mark for each, up to a maximum of 3 marks)

5 *Track 45*

5.1 Cadenza *(1 mark)*

5.2 i) Classical *(1 mark)*

ii) Any one of:
- The concerto is a common Classical form.
- There is a complicated cadenza for the soloist to show off their skills.
- The soloist is accompanied by a standard Classical orchestra.
- The phrases in the orchestral section are balanced.
- The harmonies are simple.
- The texture is homophonic.
(1 mark)

Track 46

5.3

(1 mark for each correct note or correct interval between two adjacent notes, up to 6 marks)

5.4 Begins major, then modulates to minor *(1 mark)*

6 *Track 47*

6.1 i) Horror *(1 mark)*

ii) Any two of:
- It uses low-pitched instruments.
- It's in a minor key.
- It has a slow tempo.
- Monophony makes it sound empty/scary.
- The tolling bell sounds ominous.
(1 mark for each, up to a maximum of 2 marks)

6.2 Monophonic / playing in unison / octaves *(1 mark)*

6.3 Any one of:
- It makes it sound alien/unnatural/other-worldly.
- It makes it feel like something is wrong.
- It makes it sound more modern.
- It is cheaper/easier to record than live instruments.
(1 mark)

Track 48

6.4 i) 3/4 or 3/8 *(1 mark)*

   ii) Waltz *(1 mark)*

6.5 Any two of:
- It starts off with a lively tempo (allegro).
- It then slows down / rall(entando).
- Finally, it returns to the original tempo (a tempo).
(1 mark for each, up to a maximum of 2 marks)

7 *Track 49*

7.1 Caribbean *(1 mark)*

7.2 The second option is correct. *(1 mark)*

7.3 Any three of:
- In the first half, the rhythm follows a 3-3-2 pattern.
- In the second half, it has a steady 4-beat pattern.
- The first half has syncopated rhythms.
- The second half has little syncopation/mainly on-beat rhythms.
- The first half has longer notes (crotchets and dotted crotchets).
- The second half mainly has running quavers.
(1 mark for each, up to a maximum of 3 marks)

7.4 Any two of:
- It's in a major key which sounds happy — this makes it suitable for a carnival.
- It has a bright, lively tempo so sounds fun.
- It's easy to dance to, which is suitable for a carnival.
(1 mark for each, up to a maximum of 2 marks)

8 *Track 50*

8.1 pianissimo/piano/mezzopiano/quiet *(1 mark)*

8.2 Any one of:
- Regular, quick rhythm
- Constant/repeated quavers (allow semiquavers)
(1 mark)

8.3 i) Minimalism *(1 mark)*

   ii) Any five of:
- Constant pulse/driving rhythm
- Repetitive cell structure/short repeated phrases/ostinatos
- No clear melody
- Gradual build up to complex texture
- Gradual build up to complex rhythm
- Notes gradually added/gradual changes in phrases
- Not atonal/music is modal (accept tonal)
- Diatonic/no dissonance
- No sudden changes in dynamics
(1 mark for each, up to a maximum of 5 marks)

Pages 180-187 — Section B

9.1 Basset horn *(1 mark)*
   Any one of:
- It could play four semitones lower than a regular clarinet.
- It was longer than a regular clarinet.
(1 mark)

9.2 Any two of:
- Typical Classical orchestra — string-dominated with pairs of woodwind.
- Orchestra has a quiet, thin texture when the soloist is playing.
- The orchestra also plays the melody at some points.
- Homophonic texture.
- Interaction with soloist.
- Simple, mainly diatonic harmony (though with some chromaticism).
(1 mark for each, up to a maximum of 2 marks)

9.3 Any two of:
- Rondo form
- Theme (A) and episodes (B and C), with B appearing twice.
- ABACABA
(1 mark for each, up to a maximum of 2 marks)

9.4 Any eight of:
Similarities:
- Lots of semiquavers used throughout.
- No change of time signature (it's all 6/8).
- No change of tempo (it's all allegro).
- Generally fairly quiet throughout.
- Keeps returning to A major.
- Chromaticism used throughout.
- Repetition of musical ideas (with slight differences) to create unity.
Contrasts:
- The theme (A) features lots of semiquaver runs that are mainly conjunct, and lots of staccato.
- Episode B feels slower as it uses longer notes (as well as semiquavers) — quavers and dotted crotchets.
- Thinner texture in episode B than in rest of movement.
- When episode B is repeated, it goes through a series of modulations creating more contrast and includes pauses.
- More call and response between soloist and orchestra in episode B, than elsewhere in the movement.
- Episode C is very disjunct, with wide leaps in pitch (sometimes more than two octaves).
- Episode C is in a minor key (to begin with), whereas the other sections start in a major key.
- Episode C has different rhythms to episode B and the main theme — a crotchet-quaver lilting rhythm.
(1 mark for each, up to a maximum of 8 marks. Contrasts should explicitly compare at least two sections. If only similarities or only contrasts have been discussed, award no more than 6 marks.)

10.1 Any two of:
- rock 'n' roll
- doo-wop
- Motown
- rock
- narrators sing in style of 60s girl groups
- narrators are named after 60s girl groups
(1 mark for each, up to a maximum of 2 marks)

10.2 Any two of:
- They finish off each others' phrases/sing in call and response.
- It's syllabic.
- Vocals are half-spoken, half-sung.
- They sing in harmony when agreeing with each other.
- It's very fast/at the speed of speech.
(1 mark for each, up to a maximum of 2 marks)

10.3 Any two of:
- It's a hook.
- It's an ostinato.
- It's repeated on low piano throughout the song.
- It links the different sections.
- It continues under dialogue sections.
- It's a pedal note, using the tonic.
- It provides emphasis on the first beat of the bar.
(1 mark for each, up to a maximum of 2 marks)

10.4 *Little Shop of Horrors* is a horror/comedy musical, and there are elements of both of these in 'Prologue/Little Shop of Horrors'.
Any eight of:
- The opening drum roll provides drama, letting the audience know the story is going to be exciting.
- Despite being in a major key, the opening chords have a sense of foreboding.
- The introduction sounds like a funeral march as the chords are played on an organ sound on the keyboard.
- The off-stage male voice is deep and booming, which sounds ominous.
- His lyrics include words like 'deadly threat' and 'terrifying enemy'.
- However, the lyrics are very over-the-top and tongue-in-cheek, which also makes it funny.
- The contrasting upbeat title track shows that the musical is also fun and a comedy.
- The 60s-style close harmony singing establishes the period of the show.
- It is in a major key, so it sounds happy.
- The dissonant chords in the final chorus reinforce the sense of foreboding created in the prologue.
- The contrast provided by the lyrics (which talk about 'horrors' and 'terrors') with the bright tempo, major key and lively piano quavers in the accompaniment also add to the humour of the song.
(1 mark for each, up to a maximum of 8 marks)

11.1 Any two of:
- delay on penny whistle solo
- bass solo copied and reversed
- Simon overdubbed backing vocals
- tape delays used on lead vocals
(1 mark for each, up to a maximum of 2 marks)

11.2 Any two of:
- lyrics tell a story (set in the American South)
- lyrics almost spoken
- slapback echo
- country rhythms
- pedal steel guitar
(1 mark for each, up to a maximum of 2 marks)

11.3 Any two of:
- The intro has a cappella singing, while the rest of the song has an instrumental accompaniment.
- The intro is in E major, but the rest of the song is in F major.
- There is call and response in the intro, but none in the rest of the song (which has a standard verse-chorus structure).
(1 mark for each, up to a maximum of 2 marks)

11.4 Any eight of:
African elements:
- A cappella/isicathimiya/mbube singing at the start.
- Call and response between Simon and Ladysmith Black Mambazo.
- Singing in Zulu.
- African drumming/percussion (African percussionists).
- Bass guitar imitates/completes vocal line, which is typical of mbaqanga.
American elements:
- Rock band.
- Electric guitars, trumpets, saxophones.
- Backing vocals.
- Instrumental sections.
- Guitar riffs throughout.
(1 mark for each, up to a maximum of 8 marks.
If only African elements or only American elements have been discussed, award no more than 6 marks.)

12.1 Any two of:
- Cimbalom
- Rich string sound
- Dotted rhythms/Scotch snap
- Syncopation
- Triplets
- Ornaments
- Variations in tempo

(1 mark for each, up to a maximum of 2 marks)

12.2 Any one of:
- Experimental/ambiguous tonality.
- Large/non-typical orchestra (varied percussion section, unusual instruments like cimbalom, inclusion of the saxophone).
- Unusual sounds/effects (e.g. orchestral 'shriek').

(1 mark)

12.3 Any three of:
- The Battle and Defeat of Napoleon mainly features brass, percussion and saxophone (with a few higher woodwind), while Intermezzo uses the full orchestra.
- (low) Brass dominate in The Battle and Defeat of Napoleon, whereas the melody in Intermezzo is mainly in the strings (but doubled by woodwind — and some woodwind solos in section B).
- The Battle and Defeat of Napoleon uses a variety of percussion instruments — e.g. cymbals, bass drum, tambourine, whereas Intermezzo features a cimbalom countermelody in Section A.

(1 mark for each, up to a maximum of 3 marks)

12.4 Any of:

Tempo:
- Section A is in 2/4 and has a tempo of ♩ = 108, suitable for a military march.
- Section B is a little slower, which is more appropriate for a processional march, and is in 4/4.
- Section C is much slower (half the speed of A), which is fitting for a funeral march.

Tonality:
- The main melody of Section A is largely diatonic (in C major), although some chromatics and dissonance are added at the end of each repetition of the main theme.
- The tonality in Section B is more ambiguous — it starts in C major, but then moves between C major and C minor, with a few bars in B major.
- Other than the saxophone, the instruments only play B♭ and F in Section C, making the tonality even more ambiguous.

Texture:
- Section A starts off monophonic, with the melody being played in unison or octaves.
- When the theme is repeated, it is accompanied so the texture is melody with accompaniment, and there are a few homophonic bars too.
- Section B has some bars of polyphony, where the trumpets and trombones are playing polyrhythms.
- Section B has a much fuller, thicker texture.
- Section C is melody with accompaniment.
- Section C has a much thinner texture.

Other:
- Sections A and B focus mainly on brass and percussion, whereas the saxophone is the main instrument in section C.
- Section A has mainly quavers and semiquavers in the melody, whereas B introduces triplets against a quaver melody and C has longer notes.
- Section C is very quiet, whereas the other sections have more varied dynamics.

(Award 1 mark for a correct statement about one section, and award a further mark for a correct comparison with another section, up to a maximum of 8 marks)

Index and Glossary

Index and Glossary

Index and Glossary

D

da capo aria An **aria** in **ternary form**. 56

danzón A Cuban dance developed from the **habanera**. 143

Debussy 100, 155

decoration A way of making music more interesting by adding extra notes. 41, 84

delay An electronic effect that delays the output of sound. 75, 116, 138, 140

descant A type of vocal harmony that's higher than the melody. 109

development The second section of **sonata form** where ideas are developed. 92

Diamonds on the Soles of Her Shoes 140

diatonic Music that uses notes from a **major** or **minor scale**. 27, 41, 90, 118, 159

diatonic decoration **Decoration** that belongs to the key of the melody. 41

diegetic music When the characters in a film can actually hear the music. 123

Dies Irae 103

diminished chord 35, 36

diminished triad A **triad** that has three **semitones** (a minor third) between the bottom and middle notes, and the middle and top notes. 35

diminuendo Get quieter gradually. 19

diminution Shortening the length of the notes to make the music sound quicker. 18

discordance Horrible sound that you get when notes that don't fit together are played at the same time. Also called **dissonance**. 34

disjunct When there are big jumps between the notes of a melody. The opposite of **conjunct**. 28, 54

dissonance Another name for **discordance**. 34, 41, 99, 119, 120, 152-155, 158

distortion A guitar effect that distorts the note. 75, 110, 112, 113

DJ Disc jockey. Chooses which tracks to play on the radio or at a club. 73

djembe Single-headed African drum, played with the hands. 133

dolce Play sweetly. 18

dot A symbol that makes a note or rest one-and-a-half times its normal length. 17

double flat A symbol that tells you to lower a note by two **semitones**. 11

double sharp A symbol that tells you to raise a note by two **semitones**. 11

double-stopping Playing two notes at the same time on a **string instrument**. 64

drone A long, held-on note, usually in the bass. 39, 134

drum fill A short drum solo in between sections of a piece, usually found in **pop** music. 14, 140

drum machine An electronic instrument used instead of live drums. 72, 73, 110

drum pad An electronic drum kit. 110

duet A piece for two players or two singers. 68, 70, 118, 120

dynamics How loud or quiet the music is. 19, 80, 88, 99

E

electronic effects Effects used to change the timbre of instruments. 75, 109

energico Play energetically. 18

enharmonic equivalent Notes which sound the same but are written differently (e.g. C♯ and D♭). 11, 101

episode A section in a **rondo** that contrasts with the main theme. 93, 96, 97

ethnomusicology The study of music from different cultures. 155

étude Piece of music designed as an exercise. 101

exposition The first section of **sonata form** where ideas are introduced. 92

expressionism 20th century music that ignores conventional forms and focuses on expressing emotions. 153

extra-diegetic music Music in a film that can't be heard by the characters. 123

F

falsetto When male singers sing notes in the female vocal range — much higher than their normal range. 68, 85, 109, 115, 116

fanfare A flourish, usually performed by **brass instruments**. 62, 98, 124, 156

fantasia A composition with an **improvised** feel. 82

Fauré 103

feedback The noise you get when you stand too close to a speaker with a guitar or microphone. Sometimes used deliberately in **rock music**. 112

Feed Me (Git It) 120

figured bass A type of notation often used for **continuo** parts. The bass notes are written on the **stave**, then numbers written underneath the notes tell the performers which chords to play. 57

film music 121-123, 159

first inversion An **inversion** of a **triad** with the third at the bottom. 37

flanger A guitar effect that sounds a bit like a **phaser** but more intense. 75, 110

flat A symbol that tells you to lower a note by one **semitone**. 11, 24

folk music Music played by ordinary people. It wasn't usually written down — it was passed on aurally. 111, 112, 114, 136, 144, 145, 150, 155, 157, 158

forte, *f* Loud. 19

fortissimo, *ff* Very loud. 19

free jazz A type of jazz from the 1950s and 60s with lots of improvisation. It didn't stick to set tempos or rhythms. 131

fugue A popular Baroque structure. It usually involves **imitation** and **counterpoint**. 81

fusion A musical genre formed by mixing the elements of two or more different musical styles. 132, 137-140, 143

fuzz Fuzzy-sounding **distortion**. 110

G

Gaelic Traditional Celtic language spoken in Scotland and Ireland. The two main types are Scots Gaelic and Irish Gaelic. 144

game music 124

giocoso Play in a light-hearted, joky way. 18

glissando A slide between notes. 20, 110, 133, 156

gospel 111

Graceland 139, 140

grand opera A serious opera, set entirely to music. 86

grandioso Play very grandly. 18

ground bass A way of playing **variations** with a strong repeating bass part as the main **theme**. 57, 82, 83

Index and Glossary

Index and Glossary

Index and Glossary

rondo A musical structure where you start with a main **theme**, go to a different **episode**, go back to the main theme, then to another episode, back to the main theme, then an episode... as many times as you like. **81, 92-97, 158**

root chord Chord with its **root note** at the bottom. **38**

root note The note a chord originates from, e.g. in a C major chord, the root note would be C. **37, 38**

root position A **triad** that hasn't been **inverted** (the root note is at the bottom). **37**

round Another name for a **canon**. **46**

rubato, or *rub*. Be flexible with the pace of the music. **18, 99**

rumba An Afro-Cuban dance accompanied by **percussion** and **voices**. **143**

S

sabar An African drum <u>or</u> the traditional music played with the drum. **134, 137**

sacred music Church music. **85, 103**

salsa A type of Latin American dance music. It's a fusion of **jazz** and Cuban **son**. **132, 141**

samba A type of Brazilian carnival music. **142**

sampler Electronic equipment for storing and altering sounds. **73**

sampling Adding other people's tunes, rhythms or voices to your own music. Used a lot in club dance music. **73, 75, 109, 114, 116**

scale A set pattern of notes all from the same **key**. The most common ones in Western music are **major** and **minor** scales. **24, 25**

scalic Similar to **conjunct**. A smooth melody that moves up and down a **scale**. **28, 54**

scat A type of **improvised** singing used in **jazz**, with nonsense words and syllables. **109, 119, 132**

scherzo Lively third movement of a **symphony** or **sonata**. Wakes the audience up in time for the final movement. **93**

Schumann, Clara **102**

Schumann, Robert **100, 102**

Scotch snap A rhythm used in Scottish dances where an accented **semiquaver** is followed by an unaccented dotted quaver. **17, 154, 157**

second inversion An **inversion** of a **triad** with the fifth at the bottom. **37**

semibreve A note that lasts for four beats. **16**

semiquaver A note that lasts for one quarter of a beat. **12, 16**

semitone The gap in pitch between e.g. A and A♯, E♭ and E or B and C. On a piano keyboard, any two notes, black or white, immediately next to each other are a semitone apart. **9, 24, 25, 27**

septet Piece in seven parts or group with seven players. **70**

sequence A repeated musical pattern where the starting note moves up or down each time. **83, 97**

sequencer Electronic equipment which can record, edit and play back MIDI files and usually audio. **72**

serialism 20th century music that uses precise orders of notes. **151, 153**

sextet A piece for six players or six singers. **70**

sforzando, *sfz* A sudden, strongly accented note. **20, 99**

Sgt. Pepper's Lonely Hearts Club Band **114**

sharp A symbol that tells you to raise a note by one **semitone**. **11, 24**

Simon, Paul **139, 140**

simple time Time signature with two, three or four basic beats. **13**

sitar Large, long-necked string instrument used in Indian music. **114**

ska **132, 138**

skank rhythm **138**

slapback echo A recording effect that is a type of **delay**. **139**

slur Curved line joining notes of different pitch. Means you should go smoothly from one to the next. **19**

solo character song A song in a **musical** sung by one character. A bit like an **aria** in an **opera**. **118**

son Dance style which combined Spanish and African music, based on rhythm patterns called claves. **Salsa** evolved from son. **136**

son clave A **clave** rhythm used in **son** — the beats are grouped into a 3 and a 2, or the other way round. **141**

sonata Piece of music in three or four movements for a soloist or duet. **88, 91, 92, 100**

sonata form Piece of music with an **exposition**, a **development** and a **recapitulation**. **88, 92, 94, 95, 158**

song cycle A collection of **Lieder**. **102**

sonority The nature or quality of a sound. **74**

soprano Voice that sings roughly in the range from middle C to two octaves above that. Some singers can go even higher. **68, 85**

sospirando Play or sing in a sighing sort of way. **18**

staccato Play each note short and detached from the ones either side. **19**

stave The five lines that music is written on. **9**

steel pans **135**

stepwise When a melody moves in steps. **28, 54**

string instruments Instruments with strings. Fairly obvious really. **64, 65, 71, 74, 80, 89**

string quartet Two violins, a viola and a cello. **70**

string trio A violin, a viola and a cello. **70**

strophic form Type of structure where the music is the same in every verse. Only the lyrics change. **56, 102, 111, 135, 136, 144**

structure The way a piece of music is organised. **56, 81, 82, 88, 91-93**

strumming On a guitar, playing more than one note at a time. **65**

surdo drums Drums used in **samba** to set the beat. **142**

suite A set of dances from the Baroque period, or an orchestral arrangement of music from an opera or ballet. **81, 91, 155**

suspension A series of three notes that clash with the chord then lead back into a harmony. It is also the name of the second note in the series. **41**

swing music A type of **jazz** from the 1930s and 40s that could be danced to. **69, 117, 131**

swung rhythm **129, 132**

syllabic Every syllable of text is sung to a single note. The opposite of **melismatic**. **87, 109, 120**

symphony Long piece of music, in three or four movements, for a full orchestra. **88, 91, 92, 94, 95, 98**

syncopation The accents are shifted from the main beat to a weaker beat. E.g. in 4/4 time the main accent usually falls on the first beat — in syncopated 4/4 time you could move the accent to, say, the second beat. **119, 129, 132, 139, 140, 157**

synthesizer Electronic equipment for creating new sounds. **72, 75, 109, 110, 124**

Index and Glossary

MUAS42